I0234455

Tim van der Heijden and Aleksander Kolkowski
Doing Experimental Media Archaeology

Tim van der Heijden and Aleksander Kolkowski

Doing Experimental Media Archaeology

Practice

DE GRUYTER
OLDENBOURG

This book is the twin volume to *Doing Experimental Media Archaeology: Theory* (ISBN 978-3-11-079580-6), authored by Andreas Fickers and Annie van den Oever, volume 1 in this paired set. For ease of cross-referencing, in-text references will be used, preceded by ▶ Theory.

ISBN 978-3-11-079581-3
e-ISBN (PDF) 978-3-11-079976-7
e-ISBN (EPUB) 978-3-11-079980-4
DOI https://doi.org/10.1515/9783110799767

(cc) BY

This work is licensed under the Creative Commons Attribution 4.0 International License. For details go to https://creativecommons.org/licenses/by/4.0/.

Creative Commons license terms for re-use do not apply to any content (such as graphs, figures, photos, excerpts, etc.) not original to the Open Access publication and further permission may be required from the rights holder. The obligation to research and clear permission lies solely with the party re-using the material.

Library of Congress Control Number: 2022945598

Bibliographic information published by the Deutsche Nationalbibliothek
The Deutsche Nationalbibliothek lists this publication in the Deutsche Nationalbibliografie; detailed bibliographic data are available on the internet at http://dnb.dnb.de.

© 2023 Tim van der Heijden and Aleksander Kolkowski, published by Walter de Gruyter GmbH, Berlin/Boston
Cover image: Original and replica Kinora motion picture viewer and reel. The Kinora replica was produced in collaboration with the Department of Engineering of the University of Luxembourg. Photo by Tim van der Heijden. Courtesy of the C^{2}DH / University of Luxembourg.
Typesetting: Integra Software Services Pvt. Ltd.
Printing and binding: CPI books GmbH, Leck

www.degruyter.com

Acknowledgements

This book is an outcome of the research project "Doing Experimental Media Archaeology: Practice and Theory" (DEMA). It was funded by the Fonds National de la Recherche Luxembourg (FNR) and hosted by the Luxembourg Centre for Contemporary and Digital History (C^{2}DH) of the University of Luxembourg. We would like to thank FNR and C^{2}DH for making this project possible and for their generous support. We are most grateful for the collaborations, support of and input from the other members of the DEMA project team, including Andreas Fickers, Stefan Krebs, Christianne Blijleven, and associative researchers Karin Bienek and Ludwig Vogl-Bienek (*illuminago*), and the members of the DEMA advisory board, including Annie van den Oever, Lori Emerson, John Ellis, Erkki Huhtamo, and Martin Loiperdinger. Our thanks also goes to all other participants at the DEMA workshops of 2019 and 2020, as well as at the conference "Doing Experimental Media Archaeology", organised at the University of Luxembourg in September 2022.

We thank our colleagues at the University of Luxembourg and the Open University of the Netherlands for their support. We are grateful to the supporting staff of the Luxembourg Centre for Contemporary and Digital History (C^{2}DH), in particular Tessy Delledera, Brigitte Melchior-Dolenc, Daniele Guido, Andy O'Dwyer, Noëlle Schon, and Lars Wieneke. We thank Claude Wolf and Gilbert Klein from the Department of Engineering of the University of Luxembourg for their collaborations, and the following student collaborators from the same department: Sunil Kumar, Tugdual Levasseur, Morgane Piet, David Schmit, and Thomas Theisen. We furthermore thank Sascha Helsper, Arno Ravasio, Nicolas Donnerup and Alexandre Germain from the Media Centre of the University of Luxembourg.

We are also grateful for the assistance of the following collectors, experts, societies and specialist repairers: John Adderley, Keith Badman, Stef van Brakel, Frank Bruinsma (Super8 Reversal Lab), Bert Cremers, City of London Phonograph and Gramophone Society, Sean Davis, Guy Edmonds, Gerald Freyer, Stephen Herbert, Howard Hope, Emiel de Jong, Marco Kröger, Sébastien Lemagnen (Antiq-Photo Gallery, Paris), Duncan Miller (Vulcan Cylinder Record Company), Paul Morris (Paul Morris Music), Onno Petersen (Onno Petersen cinematography and post production), Christopher Proudfoot (Sotheby's), Michael Rogge, Ivan Rose, Nirmal Sabarwal (Fuselodge, London), and Liz Tuddenham (Poppy Records, Bath). Our thanks also go to the following artistic collaborators: Tijs de Bie, Loz Cliffe, Loré Lixenberg, kitt price, Martin Riches, Damien Simon, and Judith Westerveld. We are grateful too to the following institutions, archives, galleries and museums: Antiq-Photo Gallery, Paris; British Vintage Wireless and Television Museum, London; Discovery Museum, Newcastle-upon-Tyne; E.M.I. Archive, Hayes; Eye Filmmuseum, Amsterdam; *Le Bon Accueil* sound art gallery, Rennes; La Cinémathèque

ᐁ Open Access. © 2023 the author(s), published by De Gruyter. [cc BY] This work is licensed under the Creative Commons Attribution 4.0 International License.
https://doi.org/10.1515/9783110799767-202

française, Paris; National Science and Media Museum, Bradford; Netherlands Institute for Sound & Vision, Hilversum; and the Science Museum, London.

We would also like to thank the members of the International Network of Experimental Media Archaeology (NEMA) and the growing community of researchers, artists, educators, cultural heritage professionals and other experts who promote hands-on approaches in the field of media history, as well as in the humanities and social sciences in general. We are grateful to Benoît Turquety for providing excellent feedback on an earlier draft of this book, Elizabeth Rankin for constructive proofreading, and Rabea Rittgerodt and Jana Fritsche at De Gruyter Publishers for their invaluable support.

Finally, we would like to thank our partners, Eefje and Anja, and our families and friends for their love and patience. Last but not least, we thank Nora for taking the starring role in our project. It has been wonderful to capture your first steps in historical moving images and sound.

Tim van der Heijden and Aleksander Kolkowski
Maastricht, the Netherlands; London, United Kingdom, July 2022

Contents

Introduction

In recent years, there has been a growing interest in the use of experimental approaches to the study of media histories and their cultures.[1] An increasing number of scholars researching at the intersection of media history and theory are breaking new ground by working with archival sources and historical artefacts in experimental ways. Examples of work in this field are given throughout this book, ranging from re-enactments of early cinema screenings, to the simulation of analogue television production practices, to reconstructions of and performances with past media artefacts. Doing media archaeological experiments, such as historical re-enactments and hands-on simulations with media historical objects, helps us to explore and better understand the workings of past media technologies and their practices of use. Knowledge and skills that used to be part of daily life not so long ago have been rapidly disappearing in today's digital cultures, characterised by an increased black-boxing and (planned) obsolescence of media technologies. While media historical objects have been finding their ways to the vaults of national and regional archives, or have been displayed as material artefacts behind glass in museum exhibitions, their histories of use have become more difficult to preserve, document and display. Hands-on approaches can therefore play an important role in explicating the often hidden or "tacit knowledge" of past media usages as forms of immaterial heritage.[2]

---

1 Andreas Fickers and Annie van den Oever, "Experimental Media Archaeology: A Plea for New Directions," in *Technē/Technology: Researching Cinema and Media Technologies – Their Development, Use, and Impact*, ed. Annie van den Oever (Amsterdam: Amsterdam University Press, 2014), 272–278; Andreas Fickers and Annie van den Oever, "Doing Experimental Media Archaeology: Epistemological and Methodological Reflections on Experiments with Historical Objects of Media Technologies," in *New Media Archaeologies*, ed. Ben Roberts and Mark Goodall (Amsterdam: Amsterdam University Press, 2019), 45–68; Andreas Fickers and Annie van den Oever, "(De)Habituation Histories: How to Re-Sensitize Media Historians," in *Hands on Media History: A New Methodology in the Humanities and Social Sciences*, ed. Nick Hall and John Ellis (London: Routledge, 2019), 58–75; Nick Hall and John Ellis, eds., *Hands on Media History: A New Methodology in the Humanities and Social Sciences* (London: Routledge, 2019); Sven Dupré et al., eds., *Reconstruction, Replication and Re-enactment in the Humanities and Social Sciences* (Amsterdam: Amsterdam University Press, 2020).
2 Within this guide we use the term "tacit knowledge" (Polanyi) in reference to all implicit forms of knowledge invested in past media usages, including "embodied" (Merleau-Ponty) and "gestural" (Sibum) knowledge. We discuss the notion in more detail in Chapter 3.3.1. For a discussion of the terms in the framework of experimental media archaeology, see also ▶ Theory, Chapters 3.6 and 4.1.

ə Open Access. © 2023 the author(s), published by De Gruyter. [cc) BY] This work is licensed under the Creative Commons Attribution 4.0 International License.
https://doi.org/10.1515/9783110799767-001

By systematically reflecting on the methodological underpinnings of experimental media archaeology, this book aims to serve as a practical guide for doing such media archaeological experiments. It is written as a companion to the theoretical volume *Doing Experimental Media Archaeology: Theory*, authored by Andreas Fickers and Annie van den Oever. The two books refer to each other throughout and are therefore recommended to be read together.

Experimental Media Archaeology

The term "experimental media archaeology" was coined by media historian Andreas Fickers and film scholar Annie van den Oever in 2014. In their essay "Experimental Media Archaeology: A Plea for New Directions", they underlined the heuristic potential of hands-on approaches for re-sensitising scholars to the materiality of past media technologies and the tacit knowledge involved in their technical, social, and cultural usages:

> Doing re-enactments with old media technologies in an experimental media-archaeology lab produces new historical, ethnographic, and empirical knowledge about past user practices and media experiences. It advances our classical repertoire of sources generally used to study past user generations by the co-production of experimental data and ethnographic observations.[3]

Providing an object-oriented and sensorial approach to media historiography, experimental media archaeology can serve as a heuristic tool in various ways. Media archaeological experiments can generate, for instance, new insights into the functionality and temporality that is inscribed in the materiality of media technologies. Think about the limited amount of recording time of analogue sound and film-based media, or the extensive exposure time involved in early photography practices. They can also bring about more awareness of the spatial and topographical information inscribed in media practices, the role of space and location for the production and consumption of media technologies, as well as the social dynamics involved in past media usages. Furthermore, by re-enacting the historical practices of production, media archaeological experiments can enable a better understanding of the "constructivist nature" of .media-technology content, namely how films, photographs and audio recordings were produced and mediated by media technologies in the past (▶ Theory, Chapter 2.8).

---

3 Andreas Fickers and Annie van den Oever, *Doing Experimental Media Archaeology: Theory* (Berlin: De Gruyter, 2022), Chapter 1.

Experimental media archaeology aims to turn the media archaeologist and historian into an experimenter (▶ Theory, Chapter 1). Methodologically, this enables an approach that is different from, yet complements traditional historiographical approaches, such as historical discourse analysis, oral history and archival research. Experimental media archaeology draws on insights from various fields and knowledge domains, including the history of science and technology,[4] experimental archaeology,[5] experimental approaches in art history,[6] historically informed music performances,[7] and sensory ethnography,[8] in which reconstructions, reworkings and re-enactments have been widely used and recognized as helpful research methods and heuristic tools. Inspired by the experimental research conducted within these domains, Fickers and Van den Oever argue that one of the main values of the hands-on approach for both research and teaching is that it helps to foster the historical imagination by experiencing, in addition to intellectually appropriating, past media technologies and their histories of use. In other words, it offers new ways of "sensing the past" (▶ Theory, Chapter 2).

DEMA Project

While the heuristic potential of experimental media archaeology has been recognized before and several media laboratories have gathered collections of media artefacts in order to promote a hands-on approach,[9] the practical and

---

4 Olaf Breidbach et al., "Experimentelle Wissenschaftsgeschichte," in *Experimentelle Wissenschaftsgeschichte*, ed. Olaf Breidbach et al. (Munich: Fink, 2010), 13–72; Marieke M. A. Hendriksen, "Rethinking Performative Methods in the History of Science," *Berichte Zur Wissenschaftsgeschichte* 43, no. 3 (September 2020): 313–322, https://doi.org/10.1002/bewi.202000017.

5 Jeffrey Ferguson, ed., *Designing Experimental Research in Archaeology: Examining Technology through Production and Use* (Boulder: University Press of Colorado, 2010).

6 Maartje Stols-Witlox, "Flour and Starch in Preparatory Layers for Oil Painting: Reconstructions Based on Historical Recipes (Sixteenth to Nineteenth Centuries)," in *Painting Techniques: History, Materials and Studio Practice: 5th International Symposium*, ed. A. Wallert (Amsterdam: Rijksmuseum, 2016), 79–84.

7 Aleksander Kolkowski, Duncan Miller, and Amy Blier-Carruthers, "The Art and Science of Acoustic Recording: Re-enacting Arthur Nikisch and the Berlin Philharmonic Orchestra's Landmark 1913 Recording of Beethoven's Fifth Symphony," *Science Museum Group Journal* 3, no. 3 (2015), http://dx.doi.org/10.15180/150302/001.

8 Sarah Pink, *Doing Sensory Ethnography* (London: Sage, 2009); Anna Harris, *A Sensory Education* (London: Routledge, 2021).

9 Media archaeological laboratories for hands-on experimentation and enquiry include, among others, the Medienarchäologischer Fundus at Humboldt University in Berlin (https://www.musi kundmedien.hu-berlin.de/de/medienwissenschaft/medientheorien/fundus/media-archaeolog

methodological challenges of doing media archaeological experiments as a new means of knowledge production remains largely underexplored. In the project "Doing Experimental Media Archaeology: Practice & Theory" (DEMA), of which this book is the outcome, we have aimed to systematically reflect on the methodological underpinnings of experimental media archaeology as a methodological approach.[10] In studying the potential of hands-on experimentation in order to better understand and experience the materiality of past media technologies and their practices of use, two complementary studies were conducted. Each of the projects worked with different sets of analogue media technologies, one focused on vision and one focused on sound, as two modalities to mediate and explore the past. The projects involved different methods of hands-on experimentation, from playful "thinkering" with surviving media technologies and "historical re-enactment" of their usages, to the use of 3D modelling and printing for making working replicas of the original media objects.[11]

Vision: Early Twentieth-Century Home Cinema

For the DEMA project, media historian and researcher Tim van der Heijden focused on early twentieth-century amateur film technologies in his media archaeological experiments. Comparing the Kinora motion picture technology of the early 1900s and 1910s with various small-gauge recording and screening technologies of the 1920s and 1930s, the project investigated two historical *dispositifs* of home cinema.[12] The objective of the project was to better understand

---

ical-fundus [last accessed 26.07.2022]), the Media Archaeology Lab of the University of Colorado, Boulder, United States (https://www.mediaarchaeologylab.com/ [last accessed 26.07.2022]), and the Film Archive and Media Archaeology Lab of the University of Groningen, the Netherlands (https://filmarchief.ub.rug.nl/Welcome [last accessed 26.07.2022]).

10 The DEMA project (2019–2022) was funded by the Fonds National de la Recherche in Luxembourg (FNR) (C18/SC/12703137) and was hosted by the Luxembourg Centre for Contemporary and Digital History (C²DH) of the University of Luxembourg. DEMA project members include Andreas Fickers, Stefan Krebs, Aleksander Kolkowski, Tim van der Heijden and Christianne Blijleven, and associate project members Ludwig Vogl-Bienek and Karin Bienek (*illuminago*). Members of the project's advisory board include John Ellis (Royal Holloway College, University of London), Lori Emerson (University of Colorado, Boulder), Erkki Huhtamo (University of California, Los Angeles), Martin Loiperdinger (University of Trier) and Annie van den Oever (University of Groningen). For more information about the DEMA project and its activities, see the project website: https://dema.uni.lu/ [last accessed 26.07.2022].

11 We discuss the different methods of doing hands-on experimentation in Chapter 1.2.1.

12 For his studies on historicizing the home movie *dispositif* from a long-term media historical perspective, see Tim van der Heijden, "Hybrid Histories: Historicizing the Home Movie Dispositif,"

the materiality and functionality of these early twentieth-century home cinema and amateur film technologies, as well as to explore their practices of use. Historical media technologies used in the media archaeological experiments include a Kinora viewer and various reels (ca. 1907), a Pathé-Baby 9.5mm film camera, projector and various reels (ca. 1922–1930), a Ciné-Kodak 16mm film camera, projector and various reels (ca. 1923–1930), and a Ciné-Kodak 8mm film camera, projector and various reels (ca. 1932–1940).

Kinora Viewer Replica Project

The Kinora viewer was one of the first motion photography technologies designed for home use.[13] Originally invented and patented by Auguste and Louis Lumière in 1896, it was an adapted version of Casler's Mutoscope (1894), which, similarly to Edison's Kinetoscope (1889), functioned as an individual viewing machine. Like the Mutoscope, the Kinora viewer made use of a flipbook mechanism in which a series of paper-based unperforated photographs were attached to a wheel. By turning the wheel and looking through the viewer, one can watch the series of photographs in motion. Kinora viewers and reels were manufactured in France (by Gaumont) and particularly in Britain (by the British Mutoscope and Biograph company, and later by the Kinora Company and Bond's Limited in London). The Kinora evolved into a popular device for home entertainment. In the 1900s, hundreds of Kinora reels were produced and one could even make one's own "living pictures" or "animated photographs" at a photographic studio in London. A special Kinora camera for amateurs was introduced around 1908.[14]

The Kinora replica project aimed for a better understanding of the way the Kinora worked as a media technology, how it was used and made in the past. The project focused on replicating the viewer and reel. An original Kinora viewer from ca. 1907 and several original Kinora reels were purchased, so that they could be used for hands-on experimentation and serve as models for the 3D modelling and replication processes. The Kinora replica project was conducted in collaboration with the Department of Engineering of the University of Luxembourg.

in *Materializing Memories: Dispositifs, Generations, Amateurs*, ed. Susan Aasman, Andreas Fickers, and Joseph Wachelder (New York: Bloomsbury Academic, 2018), 35–50; Tim van der Heijden, *Hybrid Histories: Technologies of Memory and the Cultural Dynamics of Home Movies, 1895–2005* (Maastricht: Maastricht University, 2018).

13 Stephen Herbert, "Animated Portrait Photography," *History of Photography* 13, no. 1 (1989): 65–78.

14 Barry Anthony, *The Kinora: Motion Pictures for the Home 1896–1914: A History of the System* (London: The Projection Box, 1996), 12.

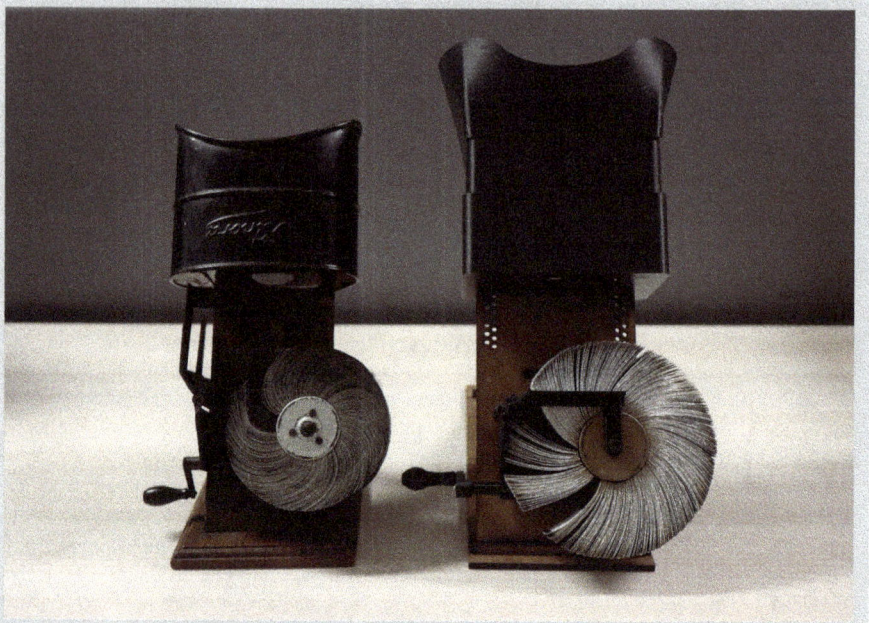

Fig. 1: Kinora viewer and reel: original and replica. Photo by Tim van der Heijden. Courtesy of the C²DH / University of Luxembourg.

Small-Gauge Experiments and Re-enactments

While there had been various attempts to produce suitable film equipment for domestic use already in the first decades of the twentieth century, it was not until the 1920s and 1930s that home cinema was popularised as an upper middle-class family practice with the releases of the 9.5mm, 16mm and 8mm "small gauges" and their accompanying equipment. The French production company Pathé Frères introduced the 9.5mm film format together with the Pathé-Baby film projector in 1922, initially for the purpose of screening reduction prints of professionally made films at home (*Le cinéma chez soi*). In the following year, the company released a hand-cranked Pathé-Baby camera, which allowed for the recording of moving images as well. The American Eastman Kodak Company introduced their 16mm film format in 1923, together with the Kodascope home projector and Ciné-Kodak film camera. In 1932, Kodak introduced the more affordable 8mm film format. Pathé's 9.5mm and Kodak's 16mm and 8mm film formats were called "small gauges", because of their smaller film width compared to the 35mm "standard" film used by professional filmmakers. They were not only more affordable, but also easier and safer to use at home, which contributed to the popularity of twentieth-century home cinema and amateur film-making and screening.

The objective of the hands-on experiments with the 9.5mm, 16mm and 8mm small-gauge technologies was to explore how these early twentieth-century amateur film technologies worked and, by historically re-enacting their practices, experience how they were used in the past. Experiments were conducted with a Ciné-Kodak 16mm film camera (model K, ca. 1930), and a Ciné-Kodak Eight 8mm film camera (model 25, ca. 1926) for re-enacting small-gauge re-cording practices. For re-enacting small-gauge projection and home cinema screening practices, experiments were conducted with a Pathé-Baby 9.5mm film projector, including both a hand-cranked model (ca. 1924) and a motor-driven model (ca. 1932). In addition, various small-gauge accessories were used, such as a Ciné-Kodak titler, a Pathé splicer and a Pathéscope projection screen.

Fig. 2: Pathé-Baby 9.5mm film projector and reel. Courtesy of the C^{2}DH / University of Luxembourg.

Sound: Histories of Use of Twentieth Century Sound Recording and Amplification Technologies

For the DEMA project, composer and researcher Aleksander Kolkowski investigated the histories of use of early to mid-twentieth-century sound recording and amplification technologies. The *HMV 2300H* portable disc recorder designed for small studios (1948), and the *Wilcox-Gay 1C10 Recordio*, a hybrid tape and disc recorder (1951) aimed at musicians seeking to make demo records, are two historical technologies that were the models for exploratory work on the practical experience of recording on disc and tape. His work with the *Cartavox* sound postcard recorder (1958) involved having to recreate the recordable postcard medium from scratch, and he re-enacted the live recording of sound postcards with members of the public. Kolkowski also drew from his previous research and experiments with air-assisted amplification technology of the early 1900s, in making working replicas of the *Stentorphone* and *Auxetophone* valved soundboxes for the gramophone. This project utilised CAD modelling and 3D printing and was made in collaboration with the University of Luxembourg's Department of Engineering in several educational projects with staff and students. The replicas were used in demonstrations and public events.

"Cartavox" Sound Postcard Recording Apparatus (1958)

The "Cartavox" is a rare and short-lived sound recording device, designed for making instantaneous voice recordings directly onto proprietary picture postcards playable on a turntable. This semi-automatic apparatus is closely based on the disc recording systems found in public coin-operated voice recording booths that were found in Europe and the USA from the 1940s until the 1970s, but requires some limited manual operation. Because of the extreme paucity of surviving recordable media for the device and no modern equivalent, new "blank" sound postcards had to be made from scratch through a self-designed process that used lamination instead of a chemical lacquer for the recordable surface (see Chapter 2.5.1).

The project also re-enacted a sound postcard recording station by installing the Cartavox in a public space where visitors were invited to make personal voice recordings onto the specially made postcards, and where this remarkable system of voice messaging could be simulated and investigated. After recording was completed and played back on a separate turntable, each visitor wrote a message to a recipient along with their address on the reverse of the card, which was later franked and delivered through the postal system. Additionally, the visitors and recipients of the sound postcards each received an MP3-transfer of the recording via email, in case they had no suitable equipment with which to play them back. Thus, the entire cycle of recording a voice message on a sound postcard, delivery through the post and its eventual playback (or listening to) by the recipient was completed and documented. The project also examined the skills needed to operate the apparatus and the interaction with the visitor "recordees". In addition, it studied the multi-sensory nature of the recording and playback processes and undertook a contextual inquiry to gain a deeper understanding of the sound postcard recording experience.

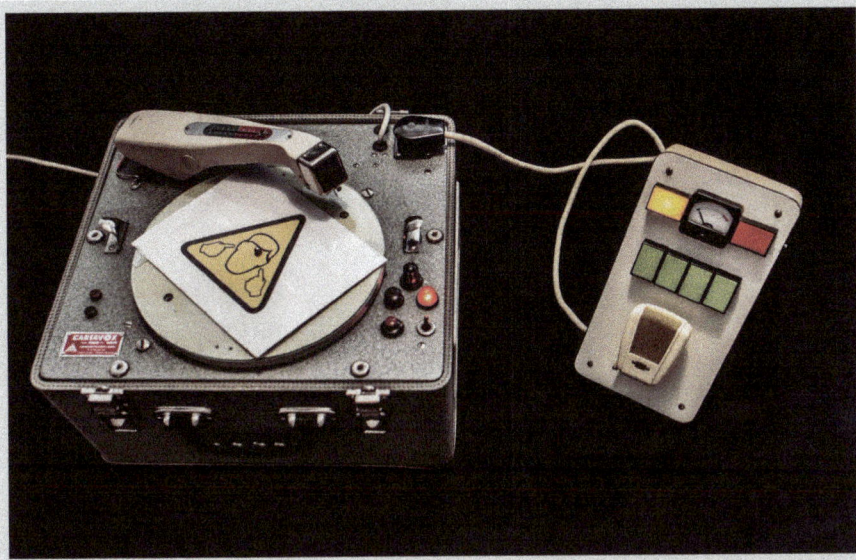

Fig. 3: The Cartavox sound postcard recorder and console. Courtesy of Leza Joe.

Auxetophone and Stentorphone Pneumatic Gramophone Soundboxes (1908; 1913)

The air-powered Auxetophone and Stentorphone gramophones were the first sound reproduction devices that brought recorded music and speech to the masses in parks, stadia and large public spaces during the pre-First World War period. They are the link between mechanical-acoustic and electrical sound amplification and there is a strong similarity between the systems. The Auxetophone-Gramophone of Charles Parsons and Horace Short was commercially manufactured from 1907, and the same compressed air and valved sound box system was used to amplify stringed instruments in orchestral concerts from 1906. Harry A. Gaydon's Stentorphone (ca. 1910–1922) is a direct descendent of the Auxetophone, but its design made it more accessible and offered possibilities for its adjustment. The Stentorphone was used to reproduce music in open air festivals and for advertising through public address. In 1921, an automatic and fully pneumatic version was installed in the London Underground to play pre-recorded safety messages on disc.[15]

Original and rare examples of both types of pneumatic gramophone sound boxes were loaned to the DEMA project by a collector, and were restored, repaired and revived to a working condition. They formed the basis of three separate replication projects using CAD

---

15 Aleksander Kolkowski and Alison Rabinovici, "Bellowphones and Blowed Strings: The Auxeto-Instruments of Horace Short and Charles Algernon Parsons," in *Material Culture and Electronic Sound*, Series Artefacts: Studies in the History of Science and Technology 8, ed. Frode Weium and Timothy Boon (Washington, D.C.: Smithsonian Scholarly Press, 2012), 1–42.

modelling and 3D printing techniques undertaken by students at the University of Luxembourg Department of Engineering. The originals and the replica models were fitted to a gramophone, tested, compared, analysed and were later used in public demonstrations. The project focused on the internal workings of both pneumatic soundboxes, and investigated the sound produced by them and their manual operation.

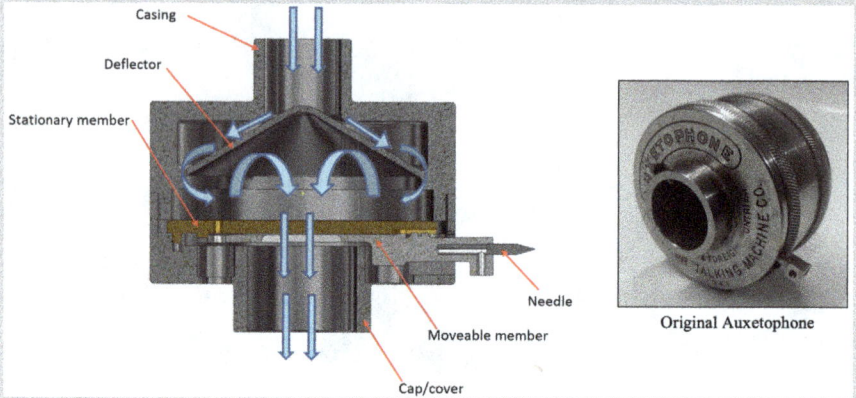

Fig. 4: Auxetophone soundbox and internal view showing airflow and sound output. Courtesy of Sunil Kumar.

Fig. 5: The restored original Stentorphone soundbox showing new front section, replacement bell-crank levers and torsional screw. Courtesy of the C^{2}DH / University of Luxembourg.

HMV 2300H Portable Disc Recorder (1948)

In modern terms, the word "portable" is a misnomer as a description for the HMV 2300H disc recorder, which, weighing nearly 60kg, would be better described as "transportable". The recorder was the first model manufactured by the EMI company that was made available to the public and was aimed primarily at small sound recording studios, laboratories and educational institutions, and for recordings made on location. The apparatus was capable of recording discs to a high enough standard that they could be used as masters for duplication via electroplating and pressing. The project examined some of the practical techniques involved in cutting records, and the device was used in experiments that included collaborations with artists and filmmakers.

Fig. 6: The HMV 2300H: recording unit, amplifier, loudspeaker and microphone. Photo by Aleksander Kolkowski. Courtesy of the C^{2}DH / University of Luxembourg.

Wilcox-Gay 'Recordio' 1C10 Portable Tape and Disc Recorder (1950)

This unusual hybrid tape and disc recording machine enabled recording from magnetic tape to lacquer disc and vice versa, all on one machine. It could play pre-recorded tapes and discs, came equipped with a microphone, had auxiliary inputs and an internal loudspeaker, and could also function as a public address system. Unlike the HMV 2300H, it was not intended for small recording studio applications or for semi-professional recordists, but was marketed mainly to musicians and music students for editing and making demo recordings. This project explored the hybridity of the device, the interchange of media and the tacit skills required to use the apparatus.

Fig. 7: Wilcox-Gay Recordio: recording from tape to disc. Photo by Aleksander Kolkowski. Courtesy of the C²DH / University of Luxembourg.

In addition to the two research projects, various workshops, hands-on events and public demonstrations were organised within the context of the DEMA project. Hands-on demonstrations involved the HMV 2300H disc-recording apparatus, original and replica Kinora viewers, and the Cartavox Sound Postcard machine. Two project-related workshops were organised, which specifically focused on the topics of documentation and dissemination of media archaeological experiments.[16]

Experimental System

Conducting our studies for the DEMA project, we aimed to develop an experimental system for doing media archaeological experiments, including their preparation, research, analysis, documentation and dissemination. This ambition was

---

[16] For more information about the DEMA public events and workshops, see https://dema.uni. lu/category/events/ [last accessed 26.07.2022]. Two detailed workshop reports can be found on the DEMA website: see Tim van der Heijden and Aleksander Kolkowski, "Documenting Media Archaeological Experiments," *DEMA* (blog), 15 July 2020, https://dema.uni.lu/documenting-media-archaeological-experiments-report/ [last accessed 26.07.2022]; Aleksander Kolkowski and Tim van der Heijden, "Performing Media Archaeological Experiments," *DEMA* (blog), 23 May 2021, https://dema.uni.lu/performing-media-archaeological-experiments-report/ [last accessed 26.07.2022]. Some fragments of the workshop reports have been re-worked in this book.

inspired by the German historian of science Hans-Jörg Rheinberger, whose notion of an "experimental system" adopts a situated and practice-driven view on scientific research.[17] According to Rheinberger's definition, "[e]xperimental systems stand for the integral of all ingredients, materials, research technologies, laboratory environment, collective experience necessary in order to set an experimental process in motion and to keep it in ongoing transformation."[18] To understand how experimentation creates new knowledge, one should consider the relation between *epistemic objects* and *technical objects*. Epistemic objects are the objects of study within the experimental setting of knowledge production. These involve concrete material objects, such as a media historical artefact but, depending on the type of experiment, epistemic objects may also include immaterial aspects, for instance, the media historical object's histories of use, the tacit knowledge involved in its operation, its performative qualities, etc. Technical objects, on the other hand, are the technical conditions of the experimental process and instruments used during the experiment. Technical objects are thus the instruments, apparatuses and devices that confine the study of epistemic objects within the experimental system. Rheinberger argued that the status of the object of study may change from epistemic object to technical object, depending on the perspective of the researcher and the questions central to the experiment. Conversely, a technical object or instrument may become an epistemic object during subsequent studies and can therefore raise further questions. For doing experimental media archaeology, this means that media historical devices can be studied as epistemic objects, but are turned into technical objects once they are used, for instance, in a public performance. The performative and aesthetic aspects of this performance then become the epistemic objects of the experiment. Media historical objects can thus turn into either epistemic or technical objects in media archaeological experiments, depending on the type and objective of the experiment. Accordingly, we have devised a system that employs three types of media archaeological experiments (▶ Theory, Chapter 4.2).

---

17 Hans-Jörg Rheinberger, *Experiment, Differenz, Schrift: Zur Geschichte Epistemischer Dinge* (Marburg an der Lahn: Basilisken-Press, 1992); Hans-Jörg Rheinberger, *Toward a History of Epistemic Things: Synthesizing Proteins in the Test Tube* (Stanford, CA: Stanford University Press, 1997).
18 Hans-Jörg Rheinberger, "Epistemics and Aesthetics of Experimentation: Towards a Hybrid Heuristics?", ed. Philippe Sormani, Guelfo Carbone, and Priska Gisler (New York: Routledge, 2019), 240.

Three Types of Media Archaeological Experiments

Within the experimental system, three entangled experimental arrangements or types of media archaeological experiments can be distinguished: basic experiments, media-technological experiments, and performative experiments.

Basic Experiments

Basic experiments study the media historical objects as epistemic objects. They focus on the technical functions and usability of the object, measure its performative capabilities and indicate the need for repair, restoration and maintenance, as well as the physical conditions under which they can operate. By measuring luminosity, loudness and dynamic range, for example, they examine the technical conditions of surviving artefacts and the physical conditions under which they can or must operate (e.g., the brightness/darkness or noisiness/calmness of the environment). They will also identify restrictions for experiments, such as safety, conservation and missing parts, and test suitable substitutes for lost or unusable components.

Media-Technological Experiments

Media-technological experiments focus on the object affordances and object-user interaction. They allow for an exploratory examination of the objects and the tacit or embodied knowledge required to operate them. As such, they study the user-friendliness and the aesthetic qualities produced by surviving media-technological artefacts and their replicas, for instance, experiments with historical projection and sound reproduction apparatuses. Failures and unexpected problems are an important part of media-technological experiments as they can produce "creative uncertainties" that are at the heart of "thinkering" as an experimental mode of knowledge production.

Performative Experiments

Performative experiments are an examination of historical media performances through re-enactments, public presentations and demonstrations. Here the focus is on the interaction between the object, user, location and a modern audience or participants. The performance or live action, in its entirety, becomes the epistemic object under scrutiny.

Distinguishing between these three types of media archaeological experiments makes it possible to analyse media technologies both as epistemic objects and technical objects, both inside the laboratory and outside in the performance venue. It provides a useful framework for doing media archaeological experiments in an experimental system of knowledge production and dissemination, and thus for developing and refining a methodology for doing experimental media archaeology in practice, which is the purpose of this guide.

How to Use This Guide

Using two distinctly different media technologies as case studies – one visual and one auditory – we have conducted various media archaeological experiments and investigations. This helped us to develop and test the generic methodological framework presented within this guide. While each of the case studies had its own specific objectives, their general purpose was to contribute to the construction of a methodological toolkit and experimental system for doing experimental media archaeology. The aim of this book is to provide a practical guide on doing media archaeological experiments and a methodological framework for planning, organising, conducting, analysing, documenting and disseminating media archaeological experiments. It is written for academic researchers, teachers, artists, heritage specialists and everyone else interested in working with media historical artefacts in hands-on and experimental ways. The book is structured in four parts, corresponding to four central practices: the preparation, research, documentation, and dissemination of media archaeological experiments.

1) *Preparation*: how to prepare and set-up a media archaeological experiment. In this chapter we recommend an initial preparation phase, beginning with the formulation of a research question, definition of the objective(s) of the experiment and the selection of a suitable approach and research method. Further recommendations are given on how to draw inspiration from both historical and modern sources, and how to gain access to media historical objects and knowledge about them.
2) *Research*: how to conduct media archaeological experiments as forms of knowledge production and/or as an artistic research practice. This chapter looks at the various aspects of the research phase, including the inspection of objects; their testing, repair and maintenance; the experimentation itself;

and the subsequent analysis, interpretation and reflection on the media archaeological experiment. Also discussed are the recreation or substitution of past media formats; how to involve experts and the public in the experimental research practice; the investigation of sensorial perception within experiments; and the evaluation of acquired skills and performance.

3) *Documentation*: how to document a media archaeological experiment. Here we explore the practices of documenting the experiment, including different methods and tools of documentation, and how to create a documentation set-up and formulate the aims, strategies and protocols of documentation. Reflections are given on both the opportunities and challenges of documenting the media archaeological experiment and on different strategies in dealing with these.

4) *Dissemination*: how to disseminate and perform media archaeological experiments and the (tacit) knowledge produced within them. The last of our four central questions focuses on the dissemination of media archaeological experiments, discussing various modes of dissemination (on site, online, hybrid) and types of dissemination of media archaeological experiments, such as experimental reports, blog posts, video demonstrations, video essays, and – last but not least – media archaeological performances. Moreover, recommendations are given for implementing hands-on approaches in teaching practices, such as object lessons.

By exploring these four central practices, each chapter draws on practical insights from other experimental projects as well as our own hands-on experiments and experiences within the DEMA project. These examples are given throughout the following chapters to illustrate reflections and recommendations. Ultimately, we hope this practical guide will inspire scholars of historical media and communication technologies to conduct and perform their own media archaeological experiments. As such, this guide aims to contribute to the use and application of experimental media archaeology as a methodological approach in media historical research and teaching.

Chapter 1
Preparation

This chapter looks at how to prepare for and arrange or set up a media archaeological experiment. The following sections attempt to identify some basic principles, such as establishing the central research question; what is being explored, learnt or produced; the objective; and the most suitable approach for the experiment.

1.1 Defining the Research Question, Objective and Approach

1.1.1 Research Question and Objective

Before embarking on a media archaeological experiment, it is useful to establish questions about what is being tested, reconstructed, verified or explored, and establish the most suitable approach to take. This might have to do with the functioning of an object, an examination of its usage, or the skills or conditions necessary for its operation. The research question should be clear and concise. Alongside the research question is the identification and listing of all the parameters or variables that are inherent to, or that can have an effect on the experiment. Parameters may be predetermined, while variables may be dynamic or subject to constant change. For instance, if an experiment involves making a sound recording of a voice reading from a script or a performance of a set piece of music, then the parameters include the duration, the type of recording being made (through acoustic, analogue or digital means) and the specific media format. Variables that can be controlled in this example are sound input levels and other adjustments that may be made in advance to achieve a satisfactory recording using the technology at hand and to avoid distortion. Dynamic changes can occur during an experiment, and often necessitate having to make adjustments "on the fly", such as adjusting sound levels when dealing with unexpectedly loud sound sources, or camera settings in diminishing light conditions. The mastering of technical operations and the identification or discovery of parameters and variables may also form part of an experiment's objectives.

∂ Open Access. © 2023 the author(s), published by De Gruyter. [cc) BY⎯] This work is licensed under the Creative Commons Attribution 4.0 International License.
https://doi.org/10.1515/9783110799767-002

Kinora Replica Project

The objective of the Kinora replica project was to make a working replica of the Kinora motion picture system of the early 1900s and 1910s by using the latest 3D modelling and desktop manufacturing techniques. Making a *working* model enabled an examination of the functioning of the apparatus' internal mechanism. The research question was: How could the 3D replication process be used as a heuristic method to explore and better understand the design, functionality and use of the Kinora as an early twentieth-century motion picture technology? Explicating the research objective and question was helpful in determining that the goal of the project was not to produce an "authentic" copy of the original Kinora, but rather a 3D printed model that allowed for experimenting and testing various predefined parameters, including (1) the optimal distance between the lens and the image; (2) the optimal magnification of the lenses and distance between them in the viewer; (3) the optimal thickness of the paper of the Kinora image cards for smooth rotation; and (4) the optimal relation between the recorded frame rate and the viewer's speed of rotation.[19]

---

19 Tim van der Heijden and Claude Wolf, "Replicating the Kinora: 3D Modelling and Printing as Heuristics in Digital Media History," *Journal of Digital History*, no. 2 (2022), https://journal ofdigitalhistory.org/en/article/33pRxE2dtUHP [last accessed 26.07.2022].

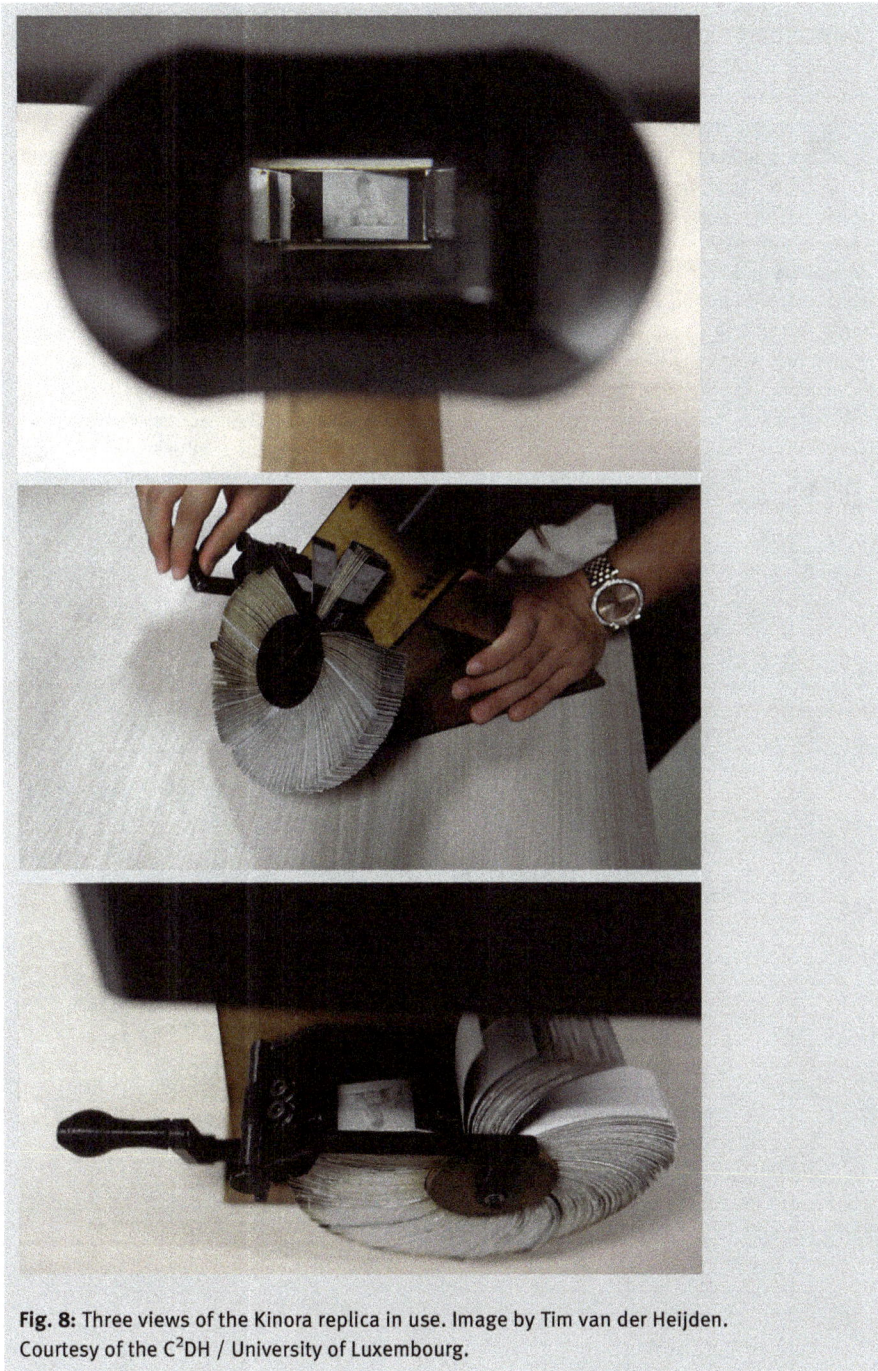

Fig. 8: Three views of the Kinora replica in use. Image by Tim van der Heijden. Courtesy of the C^{2}DH / University of Luxembourg.

HMV 2300H Portable Disc Recorder (1948)

How much skill and experience does it take to successfully "cut" a record, and can such knowledge be acquired without an instructor? The HMV 2300H portable recorder is designed for ease of use: the technical operations are simplified and there are only a few controls and switches to manage. Nevertheless, a basic knowledge of disc recording is a prerequisite, and a careful study of the operating manual is required before one can begin recording with the machine. Thereafter, the aspiring disc-recordist must learn how to master techniques and determine parameters, such as adjustments for the correct "depth of cut" of a sound groove; controlling and brushing away the threads of swarf that are removed when cutting the groove during recording; and recognising defects on a recorded disc through a visual inspection of the spiral groove using a magnifying loupe or microscope. Together, these skills involve the visual, tactile and aural senses, and the whole process of recording, from set-up to the final inspection and playback, can be seen as a pattern or choreography of actions and gestures, performed in a sequence that is learnt through constant repetition. This project saw the recordist/experimenter make numerous live direct-to-disc recordings using the HMV disc recorder in a variety of settings, while acquiring and documenting the necessary skills to achieve consistently satisfactory results.

Fig. 9: Cutting a record on the HMV 2300H Portable Disc Recorder.
Courtesy of the C^{2}DH / University of Luxembourg.

Improved Phantasmagoria Lanterns: A Series of Experiments

The objective of the media archaeological experiments performed by the *illuminago* project, founded by Karin Bienek and Ludwig Vogl-Bienek, is to explore the historical "art of projection". This term was shaped in the 1870s by trade literature on technical and aesthetic practices with projection devices called "magic lanterns".[20] The media archaeology of the art of projection explores a hybrid medium that belonged equally to the visual media and the performing arts. The surviving artefacts and written or pictorial documentations are connected through their symbiotic relationship within the performances. These examinations of media archaeological relics offer insights into contemporary variations in the use of magic lanterns and projected images since the seventeenth century, into the development of the art of projection as a mass medium in the nineteenth century, and into the cultural establishment of the "screen" within the context of live performances.[21] The research questions addressed the use of "Improved Phantasmagoria Lanterns". This type of projection device was introduced in the 1820s by the English optician Philip Carpenter (1876–1833). Apart from the current state of research on the history of the art of projection, the project's questions were based primarily on one of Carpenter's surviving sales catalogues.[22] The experiments were conducted with three surviving Improved Phantasmagoria Lanterns and with four copperplate sliders (each containing four glass slides) from the *illuminago* collection.

---

20 See, for instance, Abbé François Moigno, *L'art des projections* (Paris: Gauthier-Villars, 1872). See also Paul E. Liesegang and Franz P. Liesegang, *Die Projektions-Kunst für Schulen, Familien und öffentliche Vorstellungen: mit einer Anleitung zum Malen auf Glas und Beschreibung chemischer, magnetischer, optischer und elektrischer Experimente* (Leipzig: Liesegang, 1909); this is the 12th and last edition, but the explanations on the concept of 'Projektionskunst' (the art of projection) are also included in all known editions up to 1876. See An Expert, *The Art of Projection and Complete Magic Lantern Manual* (London: E. A. Beckett, 1893).

21 Ludwig Vogl-Bienek, "Performative Configurations of the Historical Art of Projection. A Media-Archaeological Approach to the History of the Magic Lantern and the Screen in Live Performance," *eLaterna*, 2022, http://elaterna-companion.uni-trier.de/en/sections/performance/performative-configurations-of-the-historical-art-of-projection-a-media-archaeological-approach-to-the-history-of-the-magic-lantern-and-the-screen-in-live-performance [last accessed 26.07.2022].

22 Philip Carpenter, *Elements of Zoology: Being a Concise Account of the Animal Kingdom According to the System of Linnaeus* (London: Rowland Hunter, 1823).

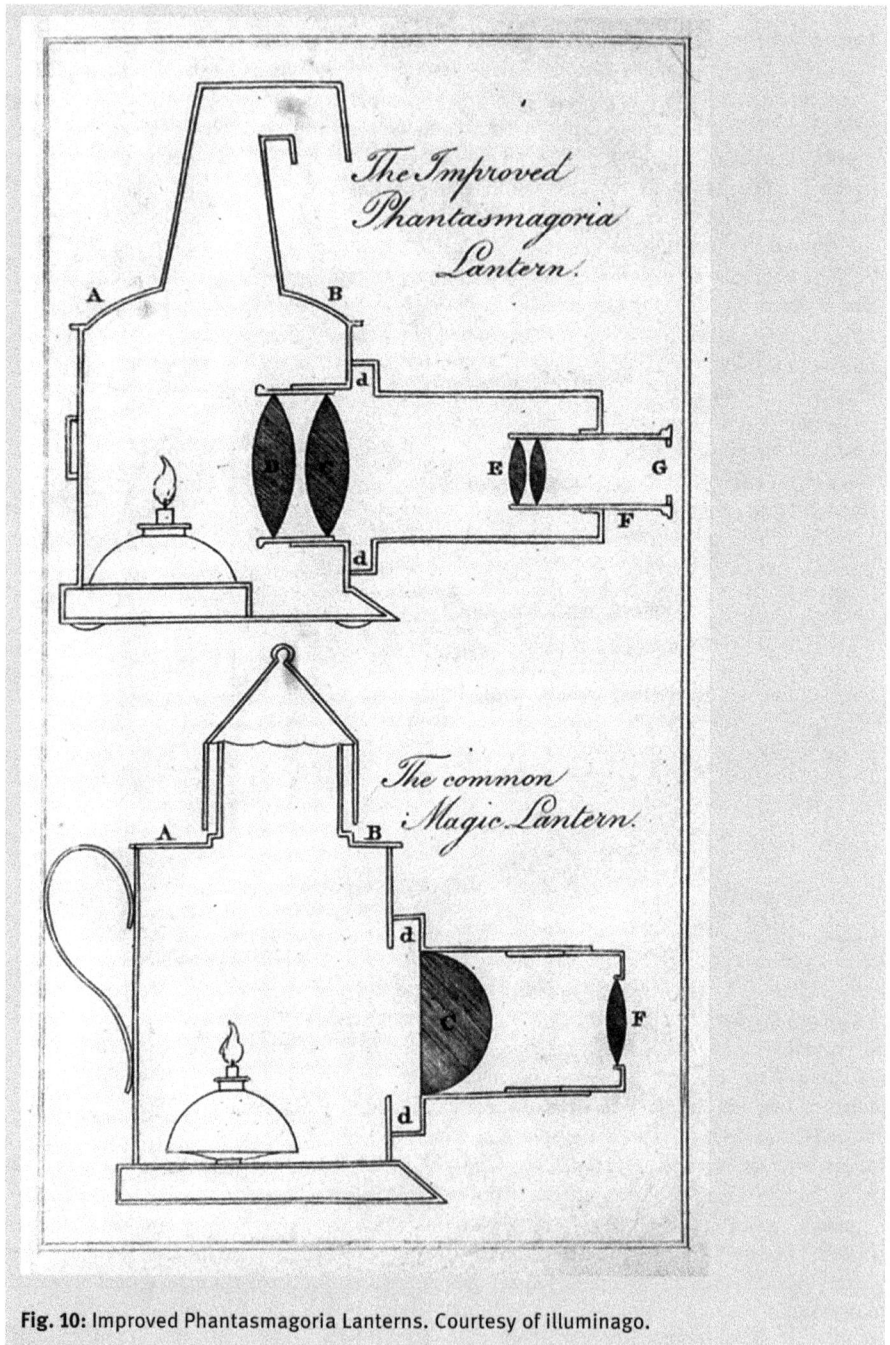

The Improved
Phantasmagoria
Lantern.

The common
Magic Lantern.

Fig. 10: Improved Phantasmagoria Lanterns. Courtesy of illuminago.

1.1.2 Approach: Deductive Versus Inductive

Besides formulating a clear and concise research question, one should define the approach taken in the media archaeological experiment. Settling upon an approach for a media archaeological experiment depends on how theory and practice inform each other. In general, we can distinguish between deductive, inductive and integrative approaches.

Deductive Approach (top-down)

A deductive or top-down approach lets an experiment be guided by theory; questions and objectives are formulated in advance. Historical sources, literature and user manuals are studied prior to the experiment and questions that arise on studying these sources will inform the hands-on experimentation. Here, the approach sets the objective of the experiment and serves to explicate certain dimensions of past media technologies and/or their usages, whether they be technological, sensorial, social or performative.

The HMV 2300H Portable Disc Recorder

In this project, the apparatus was acquired complete with a detailed user's manual, full service records, service sheets and instructions for making up-to-date technical modifications. Although the experimenter had prior knowledge and skill in analogue disc recording, operation of the apparatus required an understanding of the controls and functions particular to this device, which were gained by studying the accompanying documentation in advance of any hands-on experimentation. The investigation of tacit knowledge in this case, was guided by references to written sources (manual, service notes) and by positioning the HMV 2300H in the context of contemporaneous or earlier portable disc recording devices, through a study of technical features and affordances.

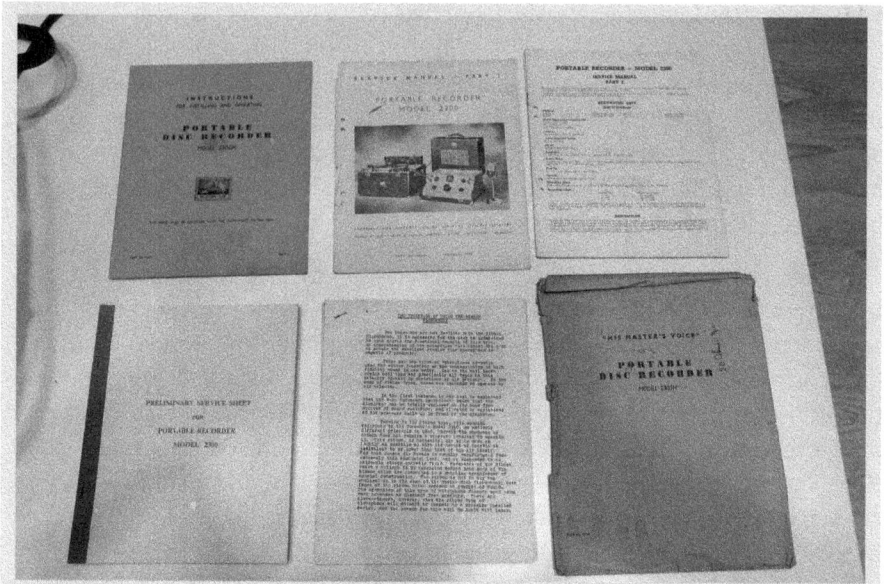

Fig. 11: Some of the accompanying HMV 2300H paper documentation.
Courtesy of the C^{2}DH / University of Luxembourg.

Inductive Approach (bottom-up)

An inductive or bottom-up approach lets the experiment be guided by practice, exploratory experimentation and sensorial "thinkering". Here the experiment may be started from scratch and questions that arise from the hands-on experimentation will elicit further examination of historical sources and literature. Such an approach may not be considered "scientific", since it forgoes scientific procedures and planned objectives and is, by its nature, improvisatory. However, it is experimental in the broader sense of being an "action [that] is done in order to see what it is like, or what effect it has".[23]

Cartavox Sound Postcard Recorder

The Cartavox machine was acquired with no documentation, user manual or instructions and no recordable media. Very little background information on the device existed. Here, using an approach not dissimilar to that of ethnographic or sociological fieldwork, the experimenter had to learn by observing the electro-mechanical workings and physically operating the device

---

23 Collins English Dictionary, "Definition of 'Experimental'," 29 June 2022, https://www.collinsdictionary.com/dictionary/english/experimental [last accessed 26.07.2022].

and making adjustments purely through trial and error. The technical affordance of the Carta-vox recorder was discovered only through practical experimentation. Additionally, it was necessary to recreate the recordable sound postcard media for this project (see Chapter 2.5.1).

Film Archive and Media Archaeology Lab, University of Groningen

The Film Archive and Media Archaeology Lab of the University of Groningen hosts a collection of film historical apparatuses to which film students are introduced during the first year of their studies. Annie van den Oever, director of the Film Archive and Media Archaeology Lab, explains how the bottom-up hands-on exploration directly triggers a sensorial relationship with the film historical objects and their historical usages: "After a tour through the archive, we present a series of devices to students as part of their introduction to film and media studies. They are invited to touch, operate, and 'play' with some of the historical devices in the archive, a magic lantern, lantern slides, a Zeiss Ikon 35 mm projector, an anamorphic lens, a replica of a 19th-century stereoscope, and a series of optical toys [. . .] It should be stressed here that most of the actions by the students in this specific introductory class are not framed for them to experience the technology's proper place in history or to learn how to operate it in terms of former use. Students are simply invited to touch, smell, hear, look, experience, and play with the device . . . " (▶Theory, Chapter 2.6). The archive serves as a good example of the pedagogical value of a bottom-up approach to experimental media archaeology. (See also Chapter 4.3 in the present volume.)

Integrative Approach (mix)

In practice, an integrative approach, one that combines the deductive with more improvisatory, inductive ways of working, will often provide the most satisfying results. Broad questions can be useful as a starting point, but when other factors come into play within the experimental process, it becomes possible to reshape the research question or approach. Research, including hands-on experimentation, is an iterative process where the research questions and other factors along with practical issues may change during the course of the experiment. New insights or problems may emerge that lead to the adoption of new approaches. Sometimes, where some research into the usage of an apparatus takes place but no specific user manual exists for the operation of a particular device, one discovers as much as one can through practical experimentation. Prior research can offer insights into differences, special features or limitations of the device being experimented upon. Where a lot of information already exists on how to operate a device, one can also choose to ignore this completely so that the experimentation becomes a process of discovery. However, this could lead to accidental damage of the object and is better done under the supervision of an experienced or expert user.

Replicating Auxetophone Soundbox for Gramophone

Prior to the replication project, considerable research had been undertaken by the experimenter on the Auxetophone-Gramophone. The technical workings and history background were studied through an examination of patents, historical sources and the examination of surviving examples in museum collections. However, only limited practical work had been done with a historical prototype version of the Auxetophone soundbox prior to the DEMA project. Through hands-on experimentation, it was possible to recover and reveal the tacit knowledge required to successfully adjust the valved soundboxes to attain the desired amplitude of sound with a minimum of distortion and fullness of range. Different types of air compressor were tried and tested to determine the correct degree of air pressure and air flow for the sound amplification, and the performance of original and replica models were compared and analysed along with their components and materials.

1.2 Selecting the Research Method, Type of Experiment and Location

Once the research questions, objectives and approach have been established, the next step is to choose the research method, type of experiment and location where the experiment takes place.

1.2.1 Research Method

Within the framework of experimental media archaeology, we can distinguish between various methods and types of experimentation, including thinkering, simulation, re-enactment, replication, and creative or artistic research practice. Each of these research methods has different purposes, varying from playful and creative explorations to reconstructions of methodological procedures and practices of use.

1) Thinkering

"Thinkering", a term coined by media archaeologist and collector Erkki Huhtamo, can be defined as a method of playful exploration that focuses on the materiality of past media technologies.[24] While it aims to recreate the experience of their practices of use, thinkering also explores the objects as they are in themselves. As a

---

24 Erkki Huhtamo, "Thinkering with Media: On the Art of Paul DeMarinis," in *Paul DeMarinis: Buried in Noise*, ed. Ingrid Beirer, Sabine Himmelsbach, and Carsten Seiffairth (Heidelberg and Berlin: Kehrer Verlag, 2010), 33–46.

research method, thinkering is a heuristic approach that is closely related to artistic research and also encompasses the creative reuse of past media technologies (▶ Theory, Chapters 2.6 and 5.2). Thinkering is, moreover, valuable as an approach in teaching experimental media archaeology (see Chapter 4.3). Huhtamo has emphasised the importance of "thinkering" with media historical objects while showing how media archaeology may be practised through the objects themselves. An example from Huhtamo's thinkering research is his work with the Spirograph, a rare moving picture technology from the early 1900s, which utilised spinning discs onto which micro-photographs are arranged in a spiral. Although the Spirograph was meant as a radical departure from existing forms of moving picture technologies at the time, Huhtamo posits it as an example of a "failed moving picture revolution".[25] Devices like the Spirograph are interesting for doing media archaeological experiments, but they also have their limitations. First, researching a device in this way can be very work intensive (Huhtamo's study of the Spirograph took almost ten years). Second, the "hardware" (i.e., the device's housing and internal mechanism) can be very fragile, and the "software" that the device once used (i.e., the spiral disc medium in the case of the Spirograph) can have deteriorated or no longer be accessible. The only way to research and demonstrate the device, Huhtamo argues, is to disassemble and reassemble it – literally opening up the "black box". Such a hands-on approach is crucial for getting a better understanding of how a device works, and even how it may have worked in the past.[26]

Thinkering with the Ciné-Kodak 16mm and 8mm Film Cameras

The method of thinkering was used in the hands-on experiments with various small-gauge technologies, including a Ciné-Kodak 16mm film camera (model K) from ca. 1930 and a Ciné-Kodak Eight 8mm film camera (model 25) from ca. 1934. The small-gauge experiments, conducted both indoors and outdoors, aimed to historically re-enact the recording practices associated with these original home movie technologies. Among others, this brought forward all kinds of practical questions about how, for instance, to insert the film in the camera, how to set the focus, how to measure the light, and how to manually control the exposure. The thinkering method enabled the experience of some of the cameras' affordances and constraints, including the functioning of the spring-motor mechanism, the viewfinder and the associated "parallax effect" (difference between what the filmmaker sees through the viewfinder and what is actually captured through the camera's lens), as well as the particular sounds the cameras make during the recording processes. The small-gauge experiments furthermore explicated the camera's size and weight, and clarified in what ways this matters for the recording practices.

---

25 Erkki Huhtamo, "The Dream of Personal Interactive Media: A Media Archaeology of the Spirograph, a Failed Moving Picture Revolution," *Early Popular Visual Culture* 11, no. 4 (November 2013): 365–408, https://doi.org/10.1080/17460654.2013.840247.

26 Van der Heijden and Kolkowski, "Documenting Media Archaeological Experiments."

Fig. 12: Ciné-Kodak 16mm film camera in use. Still from film developed and scanned by Onno Petersen and reproduced by Tim van der Heijden. Courtesy of the C²DH / University of Luxembourg.

Wilcox-Gay 1C10 Recordio Tape and Disc Recorder "Signal-to-Noise"

This hybrid magnetic tape and disc recording device from 1951 was used in a re-interpretation of Alvin Lucier's seminal electro-acoustic composition "I am Sitting in a Room" (1969), in which a narrating voice is recorded onto tape and played back into the room. The recording is re-recorded repeatedly until the natural acoustic resonances of the room are so reinforced that they overwhelm the speech. In "Signal-to-Noise", however, the speech is recorded onto tape, transferred onto a lacquer disc and back again to tape, all done on the same machine. This cycle is repeated until the voice becomes subsumed and buried under layer upon layer of tape hiss, resonances from the tape heads and surface noises from the disc. Here, the room resonance from Lucier's piece is replaced by the noise produced by media format conversion and generation loss from the repeated transfers.

"Signal-to-Noise" exploits the obsolete recording technology of the Wilcox-Gay Recordio to create a contemporary noise composition that refers not only to Lucier, but also to the works of John Cage, Edgard Varèse and *musique concrète*. At the same time, it is a playful media-archaeological exploration or "thinkering" experiment, which delves into the usage and functions of this historical audio technology, highlighting its hybridity and the noises inherent to tape and disc media technologies.[27]

---

27 Kolkowski and Van der Heijden, "Performing Media Archaeological Experiments."

Thinkering at the Media Archaeology Lab (MAL), University of Colorado, Boulder
The Media Archaeology Lab (MAL) of the University of Colorado, Boulder, founded by media archaeologist Lori Emerson, provides access to thousands of items of still functioning media technologies, ranging from the late nineteenth century until the late twentieth century. Visitors to the MAL are encouraged to actively tinker and experiment with the historical media objects. Besides researchers and students, the MAL also works with artist residencies to emphasise the point that the objects are meant to be used. In that sense, it functions not like a museum, in which the objects are often behind glass, but more like an "anti-museum". Currently, twelve volunteers and four PhD students are working for the MAL.[28]

2) Simulation

Simulation involves a systematic reconstruction that focuses on simulating the user-object relationship and foregrounding the tacit knowledge involved.[29] This is achieved by working with actual practitioners/experts, be they active or retired. A working simulation can additionally serve as a form of oral history methodology – as exemplified by John Ellis' ADAPT project on analogue television production practices, and Roger Kneebone's simulation-based re-enactments of keyhole surgery practices.

The ADAPT Project: A Hands-On Approach to Analogue Television Production
The ADAPT project, led by television historian John Ellis, explored the history of analogue television production by means of a hands-on approach. Between 2013 and 2018, the project team carried out a series of historical "simulations", in which they reunited retired BBC television producers with now obsolete television production equipment, including flatbed editing tables and electronic broadcast cameras. The project aimed to document these simulations through numerous multicam video demonstrations (over 260 videos were produced in total, covering 12 hours of footage), as well as to reflect on doing hands-on media history as a methodological approach.[30]

---

28 For more information about the Media Archaeology Lab, see https://www.mediaarchaeolo gylab.com/ [last accessed 26.07.2022].
29 Multiple users can be involved in this user-object relationship, both on the side of media production (e.g., a projectionist or broadcaster) and media consumption (e.g., a spectator or listener).
30 For more information on the ADAPT project, see https://www.adapttvhistory.org.uk/ [last accessed 26.07.2022]. See further Hall and Ellis, *Hands on Media History*.

Documenting the Early Days of Keyhole Surgery through Simulation-Based Re-enactment

In his project on historical keyhole surgery practices, Professor of Surgical Education Roger Kneebone reunited a distinguished team of (retired) professionals to re-enact a surgical procedure, performed in public at the London Science Museum. Using physical simulation, they aimed to get a sense of and insight into the landscape of surgery of the kind Kneebone himself experienced as a junior surgeon, and of the instruments used. Kneebone's project combined the methodology of historical re-enactment with "the use of simulation within present-day surgical education".[31]

3) Re-enactment

Re-enactments aim to play on the historical imagination of the practitioners and their audiences. When applied to events " . . . which no longer fall within living memory, [they offer] a means of engaging the public with their pasts".[32] Unlike the method of simulation, no surviving practitioners usually take part in re-enactments. As far as possible, a re-enactment aims to recreate historical practices, and examines the workings and outcomes of the technological object in action. The term "historical re-enactment" was used by historian and philosopher R. G. Collingwood in his seminal study *The Idea of History* (1946), in which he wrote about the practice of historiography as an "activity of thought".[33] In line with Fickers and Van den Oever's framework, we expand on Collingwood's idea of experiencing history by doing media archaeological experiments not only as an activity of thought, but by means of actual *hands-on* re-enactments. As a hands-on activity, re-enactment can consequently relive the historical experience and stimulate a "dialogue with the past".[34]

---

31 Roger Kneebone and Abigail Woods, "Recapturing the History of Surgical Practice Through Simulation-Based Re-enactment," *Medical History* 58, no. 1 (January 2014): 111, https://doi. org/10.1017/mdh.2013.75.

32 Kneebone and Woods, "Recapturing the History of Surgical Practice," 111. See also Nick Hall, "Bringing the Living Back to Life: What Happens When We Reenact the Recent Past?" in *Hands on Media History: A New Methodology in the Humanities and Social Sciences*, ed. Nick Hall and John Ellis (London: Routledge, 2019), 26–42.

33 R. G. Collingwood, *The Idea of History* (Oxford: Oxford University Press, 1946), 218. See ▶ Theory, Chapter 1.1.

34 In their presentation at the DEMA workshop 2020, Stefan Höltgen and Shantiro Miyazaki argued that, when repairing a broken computer, you build a dialogue between yourself and the object, which gives you insights for both historical and contemporary media. The hands-on approach offers a playful kind of learning, which is not based on learning from theory but rather from practice. See Kolkowski and Van der Heijden, "Performing Media Archaeological Experiments."

The Art and Science of Acoustic Recording: Re-enacting Arthur Nikisch and the Berlin Philharmonic Orchestra's Landmark 1913 Recording of Beethoven's Fifth Symphony

This collaborative project involved musicians, researchers, historical recording experts and sound engineers. It used replicated recording technology, media and techniques of the early twentieth century to record a Beethoven symphony onto wax discs. The aims were primarily to investigate the processes and practices of the acoustic sound-recording studio. Surviving documents, photographs and first-hand accounts relating to acoustic studio practices tell us little about the precise methods of recording, which were shrouded in secrecy and had largely been developed through tacit knowledge. The recording studio technicians (known as "experts") had also made or designed much of their own equipment and developed recording techniques that were guarded as trade secrets from competitors. In keeping with historical practices, the project used a newly constructed acoustic recording machine and recreated a formula for the recording wax. Furthermore, the project sought to gain insights into the musicians' experience of recording acoustically.[35]

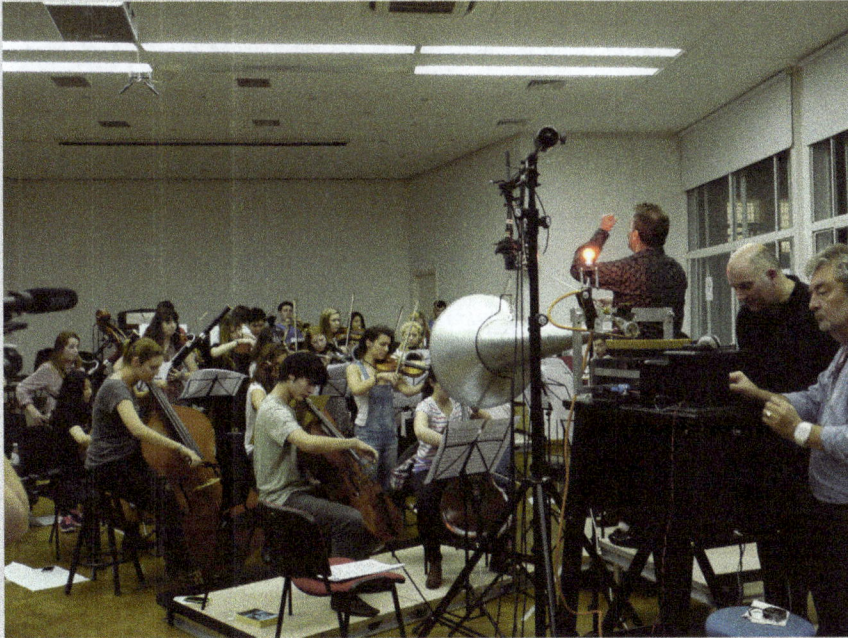

Fig. 13: Re-enactment of an orchestral acoustic recording on a wax disc. Courtesy of Amy Blier-Carruthers.

---

35 Kolkowski, Miller, and Blier-Carruthers, "The Art and Science of Acoustic Recording."

Re-enacting a Dummy Head (Kunstkopf) Recording

The research project "Failure and Success of Dummy Head Recording: An Innovation History of 3D Listening", led by historian of technology Stefan Krebs, used historical re-enactment as a methodology to investigate the history of Kunstkopf-stereophony and why this innovative binaural recording technology of the 1970s (also known as the Dummy Head) did not become the new standard of audio production and listening. The radio play "Glanz und Elend der Kunstkopf-Stereophonie" is a historical re-enactment and reflexive performance, in which Krebs, together with actor Hans Peter Hallwachs, journalist Stephan Wufbaum and media historian Andreas Fickers, made use of an original Dummy Head to re-enact and reflect on the history of this fascinating binaural recording technology.[36]

illuminago's Magic Lantern Performances

For their media archaeological experiments, Karin Bienek and Ludwig Vogl-Bienek have drawn from long experience in performing historically informed magic lantern shows under the title of *illuminago*. Formed in 1986, the duo has performed internationally, presenting historical re-enactments of lantern shows that vary from adaptations of Richard Wagner's opera cycle *Der Ring des Nibelungen* (1876), to the "lantern lectures" of Armin T. Wegner (1919). Their experimental re-enactments and creative re-use of magic lanterns and slides often involve musicians, actors, and other performers. For *illuminago*, the aforementioned concepts cannot be applied separately; every re-enactment entails some measure of creative re-use, just as every creative re-use automatically involves some form of re-enactment. Their productions also show various ways in which the results of media archaeological experiments can be incorporated into today's cultural productions.[37]

4) Replication

Where a historical object may not be used or is unavailable, it may be substituted with a replica. The construction of a working replica can serve as a heuristic method: it provides insights into the materiality of the object and a fuller understanding of its design and functions. The Kinora viewer and the Stentorphone soundbox, for example, were replicated and their functionality simulated. Our historical inquiry within DEMA combined a hands-on and technical approach, involving the latest 3D modelling and desktop manufacturing engineering

---

36 Stefan Krebs, "'Glanz und Elend der Kunstkopf-Stereophonie'. Eine technik- und medienarchäologische Ausgrabung," in *Jeux sans Frontières? – Grenzgänge der Geschichtswissenschaft*, ed. Andreas Fickers et al. (Bielefeld: Transcript, 2017), 57–69, https://doi.org/10.14361/9783839441053. See further https://binauralrecording.wordpress.com/ [last accessed 26.07.2022] and https://www.c2dh.uni.lu/data/glanz-und-elend-der-kunstkopf-stereophonie [last accessed 26.07.2022].

37 For more information on the *illuminago* project, see https://linktr.ee/illuminago [last accessed 26.07.2022].

techniques. The aim of the Kinora replica project was to use 3D replication as a heuristic method to better understand how the Kinora worked and was used in the past as a historical motion picture mechanism.[38] With the Stentorphone and Auxetophone soundbox replicas, the heuristic inquiry was complemented by technical analyses of sound spectra, airflow, dynamic range, and the precise determination of material properties under high air pressure.

3D Replica Lumière Cinématographe
In 2015–2016, the Film Archive and Media Archaeology Lab of the University of Groningen, led by film scholar Annie van den Oever, initiated a project which aimed to produce a 3D replica of the Lumière Cinématographe. The 3D model replicated the basic mechanical elements and appearance of the original historical object, so that it could be used for hands-on study purposes in a classroom setting.[39]

5) Creative or Artistic Research Practice

Creative experimentation and artistic research are effective means of exploring the affordances of the media historical object and testing the perceived limitations of its performative qualities. The object is used in ways not intended or imagined by its inventors or during its lifetime: it may be partly or entirely redesigned using new materials, combined with other technologies, old or new, repurposed, or brought to life in unusual and imaginative ways.

Artists have ploughed the furrow of media archaeology for as long as the field has existed in literature or academia. As with its literary counterpart, the origins of media-archaeological art reach back to the first half of the twentieth century, to be found in the work of artists such as Marcel Duchamp, Max Ernst, Francis Picabia and others.[40] In more recent times, the oeuvres of Paul DeMarinis, Toshio Iwai, Lynn Hershmann Leeson and Martin Riches in particular, have inspired and informed the writings and research of media archaeologist Erkki Huhtamo, who has himself curated numerous international exhibitions of

---

38 We discuss some of the affordances and limitations of 3D replication as a methodological approach in Chapter 2.3.2. See also Van der Heijden and Wolf, "Replicating the Kinora."
39 Annie van den Oever, André Rosendaal, and Bernd Warnders, "Media Heritage – Final Report," 2010, https://www.researchgate.net/publication/331283592_Media_Heritage_-_Final_Report [last accessed 26.07.2022]. For the Lumière Cinématographe 3D model, see https://sketchfab.com/3d-models/cinematograph-8df1355e552041ada0223acb696abc95 [last accessed 26.07.2022].
40 Erkki Huhtamo, "Art in the Rear-View Mirror: The Media-Archaeological Tradition in Art," in *A Companion to Digital Art*, ed. Christiane Paul (Chichester, West Sussex: Wiley, 2016), 71, https://doi.org/10.1002/9781118475249.ch3.

media art. He argues that such work can "suggest radically different ways of conceiving media history".[41]

The multitude of artistic approaches to media archaeology make it nigh on impossible to classify as a coherent genre, and a guide to making media-historical art would be a narrow and futile conception of creativity.[42] Instead, the examples given in this volume serve to illustrate ways in which creative research by artists may complement media archaeological experiments and open the mind of the experimenter to new approaches and practices. For the purposes of this guide, artistic research that is deemed to be "experimental media archaeological" will always refer to the original historical sources that serve as the inspiration or *raison d'etre* for the artistic work, whether the references are made explicit or remain hidden.

Paul DeMarinis "The Edison Effect" (1989–1996)

"The Edison Effect" is an audio-visual installation comprising up to thirteen individual, interactive and self-contained works that DeMarinis calls "sculptures". Laser beams are used to reproduce the sounds contained in aged disc and cylinder records, or newly engraved ceramic cylinders and dinner plates overlaid with spiralling optical soundtracks. The records are played back using light instead of a physical stylus and the media objects become holographic. DeMarinis writes that "Each *Edison Effect* player is a meditation on some aspect or the relations among music, memory and the passage of time. Our sense of time, memory and belonging have all been changed by the exact repetition implicit in mechanical recording."[43] This "meditation" on the meanings of media technology is by its nature discursive: "The dense discursive veil that surrounds the work becomes part of its signification. Eras, technologies, and the relationship between sound and visual media [. . .] are brought together while the work itself bridges gramophony, lasers, and holography."[44]

Martin Riches "Serinette" (2003)

In his "exploded" version of the serinette, an eighteenth-century music player used to train or entice captive songbirds to sing, the artist and machine builder Martin Riches chose to radically reinterpret the design of the instrument. His construction was based on extensive research of the serinette and retained essential elements of the original, including bellows and pipes, and the mechanical method of its sound reproduction. Like the original, Riches' serinette is hand-cranked and the only one of his music machines not to use electricity. This

---

41 Huhtamo, "Art in the Rear-View Mirror," 89. See also ▶ Theory, Chapter 5.2.

42 See Jussi Parikka, *What Is Media Archaeology?* (Cambridge, UK; Malden, MA: Polity Press, 2012), 136–158.

43 Paul DeMarinis, "Installations 1973–2010," in *Paul DeMarinis: Buried in Noise*, ed. Ingrid Beirer, Sabine Himmelsbach, and Carsten Seiffairth (Heidelberg, Berlin: Kehrer Verlag, 2010), 172.

44 Huhtamo, "Art in the Rear-View Mirror," 94.

instrument was created for the composition and performance of *Mechanical Landscape with Bird* (2003), by Aleksander Kolkowski, in which the serinette was combined with live singing canaries, a Stroh (horned) string quartet and Edison phonographs.[45]

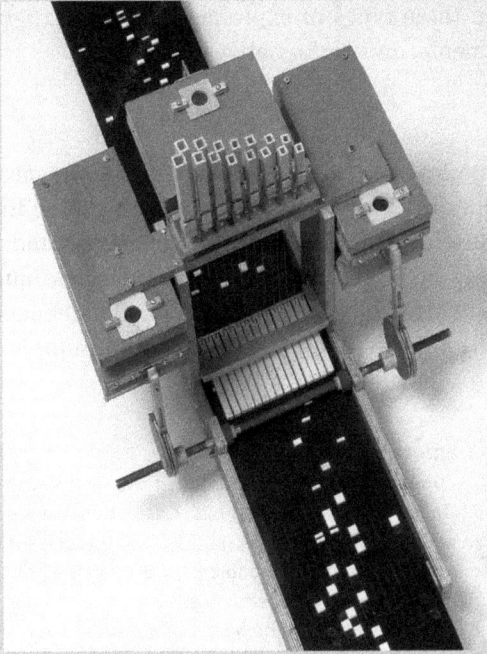

Fig. 14: Martin Riches' Serinette. Courtesy of Roman März.

Dawn Scarfe "Listening Glasses" (2008)

For her "Listening Glasses" installation, the sound artist Dawn Scarfe created glass sculptures modelled on the hollow spherical resonators developed by Herman von Helmholtz in the 1850s. The Helmholtz resonators were scientific instruments used to detect and identify specific frequencies from a sound source in laboratory experiments in acoustics, such as the specific partial tones of a musical instrument. Drawing on Helmholtz's writings on using the resonators to hear tones in the wind or in the rattling of carriage wheels on the road, Scarfe invites people to listen through them to the surrounding environment. The glass instruments filter the noise of traffic or sounds from within a room, directing the listener to hear in a new way.[46]

---

45 For more information, see https://martinriches.de [last accessed 26.07.2022].
46 Lutz Koepnick, *Resonant Matter Sound, Art, and the Promise of Hospitality* (London: Bloomsbury Academic, 2021), 122–126.

1.2.2 Type of Experiment

Besides thinking about the type of research method, one may think about what type of media archaeological experiment to pursue or embark on. In the DEMA project, we distinguished between three types of experiments: basic experiments, media-technological experiments, and performative experiments.

1) Basic Experiments

Basic experiments study media historical objects as epistemic objects. By measuring, for example, luminosity, loudness, dynamic range, they examine the technical conditions of surviving artefacts and the physical conditions under which they can or must operate (e.g., the brightness/darkness or noisiness/quietness of the environment). They will also identify restrictions for experiments, such as safety, conservation, missing parts, and test suitable substitutes for lost or unusable components.

Testing the Ciné-Kodak 8mm Film Camera

In this basic experiment, the technical functions and recording abilities of the Ciné-Kodak Eight 8mm film camera were tested in both indoor and outdoor settings. Characteristic for a standard 8mm film camera is that the film spool needs to be reversed half-way through the recording process. The 8mm film, also known as "regular 8" or "double 8", works on the principle that a 25-foot roll of special 16mm film is exposed in two parts: "Each picture or 'frame' exposed in the Ciné-Kodak Eight is only half the width and half the height of a standard frame of 16mm film. After the 25 feet of film is run through the camera, the spools must be reversed and the other half of the film should be exposed".[47] The Ciné-Kodak Eight is a spring-motor driven camera, which means that the spring motor is wound up manually to be able to make a recording. The camera's "fixed-focus" indicates that the focus of the lens cannot be changed, as with variable-focus (turret) cameras or post-war film cameras with zoom-lenses. With the fixed-focus lens, the picture will be sharp from a certain distance, defined by the size of the diaphragm opening. The Ciné-Kodak Eight, model 25, 8mm film camera has diaphragm openings ranging from f/2.7 (largest opening) with subjects in focus from a distance of seven feet, to f/16 (smallest opening) with subjects in focus from two feet.[48] In the experiment, a yellow filter that came as an accessory with the 8mm film camera was used.

---

47 Eastman Kodak Company, "Instructions for Use of the Ciné-Kodak Eight, Models 20 and 25," 1934, 2, https://www.browniecam.com/brownie_user_manuals/cine-kodak-20-25.pdf [last accessed 26.07.2022]. See also Alan Kattelle, *Home Movies: A History of the American Industry, 1897–1979* (Nashua, NH: Transition Pub., 2000), 95.
48 See the exposure table in the camera manual: Eastman Kodak Company, "Instructions for Use of the Ciné-Kodak Eight, Models 20 and 25," 15.

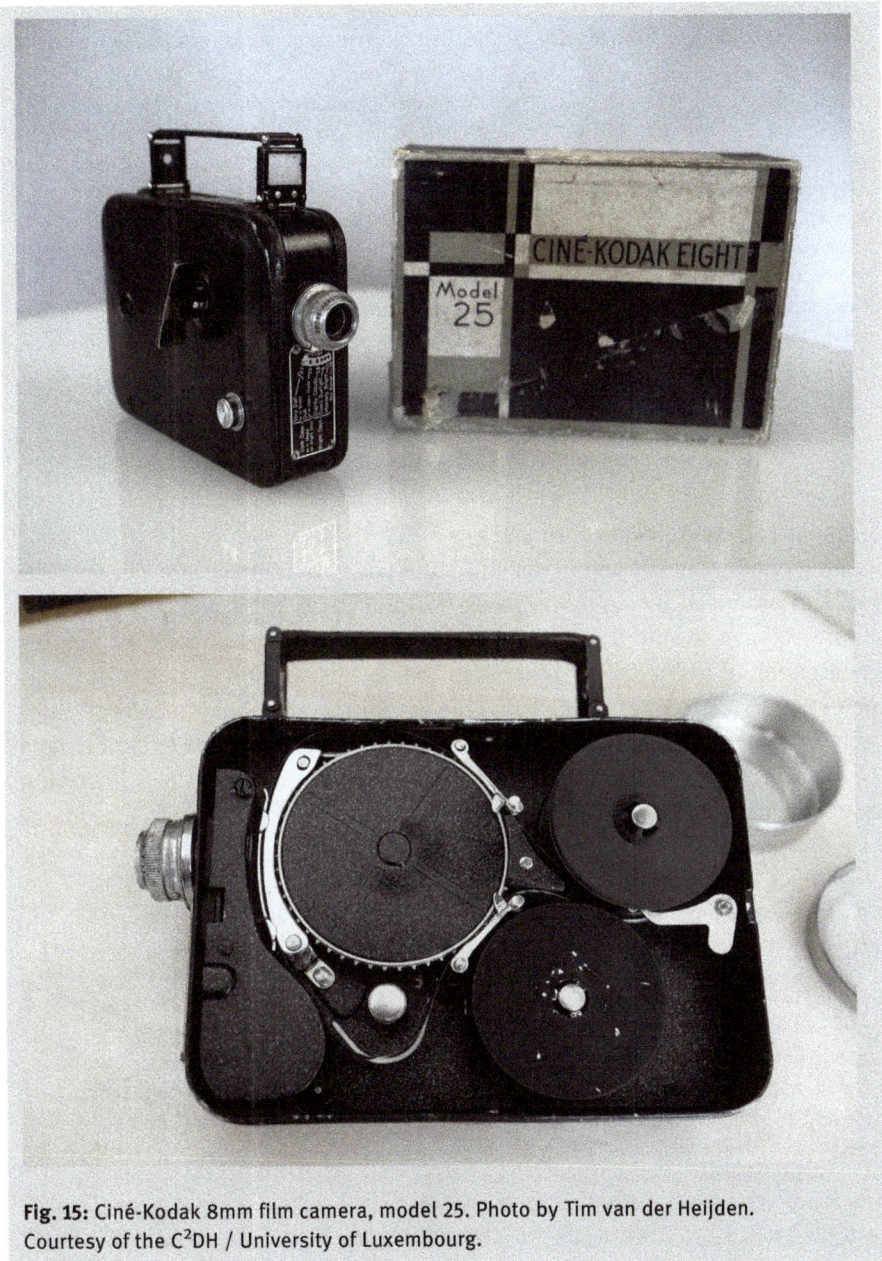

Fig. 15: Ciné-Kodak 8mm film camera, model 25. Photo by Tim van der Heijden. Courtesy of the C^{2}DH / University of Luxembourg.

Stentorphone Replica Model Soundbox – Spectral Analysis of Tests on a Gramophone

In this experiment, scientific comparisons were made between a prototype replica model of the pneumatically-driven Stentorphone soundbox and two different types of conventional gramophone soundboxes – an HMV "Exhibition" soundbox with a flat mica diaphragm, ca. 1914, contemporary with the Stentorphone, and an HMV "5A" with a louder domed aluminium diaphragm, ca. 1929. The three soundboxes were interchanged on a gramophone and each was recorded playing the same record using a measurement microphone. Through the use of audio analysis software, the frequency spectra, dynamic range and loudness of each soundbox could then be measured and assessed. Although the replica Stentorphone was an early-stage work in progress, it nevertheless performed well enough to compare favourably in its sound reproduction with both the conventional soundboxes in relation to loudness (although significantly under-driven in terms of air pressure), and it outperformed them in the reproduction of the lower frequencies.

2) Media-Technological Experiments

Media-technological experiments study the user-friendliness and the aesthetic qualities produced by surviving media-technological artefacts, such as historical projection and sound reproduction apparatuses. They allow the exploratory examination of technical affordances of the objects and, thereby, the necessary tacit knowledge to operate/manipulate such apparatuses. Failures and unexpected problems are an important part of media-technological experiments as they can produce "creative uncertainties" that are at the heart of "thinkering" as an experimental mode of knowledge production.

Making a Title Animation with the Ciné-Kodak Eight Camera and Titler

In a media-technological experiment with the Ciné-Kodak Eight 8mm film camera, model 25, the techniques of making a title animation were explored. In preparation for the experiment, the camera's instruction manual was studied in combination with a dedicated booklet containing instructions for making titles with the Ciné-Kodak Titler.[49] The titler came with a transparent frame that could be positioned in the card holder of the titler. When making the titles, the loaded film camera needs to be attached to the titler by means of a screw in the assigned place. The instructions recommend positioning the titler in such a way that "the title should be facing a window towards an unobstructed area of sky",[50] so enough daylight will fall on the card. Alternatively, artificial light can be used, which requires the use of an electric bulb. For this experiment the daylight option was chosen. After setting the right aperture and focus, the title animation can be made. For this, a blank card was used; for each recording a new character was added. Unfortunately, the Ciné-Kodak Eight camera did not allow for making single

---

49 Eastman Kodak Company, "Making Titles with the Ciné-Kodak Titler," n.d.
50 Eastman Kodak Company, "Making Titles with the Ciné-Kodak Titler," 7.

frame recordings, so only very short takes of less than a second each were taken. Although the result was a relatively slowly progressing title, the animation effect worked as intended.

Fig. 16: Ciné-Kodak Titler and title card. Image by Tim van der Heijden.
Courtesy of the C²DH / University of Luxembourg.

His Master's Vintage Voice: Experiments in Instantaneous Disc-Recording

This was a public hands-on workshop and demonstration of direct-to-disc recording on lacquer discs using the HMV 2300H portable disc recorder (1948). The workshop was supervised by Sean Davies, an internationally renowned studio engineer and authority on disc-cutting, mastering and disc-recording lathes.[51] Participants were given the opportunity to cut their own one-of-a-kind records, and the tacit knowledge of disc recording was discussed and explored. The workshop offered an opportunity to test the affordances of the newly restored disc recorder by making a variety of live recordings that included speech, recitation for both a capella and accompanied singing, a concertina solo, and an improvised crowd scene. Moreover,

---

51 For more information, see https://dema.uni.lu/his-masters-vintage-voice-experiments-in-instantaneous-disc-recording/ [last accessed 26.07.2022].

a mobile phone and a laptop were connected to the archaic recording apparatus and digital sound files cut onto disc, thus exploring the interface between digital and analogue media.

The disc recorder had been acquired with a large quantity of blank lacquer discs, originally supplied by the EMI company who manufactured the disc recorder, and also dating from 1948. These historical discs were used in the workshop to make test recordings, after gentle heating with a hair dryer to soften the lacquer surface, which had become hardened after many decades left in storage. Results with these discs were surprisingly good, given their age. The additional noises heard on playback from the surface imperfections, caused by ageing and environmental conditions, drew attention to the materiality of the medium itself, while imbuing the listening experience with a patina of nostalgia. Modern lacquer discs were also used and, as these produced less surface noise, listening attention could focus more on the quality of the recording and the capability and limitations of the recording apparatus.

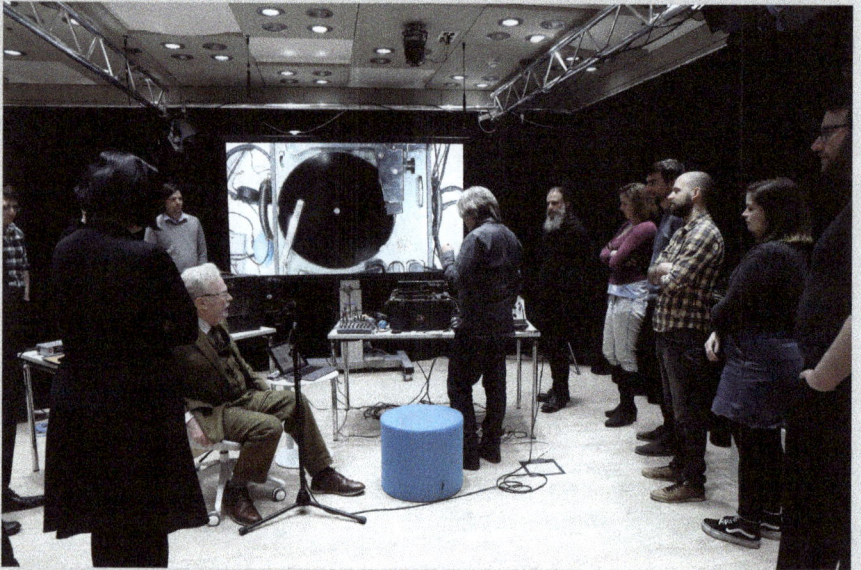

Fig. 17: His Master's Vintage Voice, Disc-Recording Workshop (Sean Davis seated). Courtesy of the C²DH / University of Luxembourg.

3) Performative Experiments

Performative experiments examine historical media performances through historical re-enactments, public presentations and demonstrations. Here the focus is on the interaction between the object, user, location and a modern audience or participants. The performance or live action, in its entirety, becomes the epistemic object under scrutiny.

Cartavox: Self-Recordable Sound Postcards
In the autumn of 2000, visitors and special invitees to the Temporary History Lab in Esch-sur
-Alzette made voice recordings directly onto bespoke sound postcards in a live simulation of a
short-lived personal voice-messaging system from the mid-twentieth century. This event took
into account the entire *dispositif* of recording, playback, public interaction and response, together with a multimodal analysis that included assessments of sensory perception and attention and an evaluation of human skill (see Chapters 2.6 and 2.7).

1.2.3 Choosing an Experimental Setting

Experiments will normally take place either under the controlled conditions of
a laboratory or workshop, or are conducted "in the field" where conditions are
more true to life. In scientific experiments, working in a lab is generally classified
as being "in situ" (in place), while experiments conducted in the field under more
environmentally natural conditions are termed "in vivo" (in the living context).[52]
Those experiments that we classify as being either basic or media-technological
will typically take place "in situ", while performative experiments will most likely
be conducted "in vivo", such as in a theatre where they are simulated for an audience, or another realistic setting that brings the re-enacted activity closer to its
original environment.

16mm and 8mm Home Movie-Making Re-enactments (in vivo)
The media archaeological experiments with the Ciné-Kodak 16mm and 8mm film cameras took
place "in vivo", specifically in or nearby a domestic setting as the natural place for making
home movies. In general, the home can be considered an ideal location for doing media archaeological experiments, because this is the place where past users appropriated and used
consumer-orientated communication and media technologies. As Fickers and Van den Oever
argue: "Since the home can be considered the privileged locus for the appropriation and use
of communication and media technologies, the arrangement of a domestic environment
seems entirely appropriate for conducting media archaeology experiments." (▶ Theory,
Chapter 2.7)

---

52 Andreas Tolk, *Ontology, Epistemology, and Teleology for Modeling and Simulation: Philosophical Foundations for Intelligent M & S Applications* (Berlin, Heidelberg: Springer, 2013),
167–168.

HMV 2300H Portable Recorder (in vivo and in situ)

Direct-to-disc recordings using the HMV recorder were made in various locations; e.g., an empty room in the experimenter's home was used as an impromptu recording studio for an independent film project featuring the device and recordings made on it, thus "in vivo". Experiments were also conducted without participants, in the controlled, uniform conditions of a university Media Lab and thus "in situ".

illuminago Experiments with Improved Phantasmagoria Lanterns for Entertaining Knowledge Transfer (in situ and in vivo)

The experiments with the Improved Phantasmagoria Lanterns were conducted in the rehearsal hall of the Antagon Theatre in Frankfurt am Main, Germany. Both the size of the space and the darkening facilities were well suited for setting up a temporary laboratory. Three areas were set up for the experiments (Lab-Space 1–3), which were further modified during the experiments. The laboratory bench in Lab-Space 1 was initially used to examine the three selected Improved Phantasmagoria Lanterns (mainly to test the function of the lamps). After completion of these basic experiments, two of the examined devices were available for media-technological and performative experiments as technical objects, which were made available in Lab-Space 1.

In Lab-Space 2, a screen-frame previously reconstructed according to Carpenter's (1823) specifications was set up and a water-soaked cloth was hung on it and smoothed out. In these basic experiments, the technical functionality of the reconstructed screen was confirmed. It was now available as a technical object for the media-technological and performative experiments. The media-technological experiments with moving back projections onto the transparent screen were carried out between Lab Spaces 1 and 2.

Lab-Space 3 was set up opposite the screen, so that audience members could watch the rear projections on the screen, and performers next to the screen could address the audience through recitations or similar performances. For the performative experiments, this setting established two fields of action typical for the *dispositifs* of live performances of the historical art of projection: the interconnection of Lab-Space 1 and Lab-Space 2 formed the field of action of the operator. Lab-Space 3 was the field of action of the audience and the performer.[53]

53 Karin Bienek and Ludwig Vogl-Bienek, *Media-Archaeological Experiments with 'Improved Phantasmagoria Lanterns' (1820–1880)* (Frankfurt am Main, 2020), https://player.vimeo.com/video/489306344 [last accessed 26.07.2022].

Fig. 18: Experimental set-up of the *illuminago* experiments with Improved Phantasmagoria Lanterns. Courtesy of illuminago.

1.2.4 Experimental Design

Borrowing again from scientific research procedures, media archaeological experiments can also benefit from adopting experimental design principles when planning an experiment. In its simplest form, an experimental design will use two types of subject group, one being a treatment and the other a control group. Using clinical trials as an example, the treatment group is given a stimulus, such as a drug that is being tested, while the control group receives no stimulus or is given a placebo. Experimental design tests a hypothesis by comparing the results from the two different subject groups.

In the context of a media archaeological experiment, the two subject groups might be drawn from an audience and participants at a performative event or a workshop, and the hypothesis would be a specific element of the research question that examines the cause-and-effect relationships between two or more variables. Such a hypothesis could be to assess the usability of a technology. In that case, one group is given step by step instructions while the other can only learn through trial and error. Another hypothesis examines the subjective qualitative judgement of two separate groups when demonstrating an original historical device and its replica model. Here, only the treatment group is told in advance which model is being operated. Experimental design is widely used in industry, agriculture, market research and any field where variables can be identified. In the humanities and social sciences, it has been used in music cognition and perception studies and by film scholars.[54]

Experimental Design in Film Studies

In the article "Film studies and the experimental method", film scholar Mario Slugan pleads for "a greater engagement with the experimental method, including experimental design and critical reading of it".[55] Despite the "longstanding disciplinary scepticism" against experimental methods in the humanities, within film studies specifically, he argues that the experimental method allows for engagement with actual practices rather than normative beliefs, empirically studying, for instance, how film audiences behave. Experimental design can be an important requirement for testing theories or assumptions about such audience behaviour. Slugan gives the example of an experiment that tests how a real-life indigenous group is represented in a fiction film and whether or not this generates real-life beliefs about the social group among the film spectators. By selecting different films for the control and treatment groups, the post-screening beliefs and narrative persuasion effects can then be measured and compared through questionnaire testing. Slugan argues that film theory can greatly benefit from such experiments. In his article, he reminds us of how Kuleshov's early twentieth-century montage experiments "have arguably been a key impetus for inauguration of film theory".[56]

Empirical Design in Musical Research

W. Luke Windsor, in "Data Collection, Experimental Design, and Statistics in Musical Research" (2004), discusses methods for the analysis and interpretation of experimental results and data in relation to musical research, which can equally be applied to experimental media archaeology. Some of the different types of quantitative data and ways of collecting it are surveyed along with methods of organising, filtering, summarising, and representing data. Windsor also discusses the difficulties in "doing controlled research in music",[57] and the problem of variables that may not be recognised in an experiment. He warns of the reductive nature of an experimental approach, where factors are scaled down to better demonstrate the differences and relationships between them: "There is always a danger that such a reductive approach changes the observed phenomenon so much that the findings are hard to apply to the

---

54 W. Luke Windsor, "Data Collection, Experimental Design, and Statistics in Musical Research," in *Empirical Musicology: Aims, Methods, Prospects*, ed. Eric Clarke and Nicholas Cook (Oxford: Oxford University Press, 2004), 197–222; Mario Slugan, "Film Studies and the Experimental Method," *NECSUS_European Journal of Media Studies* 9, no. 2 (2020): 203–224, http://dx.doi.org/10.25969/mediarep/15317.

55 Slugan, "Film Studies and the Experimental Method," 216.

56 Slugan, "Film Studies and the Experimental Method," 203. See also N. N., "Études Expérimentales de l'activité Nerveuse Pendant La Projection Du Film," *Revue Internationale de Filmologie* 16 (March 1954).

57 Windsor, "Data Collection, Experimental Design, and Statistics in Musical Research," 219.

real world."[58] Windsor concludes by positing the use of an informal approach in order to gather real-world data where inherent variables can be identified, which can be combined with an experimental study where the hypotheses can be tested under more controlled conditions. This can be taken a step further through a process of triangulation where different types of data and methods of collecting it are applied to the same research questions.

Through the practices of trial and error for the testing of hypotheses, repetition forms an important element of the experimental design. Repetition can even be used as a heuristic instrument, to test variations in the outcomes of the experimental process, for instance. In this context, art historian George Kubler speaks about a "formal sequence", which he defines as "a historical network of gradually altered repetitions of the same trait".[59] Arguably, it is exactly this repetitive character of the experimental process that makes the experiment and its results meaningful, as Ludwik Fleck states: "Every experimental scientist knows just how little a single experiment can prove or convince. To establish proof, an entire system of experiments and controls is needed, set up according to an assumption or style and performed by an expert".[60] In a similar way, media archaeological experiments can be conducted in series, depending on the research question, approach and experimental design.

1.3 Drawing from Both Historical and Modern Sources

Studying historical and modern sources is, undoubtedly, an important part of the preparation phase. It can be complementary to hands-on experimentation in the sense that it informs the experiment (deductive approach), answers questions that come forward during the experiment (inductive approach), or both (integrative approach). Historical sources include patent applications, original user manuals, service sheets and records, and surviving workshop notes, as well as magazine articles and handbooks that provide general knowledge on the object and its operation. Modern sources encompass academic research as well as information from amateur and collector societies and their publications. Internet forums and social media channels can also provide invaluable information, as these are often posted by knowledgeable enthusiasts, collectors and experts in a given field.

---

58 Windsor, "Data Collection, Experimental Design, and Statistics in Musical Research," 198.
59 Cited in Rheinberger, "Epistemics and Aesthetics of Experimentation," 239.
60 Cited in Rheinberger, "Epistemics and Aesthetics of Experimentation," 238.

Historical sources may provide useful leads for basic experiments or even parameters for media-technological experiments. Studying the historical sources is often necessary in order to reconstruct a specific historical setting, *dispositif* or circumstance, for instance, when simulating or re-enacting a media historical practice, such as a film screening or historical music performance. While the historical sources may thus serve as a heuristic tool, they often do not correspond to the actual technological objects and user practices they represent. A patent, for instance, usually differs slightly from the actual manufactured technology. Likewise, an advertisement or description of a media practice in a user manual represents an ideal type of use. The historical sources, as with any source in general, therefore need to be interpreted. As such, they can provide insights into various conceptualizations and discourses on past media usages. The type of historical source material arguably corresponds to or represents an ideal type or category of user. As historical sources, amateur magazines and handbooks represent the "amateur" user, advertisements the "configured" user, and technical reports the "expert" user. In total, Fickers and Van den Oever distinguish between eight user types, including furthermore "imagined", "remembered", "artificial", "simulated", and "re-enacted" users (▶ Theory, Chapter 2.3). Such a taxonomy is useful for the purposes of reconstructing a historical setting and also to assert or question the validity of representations in the literature of historical user practices. The modern media archaeological experimenter, in this case, becomes the "re-enacted user" who is informed by studying these historical sources.

Use of Historical Sources in the Kinora Replica Project

To inform the process of making the Kinora replica, the original Kinora patents were studied. The research phase focused on several elements of the Kinora mechanism, including the curvature of the photographic image cards of the Kinora reel, and the metal stop, positioned at the edge of the viewer's guidance. The function of the stop is to arrest and disassociate each of the curved image cards during rotation and thereby flatten them at the moment they become visible through the lens. This part of the Kinora viewer is thus essential for creating the anticipated illusion of movement when watching the images of the Kinora reel in the viewer. In the original Lumière Kinora patent from 1896, the reason for the curved shape of the photographic image cards is explained as follows: "The wheel might be formed of flat cards radiating from the centre of the shaft (A) but in such case the stop (C) would curve the pictures at the moment of vision; this is why it is preferred to curve the cards previously in order that they may be presented flat during observation."[61]

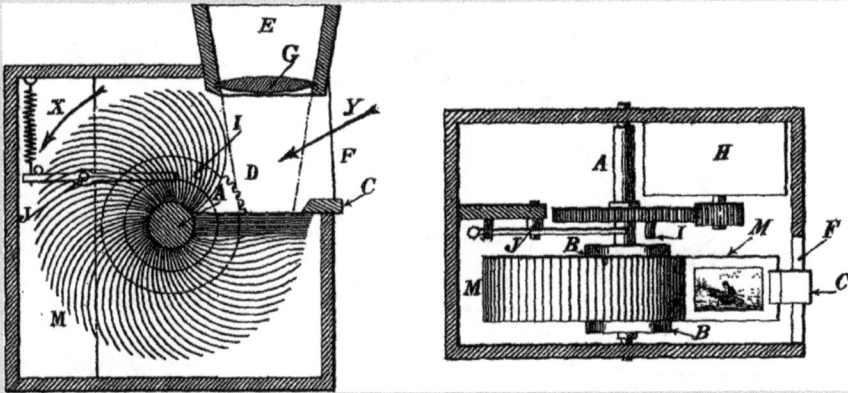

Fig. 19: Drawings of the Kinora viewer and reel mechanism from the original Lumière patent (1896).

Two Kinora patents from 1912, one describing the Kinora viewer ("Improvements in Cinematograph Apparatus") and one the Kinora reel ("Improvements in Rotary Moving Picture Apparatus") were particularly helpful for reconstructing the different parts of the original Kinora model. They describe in detail and visualise how each of the 640 photographic pictures is part of a strip which is attached to a spool. The spool contains a circular core, referred to in the patent as central tube. This central tube contains different edges or flanges, namely: the main flanges and their ends, and the binding flanges. These binding flanges have dished parts, which correspond to the incuts made on each of the sides of the image strips.

---

61 Auguste Lumière, Louis Lumière, and Benjamin Joseph Barnard Mills, "Kinora Lumière Patent: 'Apparatus for the Direct Viewing of Chrono-Photographic or Zoetropic Pictures'. British Patent No: 23,183," 1896. See also Henry V. Hopwood, *Living Pictures: Their History, Photoproduction and Practical Working* (London Optician and Photographic Trades Review, 1899), 39.

The 1896 and 1912 Kinora patents helped to identify and formulate various parameters in relation to the frame rate and optimal speed of rotation, magnification degree of the lenses, and thickness of the photographic paper. Studying the historical sources was thus an important heuristic tool for identifying the focus point of the hands-on experimentation and 3D replication in the research phase. It was also a useful exercise in comparing different patents of the same technology, which, besides providing inspiration for doing media archaeological experiments, helps understanding changes in conceptualizations of the media technology, its functionality, design and use.

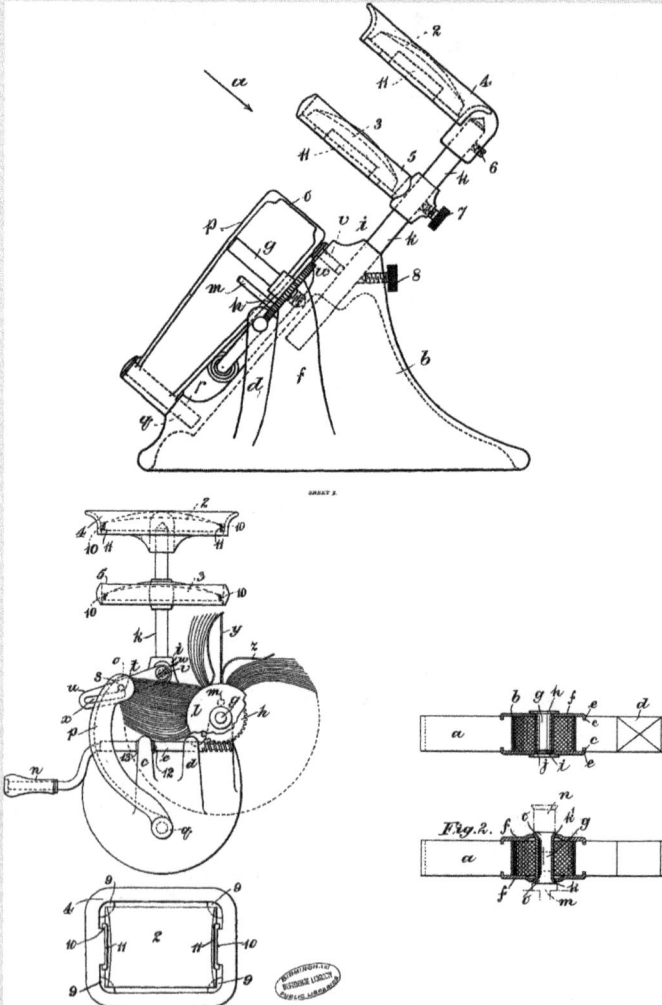

Fig. 20: Patent drawings of the Kinora viewer and reel mechanism (1912).

Historical Home Movies as Sources of Inspiration

For the film experiments with the Ciné-Kodak 16mm film camera, inspiration was taken from various historical amateur films and home movies. As documents of everyday life, the recording of children growing up is a popular and recurring theme. Arguably, one of the first "home movies" ever made was the film *Le Repas de Bébé*, 17 metres in length, recorded by Louis Lumière in 1895 with the Cinématographe. The short film depicts August Lumière, his wife and their baby daughter Andrée Lumière at breakfast. Although this particular film was recorded on 35mm nitrate-film, it inspired the domestic setting and theme for the first media archaeological experiment with the Ciné-Kodak 16mm film camera. The experimenter, Tim van der Heijden, recorded his daughter – by then almost one year old – having her meal at the living room table.

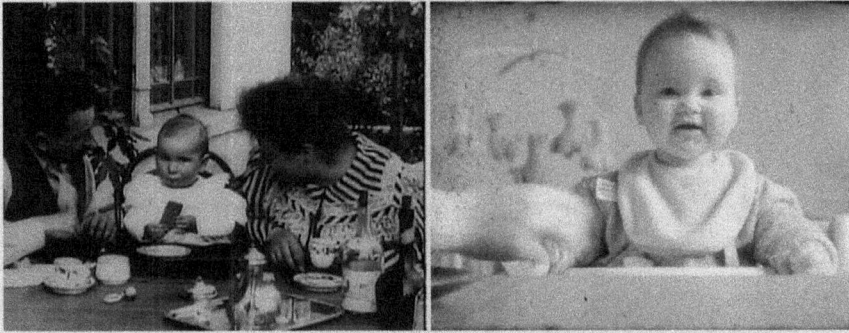

Fig. 21: Still from *Le Repas de Bébé* (Lumière, 1895) and still from 16mm film re-enactment (2020). Still from 16mm film developed and scanned by Onno Petersen and reproduced by Tim van der Heijden. Courtesy of the C^{2}DH / University of Luxembourg.

Another media archaeological experiment with the Ciné-Kodak 16mm film camera was inspired by a 16mm home movie from the Dutch amateur filmmaker Piet Schendstok (1902–1978). Schendstok documented the growing up process of his daughter, in the film *Jetty from about two weeks until her first steps* from 1941–1942.[62] In one sequence from this 20-minute film, we see Jetty taking her first steps. The experimenter wanted to re-enact this "first steps" sequence by means of using the same technology, mise-en-scène, camera angle and movement. (See Chapter 4.2.4.)

---

62 Piet Schendstok's film collection (1932–1978) has been archived by the Netherlands Institute for Sound & Vision. For a case study on Schendstok's family films, see Susan Aasman, *Ritueel van huiselijk geluk: Een cultuurhistorische verkenning van de familiefilm* (Amsterdam: Het Spinhuis, 2004), 113–135.

Stentorphone Soundbox for Gramophone

The rare Stentorphone soundbox loaned to the project required extensive restoration and had a number of missing parts that had to be remade from scratch in order to bring the soundbox to a working condition. These included a specially shaped steel spring onto which the moveable comb-like valve of the Stentorphone was mounted to control its movement, and an entire front section of the soundbox that connected it to the gramophone's tone-arm. No surviving examples of the same soundbox could be found, either in museum collections or amongst private collectors, that could be used as models from which to make the facsimiles. Instead, a search of the original patents filed by the Stentorphone's inventor H. A. Gaydon (1911) disclosed a figure in a patent drawing that gave the shape of the sought-after steel spring,[63] while an illustration in a *Popular Science* magazine article on the Stentorphone (1921) showed an exploded view of the same soundbox that included the entire front section that was missing from the loaned Stentorphone.[64] These historical sources were instrumental in informing and enabling the reconstruction, restoration and replication of the Stentorphone soundbox.

Historical Instructions for the Use of Improved Phantasmagoria Lanterns

In Carpenter's Improved Phantasmagoria Lantern sales catalogue (1823), described in section 1.1.1, the manufacturer explains for his customers the use of the Improved Phantasmagoria Lantern and the copperplate sliders. The media archaeological experiments with Improved Phantasmagoria Lanterns were guided by the instructions in this catalogue regarding the handling of the surviving devices and lantern slides. Carpenter points out that their operation requires a lot of hands-on practice. For the projection of the Phantasmagoria effects, a transparent screen was needed, for which Carpenter provides detailed building instructions. For the experiments, a screen was reconstructed according to these instructions, which functioned perfectly as described. The catalogue contains an illustration to explain the use of Improved Phantasmagoria Lanterns. This illustration shows the projection of a zebra. As there is also a copperplate slider by Carpenter with the same zebra in the *illuminago* collection, it was used for the media-technological and performative experiments.[65]

---

63 H. A. Gaydon, "Improvements in Sound Producing Devices [GB Patent 16,934]," 24 July 1911.
64 N. N., "Make the Phonograph Record Loud or Soft," *Popular Science Monthly*, September 1921.
65 Bienek and Vogl-Bienek, *Media-Archaeological Experiments with 'Improved Phantasmagoria Lanterns' (1820–1880)*.

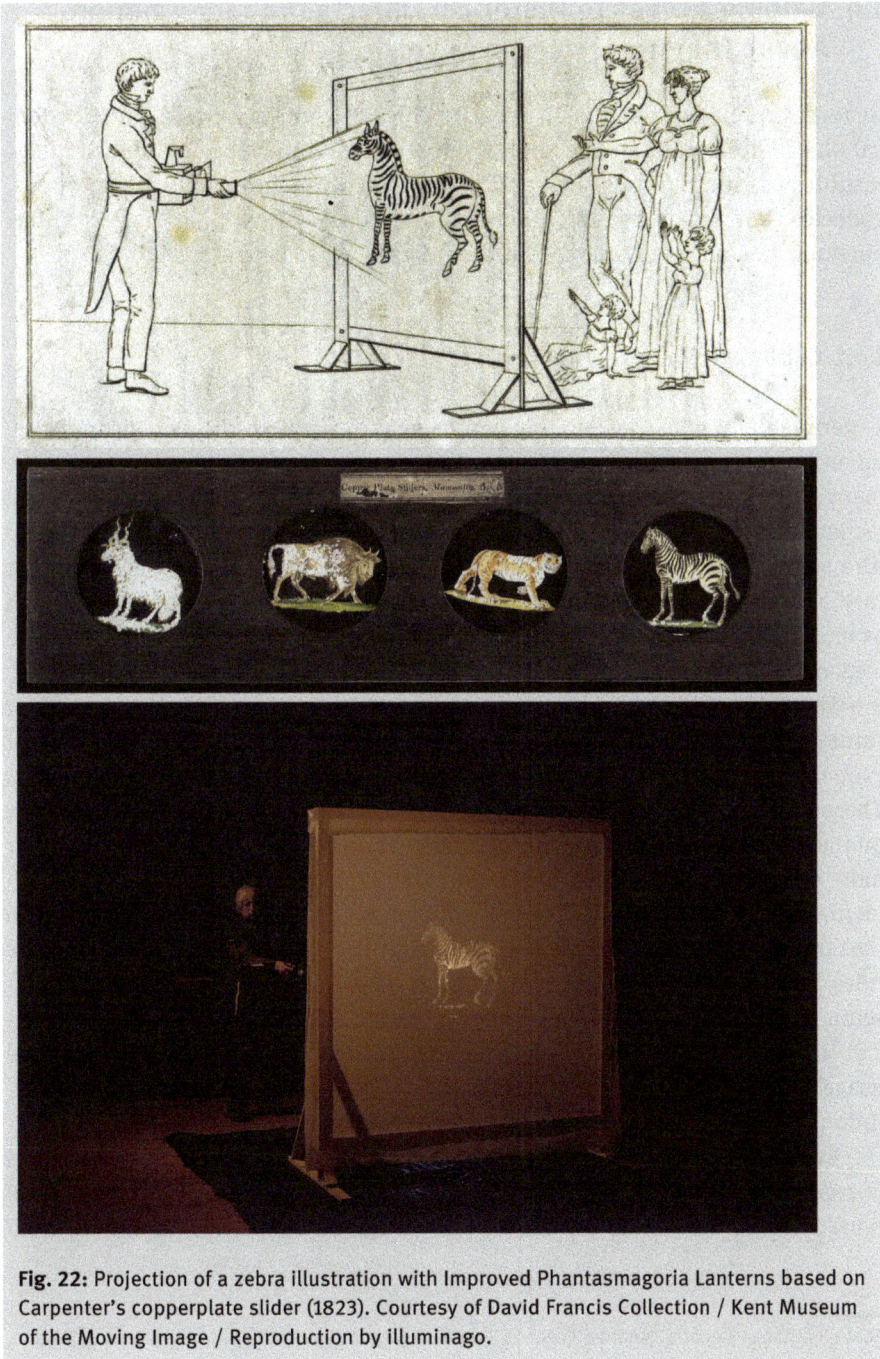

Fig. 22: Projection of a zebra illustration with Improved Phantasmagoria Lanterns based on Carpenter's copperplate slider (1823). Courtesy of David Francis Collection / Kent Museum of the Moving Image / Reproduction by illuminago.

1.4 Gaining Access to Historical Objects (And Information About Them)

Generally, there are three main ways in which to gain access or acquire historical objects for media archaeological experimentation: (1) via cultural heritage institutions, such as museums and archives; (2) through independent experts, collectors and amateurs; and (3) outright purchases through physical or online auctions, flea markets, antique shops and used equipment stores.

1.4.1 Cultural Heritage Institutions

Experimental media archaeology can be said to have, in the Derridean sense, an archival drive (▶ Theory, Chapter 1.6) – one that yearns to make use of the many collections of mute and inanimate media apparatuses stored away in collections, and to produce work with them that relates to the present and the future as much as it does to the past.[66] This section looks at ways in which the media archaeologist can work together with cultural heritage institutions, such as museums and archives who, while actively encouraging research into their collections, will only in rare instances loan out objects for hands-on experimentation.

The main objective of the museum or archive is to *preserve* the objects for future generations. Hands-on experimentation may cause wear and tear or even damage the object and so conflicts with archival and conservation rules. These rules and regulations change from time to time, and also vary depending on the institution and its individual conservation policy. Where there are two or more examples of an object, a curator may allow one to be used in an experiment, but any repairs, servicing or modifications that need to be undertaken so that the object functions as it should, would be reliant, again, on the specific rules for conservation at the institution. It may also be necessary to have museum technicians assist in some practical tasks, as they will have received special training in object handling. Essentially, any access to, and the practical usage of museum and archival artefacts, will depend on the policy of the institution, the discretion of the curators and the agreement of the conservators.

Evaluating the practical usage of historical objects is often largely viewed as of secondary importance in cultural heritage institutions. However, these institutions are able to provide invaluable knowledge and expertise, including well-

---

66 See Jacques Derrida, *Archive Fever: A Freudian Impression*, trans. Eric Prenowitz (Chicago, London: University of Chicago Press, 1996).

documented provenance of an object or collection, available meta-data and access to networks of other experts. Working alongside museum curators and having access to the objects, even without being able to operate them, will greatly help in the creation of replicas, as the original object may be probed, measured precisely, photographed and even scanned. Institutional cooperation can also facilitate the assistance of local specialist firms, e.g., 3D scanning for measuring the objects onsite or engineering services that can manufacture replica parts.[67]

The results of media archaeological experimentation around a historical object in a collection may be of great interest to museums and archives. They will add the research to their databases and use it to inform visitors and other researchers, as well as to help develop narratives for exhibitions and events. Almost all of the DEMA projects – in particular the Kinora replica viewer, Stentorphone and Auxetophone Soundboxes, and the HMV 2300H Portable Disc Recorder – were made in collaboration with, or benefited from the expertise of museums and their curators, as well as archives, individual collectors, engineers and experts in the chosen fields.

The Exponential Horn: In Search of Perfect Sound (2013–2014)

This large-scale historical reconstruction and exhibition project, which took place at the Science Museum, London, was artist-led and the result of a sound artist-in-residence programme at the museum.[68] The commissioned sound artist, Aleksander Kolkowski, worked together with the Curator of Communications, John Liffen, and the museum's own workshop staff to reconstruct a giant loudspeaker horn from 1929, which had been demonstrated at the Science Museum throughout the 1930s, and served as a benchmark for the performance of contemporary loudspeakers and high quality radio broadcast reception. Research undertaken by Liffen had inspired Kolkowski to initiate the project, which depended on a close collaboration between them, the workshop staff and museum conservators. The original 9ft initial section of the horn – the only surviving part – formed the basis of its full-scale reconstruction, while a historic Western Electric 555W loudspeaker driver, also from the museum's collection and as used in the original 1930s installation, was employed during the subsequent exhibition (see Chapter 3.5.2).

---

67 In the 2019 DEMA workshop, John Ellis argued that museums often do not have working examples of the historical media objects, but they do have access to a broad network of collectors, maintainers, tinkerers and enthusiasts, including retired professionals. These people are invaluable for your project. However, it may require good communication skills to make them collaborate and understand the purpose of your project. See Van der Heijden and Kolkowski, "Documenting Media Archaeological Experiments."

68 The Science Museum's sound-artist in residency programme was part of the *Supersonix* project delivered by the Exhibition Road Cultural Group (ERCG), and begun in January 2012. "The Exponential Horn: In Search of Perfect Sound" exhibition was commissioned by Hannah Redler, Head of the Science Museum Arts Programme, for the Science Museum's Media Space.

The reconstruction of the "Denman Horn" – named after its designer and former museum keeper Roderick Denman – took nine months to complete. It was publicised as the largest loudspeaker horn in the U.K. and is arguably the largest truly exponential loudspeaker horn that exists in the world today. It was exhibited and demonstrated at the Science Museum's Media Space, where it was featured in a wide-ranging programme of radio transmissions and receptions (both archival and modern), together with a series of live events. The artist and museum partnership was extended to include other participating institutions and actors, such as the Royal College of Art and Royal College of Music, Resonance 104.4FM arts radio station, BBC Radio 3, academics, and experts in the field of acoustics and audio electronics.[69]

Fig. 23: Aleksander Kolkowski with the reconstructed "Denman" exponential horn. Courtesy of the Science Museum, London.

69 Aleksander Kolkowski, "In Search of Perfect Sound," *Science Museum Blog* (blog), 24 April 2014, https://blog.sciencemuseum.org.uk/in-search-of-perfect-sound-introducing-britains-largest-horn-loudspeaker/ [last accessed 26.07.2022].

Stentorphone and Auxetophone Soundboxes, HMV 2300H Portable Disc Recorder

The resources for these two projects came from a mix of heritage institutions, private collectors and individual experts. The historic pneumatic soundboxes used as models for replication were loaned by the expert gramophone and phonograph collector Howard Hope. Other examples were examined in the Science Museum, London; National Science & Media Museum, Bradford; and The EMI Archive, Hayes, with the assistance of their curators. Further information was supplied by the gramophone expert Christopher Proudfoot (Sotheby's). The HMV 2300H portable disc recorder was purchased outright at auction. Expert advice on the recorder was sought from Sean Davies and the audio engineer Liz Tuddenham; the latter helped to restore the device and bring it to working order.

"Histories of Use", U.K. Science Museum Group

In his presentation at the DEMA workshop 2019, Tim Boon, Head of Research at the Science Museum, London, reflected on the "Histories of Use" project at the U.K.'s Science Museum Group.[70] The group has ambitions to develop research in this field, using objects in their collection to build an archive of the histories of how these objects were built into the lives of people in the past, at work, home and play. Such research would also be used to enhance museum displays. The investigations would involve oral history, simulation-based re-enactment, reconstruction, and replication. Tim Boon went on to recount the practical and methodological challenges of establishing a "Histories of Use" programme at the Museum. He cited opportunities that were explored in the recent past through collaborations with sound artist-in-residence Aleksander Kolkowski, which made use of objects in the Museum's collection of early sound recording and reproduction, notably in the reconstruction of the giant exponential Denman Horn and re-enactments with the Auxetophone-Gramophone.[71]

Further attempts in the sonic field, however, were not so successful and a proof of concept conducted by Christianne Blijleven at the National Science and Media Museum, Bradford, and the Science Museum, London, met with difficulties in attempting to do practical work with three electronic musical instruments, namely a 1928 Theremin, a 1970s Mellotron electromechanical sampling keyboard, and a 1980s Fairlight digital sampler and synthesiser.[72] Reasons why the project failed to deliver a public event with any of the three instruments was due to a combination of factors, including the Museum's own policy with regard to conservation, together with a lack of time and availability of experts and technicians who were needed to participate in open sessions demonstrating the operation and maintenance of the instruments. The project served to show that operating museum objects in an ethical and controlled

---

70 Objects in the Science Museum Group's collections may be viewed online at: https://collec tion.sciencemuseumgroup.org.uk/ [last accessed 26.07.2022].

71 Alison Wright, "Festival: The Art of Sound," *Nature Physics* 8, no. 6 (June 2012): 441, https://doi.org/10.1038/nphys2349.

72 Christianne Blijleven has written an Master's thesis on this topic; see Klazina Johanna Blijleven, "Conveying Histories of Use to Science Museum Audience Via Object-based Re-enactment: Practical and Ethical Considerations" (Master's thesis, University of Groningen, 2020), https:// arts.studenttheses.ub.rug.nl/25117/ [last accessed 26.07.2022].

way takes real resources. However, the intellectual and practical reasons for doing histories of use research using museum objects are incontestable.

In response to Blijleven's project, it was suggested that a better approach might have been to work with collectors of the aforementioned instruments who own functioning examples. While this is a path that the Museum is currently being forced to follow, questions remain about the exalted status given to objects in collections, putting museum objects beyond use (especially if they are not globally unique). If, for example, the Museum's theremin could be regularly played in public events (as had often been done with museum objects in the past), perhaps at some stage it might become unrepairable, but its appearance would not necessarily be radically changed, in which case the now non-working object would still be available for analysis, visual inspection and exhibition purposes. In contrast to the 1960s and 1970s, when all kinds of historical objects were being demonstrated every week, the current situation in the U.K. is that major museums are unable to operate the objects in their collections, bar a very few exceptions.[73]

1.4.2 Independent Experts, Collectors and Amateurs

Working alongside independent experts, collectors, practitioners or amateurs offers more possibilities for the loan (and sourcing) of objects, and generally allows for some careful physical manipulation and examination of their internal workings by the experimenter. This makes it possible to acquire and document the tacit knowledge necessary to operate the object, as well as the modern practical usage of such historical objects. Collectors and practitioners can be more informed about particular objects in their collections than museum curators (who possess more general knowledge) and have extensive networks that are often the same as those known to museums and archives. However, there will frequently be no documented provenance and no available meta-data.

---

73 Van der Heijden and Kolkowski, "Documenting Media Archaeological Experiments."

Bolex Project and Francois Lemai Collection

In his presentation in the DEMA workshop 2019, film historian Benoît Turquety gave two examples of projects in which experimentation with film historical objects had been undertaken, and in which collectors and amateurs played an important role as mediators and experts. The first, the research project "Bolex, Film Technology and Amateur Cinema in Switzerland" (2015–2018), was not done with the collection of the Swiss Film Archive itself but with collectors who were willing to share their expert knowledge.[74] The project has compiled a history and information on Bolex cameras, and plans to include further content from participating students about the cameras, collections and practices of use. In one case, a PhD student focused on the interaction between the machine and its users, examining cameras by weight, sound, design features and gestures when handling them. Another aspect of hands-on work dealt with the engineering history of the cameras: the student worked together with a Paillard-Bolex engineer, taking apart different models in order to compare them, examining components, design and even the noise of the machines in operation. The idea was to see what could be learnt from opening up cameras and examining their mechanisms and component parts. While this may or may not concern the user, who might be more interested in the surface of the machine and its interface, nevertheless, the internal workings of the camera should be investigated.

The second example concerned the TECHNÈS project, an international Research Partnership on Cinema Technology that connects the Universities of Lausanne, Montreal, Rennes, and the cinémathèques of Quebec, France and Switzerland, among others. This enormous project is currently developing an online encyclopaedia of film technology, hosts interviews with film-makers and technicians, and organises conferences and demonstrations by specialists. Its demonstration videos are "clean": their aim is pedagogic and mainly for lay film students. TECHNÈS has invested heavily in creating 3D scans of objects, which the viewer is able to inspect and zoom into from every angle.[75] These 3D scans are time-consuming and expensive to make, and Turquety questioned their value and what they can tell us about an object apart from surface information. Technical objects are worthless if not connected to an infrastructure and users. The 3D representation of the scanned objects gives no information as to weight, size, feel, operation or sound.

An international conference, organised by the Université Laval, Québec in 2019 and promoted on the TECHNÈS website, invited researchers to propose conference papers based on objects in the François Lemai collection. Those selected were given a day to work with a physical object together with a technician, in order to closely examine and manipulate the objects they were to present on, then have another day to re-think their paper and present at the conference in the usual fashion.[76]

---

74 For more information about the project, see https://wp.unil.ch/cinematheque-unil/pro jets/bolex-et-le-cinema-amateur/ [last accessed 26.07.2022].

75 See the project website https://technes.org/ [last accessed 26.07.2022].

76 More information on the international conference and the François Lemai collection can be found at http://technes.org/en/membres/conference-materialite-esthetique-et-histoires-des-techniques-la-collection-francois-lemai-comme-laboratoire/ [last accessed 26.07.2022].

Stef van Brakel (Collector and Expert)

Collector Stef van Brakel (1948–2020) held a remarkable collection of historical film and photography objects, including a Mutoscope, Pathé KOK 28mm film projector, and Krupp-Ernemann Kinox, as well as various magic lanterns and 35mm still photography cameras. Throughout the years, Van Brakel, who had a career as a certified cinema projectionist, built his personal home cinema where he projected his film prints. In the spring of 2020, the experimenter, Tim van der Heijden, came into contact with the collector, who was willing to share his practice-based knowledge and expertise on the history of cinema and technology. After Van Brakel's passing in November 2020, part of the collection was taken over by the Luxembourg Centre for Contemporary and Digital History, where the film historical objects are currently preserved and can be used as a resource in research and teaching activities.

Fig. 24: Collector Stef van Brakel's personal home cinema. Photo by Tim van der Heijden. Courtesy of the C²DH / University of Luxembourg.

Bert Cremers (Collector and Expert)

Netherlands-based film collector Bert Cremers owns a remarkable collection of 9.5mm and 16mm films, cameras and projectors, including many rare objects. When the experimenter bought an item via eBay for the DEMA small-gauge experiments, Cremers kindly demonstrated his Pathé-Baby 9.5mm hand-cranked film projector from the early 1920s in his own cinema at home. The demonstration was documented on video.[77] The encounter serves as an example of how collectors are often willing to provide access to historical media objects, give video demonstrations or contribute to oral history projects, uncovering both historical and contemporary media usages.

Fig. 25: Collector Bert Cremers and his collection of 9.5mm film apparatuses. Photo by Tim van der Heijden. Courtesy of the C²DH / University of Luxembourg.

---

77 For the video demonstration of the Pathé-Baby film projector by collector Bert Cremers, see https://dema.uni.lu/demonstration-pathe-baby-projector-by-film-collector-bert-cremers/ [last accessed 26.07.2022].

Howard Hope (Collector and Expert)

The esteemed gramophone and phonograph collector Howard Hope is well known in the U.K. for his vast knowledge of early sound reproduction machines and their history. The generous loan from his personal collection of two original and rare pneumatic soundboxes for gramophone from the 1900s – an Auxetophone and a seldom seen Stentorphone soundbox – made possible the replication projects described in this volume. This informal transaction benefited both parties; the objects were returned to the collector in a restored condition, while the project was able to use the historical soundboxes for CAD modelling, 3D replication and, ultimately, for hands-on experimentation.

In this relationship between the lender and loanee it was important to establish trust and confidence that the objects would not be damaged or physically altered in any way. The lender was regularly kept informed about progress on the project, especially as regards restoration and testing. Finally, both parties were able to collaborate in further experiments by fitting the original and restored soundboxes to an E.M.G. exponential horn gramophone, in preparation for a joint demonstration of pneumatically driven gramophones for the City of London Phonograph and Gramophone Society.

Both objects had been in need of extensive repair and restoration, including the remaking of missing parts, such as specially shaped steel springs and entire metal sections, and this work was undertaken through the DEMA project's collaboration with engineering students and staff at the University of Luxembourg. Here, the project benefited from having sufficient funds to pay for materials, and for parts to be milled and laser cut by external precision engineering firms. Such additional costs are often prohibitive and may limit the amount of restoration work done on an object. The harsh reality is that media archaeological experiments will often require considerable financial support.

1.4.3 Auction Houses, Repair Shops and Online Resources

Purchasing an object outright from an antique or repair shop or via an auction gives the experimenter unfettered freedom to pursue practical, hands-on research. However, the objects obtained this way will most likely require restoration, repair and recourse to expert assistance. There may be little or no documented provenance or expert knowledge to accompany the object and no opportunity to observe tacit knowledge. Once an object has been acquired, either through purchase or loan, it is urged that the experimenter seeks active cooperation from specialist practitioners, experts, museum curators, collectors and societies. Independent collectors and amateurs will often have networks of specialist repairers and sources for replacement parts, while objects can be compared with those in museum and private collections, so that valuable knowledge can be gained and shared.

Kinora Purchased at the Antiq-Photo Gallery, Paris
For the DEMA project, we had the opportunity to purchase an original Kinora viewer from ca. 1907, including five reels, so it could be used for hands-on research and experimentation. The original Kinora viewer and reels served as models for the 3D modelling and replication process. The Kinora viewer was purchased from the Antiq-Photo Gallery, based in Paris, which had advertised the viewer via eBay, as well as on the gallery's website. At the time the object was collected at the gallery in February 2020, Sébastien Lemagnen, the gallery owner, and his assistant provided a demonstration of the object in use. Besides sharing knowledge about the object, they also showcased some of the other Kinora viewer models they had on display, including a Gaumont Kinora with a completely different design. Lemagnen, who is an expert in nineteenth- and early twentieth-century film and photography equipment, furthermore provided an authenticity certificate and high quality pictures of the purchased object, which could be re-used in project-related presentations and publications.[78]

HMV 2300H Portable Disc Recorder Purchased via Hybrid Auction
The disc recording apparatus was obtained for the DEMA project via a hybrid auction (one that combines a physical auction taking place in a room and open to the public with online bidding, all done in real-time). Such auctions are fast becoming the norm as they can attract a vast number of bidders and increase international interest. The HMV 2300H was a rare find, as all its component parts were listed together in this auction. Often, the individual units that make up this apparatus, including the amplifier, main recording unit and microphone, are sold separately. Furthermore, the apparatus came with a large number of blank lacquer discs, sapphire cutting styli and complete documentation (manual, service notes, bill of sale). Unfortunately, because the seller chose to remain anonymous, it was not possible to extract any information as to the provenance of the recorder. However, correspondence included in the paperwork gave the name and address of the original purchaser in 1948.

In sum, it is highly recommended to collaborate, where possible, with institutional partners, experts, and collectors in the field of research, as they can help to inform your experiments, enrich your research questions and test or develop interesting hypotheses or subjects of investigation. Collaborating with archives and museums can also be useful in the dissemination of experimental media archaeological research. Each of the three ways of gaining access to historical objects for hands-on experimentation discussed in this subchapter comes with its own pros and cons. While cultural heritage institutions may provide the most common pathway to gaining access to media historical objects, the possibilities offered by them for hands-on experimentation will most likely be severely limited because of ethical guidelines around conservation. Consulting with independent experts and collectors can be useful for both sharing tacit knowledge and access to media historical objects, but will depend on the

---

78 For more information about the Antiq-Photo Gallery, see https://www.antiq-photo.com/en/home/ [last accessed 26.07.2022].

willingness and trust of the expert to loan or lease-lend the object to the researcher. Obtaining an object outright by purchasing it from an auction house, gallery, shop or online resource involves expense but gives the experimenter unfettered freedom to do hands-on work with it. However, the object may need extensive restoration and repair.

Where there is cooperation with collectors, expert practitioners and museum curators or archivists, it is also recommended that their knowledge be well documented and that the object is considered from different perspectives – as a collectable item with emotional, intellectual or monetary value; as an apparatus or tool used in connection with a work activity; or as an object with historical significance. Whether purchasing or loaning an object from a seller or collector, be sure to ask about the provenance of the object, dating and any other contextual information that may give evidence about how the object was used in the past. This may also provide opportunities for a demonstration of the object in use or an oral history project with the previous owner(s) or users of the object, which may then form part of the experiment's overall documentation.

1.5 Recommendations and Reflections

Within this chapter, we have discussed various aspects related to the practice of preparing media archaeological experiments. Based on the examples discussed, we can summarise the following recommendations and reflections:

- It is important to define a research question, method and approach prior to the media archaeological experiment. Nevertheless, research is an iterative process, especially in hands-on experiments, so your research questions, method, approaches and even objectives may be subject to change during the experimentation process itself (1.1).
- Selecting a suitable research method, type of media archaeological experiment and experimental setting is dependent on the objectives of the media archaeological experiment (1.2).
- Studying historical and modern sources can both inform and be informed by hands-on experimentation (1.3).
- Collaborating with institutional partners, experts and collectors is recommended as they can help to inform and enrich the media archaeological experiments and provide possibilities for their dissemination (1.4).
- Gaining access to historical objects for hands-on experimentation can be done in collaboration with cultural heritage institutions, independent experts/collectors/amateurs, or by obtaining an object outright by purchasing it from an auction house, gallery, shop or online resource. Each type of access has its own pros and cons (1.4).

Chapter 2
Research

This chapter delves into various aspects of practical research, beginning with the initial inspection of objects, their testing, repair and maintenance, leading to experimentation and the involvement of participants (including expert observers and the public), and the analysis and interpretation of and reflection on experiments. We will also discuss the assessment of sensory modalities within experiments and the evaluation of acquired skills and performance in relation to operating media archaeological objects.

2.1 Inspection and Testing

The condition of the media historical object should be assessed before commencing any hands-on experimentation. The following steps give a useful framework for inspection and testing, a central element in what we have earlier defined as "basic experiments":

- Examine the object, noting its material state and condition and, if in working order, try to determine if it will withstand repeated handling and experimentation. Assess the need for restoration, repair, servicing or any treatment for decay. Consider the amount of repair or restoration needed to bring the object to a working state.
- Carefully check if the object is safe to use, critically so if it requires electricity, heat, fuel or motive power to function. Consider any necessary safety precautions (e.g., asbestos, electric shock risks, "vinegar syndrome"[79]).
- Survey the object for any past modifications or alterations, either contemporary or modern. Confirm its authenticity – whether it is an original or a reproduction. If the latter, consider whether it is close enough to the original to be a good substitute. If part of a series, note the type, model and its place in the line of development. This may be useful in assessing special features the object may or may not have in relation to other versions.

---

79 National Film and Sound Archive of Australia (NFSA), "Vinegar Syndrome" (Canberra: National Film and Sound Archive of Australia, 8 July 2010), https://www.nfsa.gov.au/preservation/preservation-glossary/vinegar-syndrome [last accessed 26.07.2022].

∂ Open Access. © 2023 the author(s), published by De Gruyter. [cc) BY] This work is licensed under the Creative Commons Attribution 4.0 International License.
https://doi.org/10.1515/9783110799767-003

The technical appraisal, especially if the object requires electricity, should be carried out by a qualified electrician, engineer or service person. That way, the safety of the experimenter and any participants in the media archaeological experiment is guaranteed, as well as avoiding damage to the object. It may be necessary to take the object to be tested at a repair workshop or engineering lab. Where possible, it is strongly advised to use an engineer or repairer who is familiar with the type of technology you are testing, be it vintage cameras, valved units such as radios and amplifiers, transistorised electronics, televisions or computers. It may be that, given the amount and difficulty of the restoration and repair, the object you have purchased is not worth the total investment in time and cost. Whether the acquired object is a replica or reproduction, it is strongly advised to confer with an expert who is able to assess its operation and performance in comparison with an original.[80]

Inspecting and Testing the Pathé-Baby 9.5mm Film Projectors

Before using the Pathé-Baby 9.5mm film projectors in the media archaeological experiments, the objects were brought to the University's Engineering Lab in Belval to do a safety test with engineer and university teacher Gilbert Klein in his workshop. For the inspection, a transformer was needed to be able to convert the 230 voltage of the mains to the 110 voltage required for these film projectors. Two types of 9.5mm film projectors were tested, one hand-cranked (Pathé-Baby model D, ca. 1924) and one electric motor-driven version (Pathé-Baby model G2, ca. 1932). From an electronic point of view, the hand-cranked Pathé-Baby film projector is rather simple. The electricity comes in via the current contact points, one of which is directly connected to the lamp via the wiring. The other contact point is connected to the resistance, a plate located at the base of the projector with a copper wire wrapped around it. Its function is to limit and regulate the amount of voltage going to the lamp. Connecting the projector to the mains activates the electric bulb in the lamp house. To make sure there is no shortened circuit, a multimeter was used to measure the voltage on different parts of the projector and inspect the path of the in-coming voltage. Some early twentieth-century film projectors contain asbestos as a fire retardant and for noise absorption. Before using an early film projector in a media archaeological experiment, it is therefore recommended to check whether it contains any asbestos at a specialist repair shop.

---

80 Examples include reproduction gramophones and copies of rare musical instruments, whose similarities to the originals are mainly cosmetic and which function in a vastly inferior way. See, for instance, https://oldcrank.com/articles/crapophone/Introduction.html [last accessed 26.07.2022].

Fig. 26: Engineer Gilbert Klein testing the Pathé-Baby 9.5mm film projectors in the Belval Engineering Lab. Photo by Tim van der Heijden. Courtesy of the C²DH / University of Luxembourg.

illuminago's use of Oil Lamps in Historical Projection Devices

Light sources are an essential component of projection devices and, as they are difficult to handle, they occupy a considerable part of the surviving trade literature. This corresponds to the level of attention they required in basic experiments within the experimental media archaeological series on the historical art of projection. During the inspection of the objects, the existing components were recorded, and missing parts (glass chimney, wicks) were identified and added. The historical lamp oils are no longer available today and would also not be permitted from a safety point of view. Carpenter (1823) recommends whale oil or colza oil made from rapeseed. A rapeseed oil was used for the oil lamp in the first experiment with the Improved Phantasmagoria Lanterns, the other two experiments used a present-day "petroleum". The open fire required fire protection arrangements (fire extinguisher and fire blanket) to be adopted.

Wilcox-Gay 1C10 Recordio & HMV 2300H Portable Disc Recorder

As a safety precaution, both of the above units were initially powered-up using a voltage and current controller (a variable transformer or "Variac") loaned by an electrical engineer. Connecting an old and untested device to the mains supply at full power for the first time can be dangerous, causing possible component failure, electrical shorting, and risk of fire. Using intermediary test equipment such as a Variac will minimise such risks. The Variac's control unit consists of a rheostat, and voltage was slowly increased over several periods of 45 minutes duration until the full operating voltage was reached, all the time observing the drop or increase in current on the inbuilt gauge. An increase in current over time is an indication of a fault, meaning that the unit is dangerous to operate and the object is therefore in need of repair. Fortunately in this case, testing proved both units were safe to use.[81]

---

81 Some hobby electronic equipment repairs use light dimmer controllers to power up vintage electronic equipment. However, this is not safe, as the level of current drawn by some electronic units is

2.2 Repair and Maintenance

While minor repairs may be accomplished by the experimenter, it is recommended that the repair and restoration of a media archaeological object should be carried out by a specialist in the technological field of that object. Collectors and their societies, museum curators and conservators can often provide advice and contacts to expert repairers who are able to restore a device as closely as is possible to its original state. When replacing parts and materials, it may not always be possible to do so authentically, on a like-for-like basis, and modern equivalents will have to be used. The original materials that constitute a device may affect its performance considerably and substituting these materials can often change the way the device will behave under use. Where the object being repaired is "upgraded" or enhanced through the use of modern materials and components, it should be asked to what extent this limits the degree of historical authenticity of the media archaeological experiment. (See Chapter 3.5.2 for a discussion on the notion of historical authenticity.)

In some cases, the object may have already been modified by a previous owner. It might be desirable to undo such a modification, especially if it has been badly done, or simply to redo it better. However, modifications and improvements are often made to a working object during its lifespan, and they could be a relevant source when investigating histories of use.

Restoring the HMV 2300H Portable Disc Recorder
Inspection of the recorder's amplifier unit chassis showed that a previous owner had carried out modifications recommended in the service notes that accompanied the apparatus. A document from 1951 gave detailed instructions on three modifications to improve ribbon microphone performance and the tonal reproduction of discs, and to extend the high frequency response of the recorder. Although the wiring and connections were correctly done, the soldering work was messy and might have caused short circuiting and excess loading. It was decided with the electrical engineer Nirmal Sabarwal (Fuselodge Electrical Repairs, London) to remove the later-applied solder and redo the modifications to a higher standard.

---

far beyond what is needed for a light bulb. A useful guide is published online by the VPRS (Vintage Radio & Phonograph Society). See M. McCarty, "Introduction to Vintage Electronic Equipment Restoration" (Vintage Radio and Phonograph Society website, Dallas/Fort Worth, Texas, 2004), http://vrps.org/documents/IntroRestoration/IntroRestoration.html [last accessed 26.07.2022].

Fig. 27: The HMV2300H amplifier unit undergoing repairs. Photo by Aleksander Kolkowski. Courtesy of the C²DH / University of Luxembourg.

Ciné-Kodak 16mm Film Camera Repair

The Ciné-Kodak 16mm film camera used in the small-gauge experiments features a spring motor that needs to be wound manually. To test its functioning and usability, a test roll was used to see whether the take-up spool and claws were still functioning. It was furthermore checked whether the motor was running when releasing the shutter. The camera was cleaned at the analogue film and photography shop Click und Surr in Berlin.[82] The camera was loaded with a "fresh" 16mm black and white reversal film, produced by the Czech brand Fomapan. At that time, Fomapan was the only manufacturer that still produced double-sided perforated 16mm reversal film, which is required for this type of 16mm film camera. The process of loading the 16mm film camera with test film was demonstrated by the technical expert working in the film shop's workshop.[83]

---

82 For more information, see http://clickundsurr.de/ [last accessed 26.07.2022].
83 For a video demonstration of loading the Ciné-Kodak 16mm camera, see https://dema.uni.lu/demonstration-loading-a-cine-kodak-16mm-film-camera-by-marco-kroger/ [last accessed 26.07.2022].

Fig. 28: Loading the repaired Ciné-Kodak 16mm camera at the film shop. Photo by Tim van der Heijden. Courtesy of the C²DH / University of Luxembourg.

Repair and Maintenance of Pathé-Baby 9.5mm Film Projectors

Both the hand-cranked Pathé-Baby (model D, ca. 1924) and electric motor-driven Pathé-Baby (model G2, ca. 1932) were repaired, maintained and modernised by film collector and technical expert Emiel de Jong at his workshop in Tilburg, the Netherlands. The aim was to get the two projectors suitable for performative experiments and public demonstrations. Instead of using a transformer to be able to run the projectors on the recommended current of 110 volts, a low current adapter was installed to directly transmit a maximum of 12 volts to the projector's lamp. While modernising the projector, De Jong detached the original cables but did not remove them completely, so they could be reverse-engineered if needed. When opening the housing of the projector for cleaning and oiling the mechanism's internal parts, including the axles and gears, it was found that the projector's flywheel was actually made from plastic instead of the original metal, and so must have been replaced earlier by a previous owner. The modification raises all kinds of questions: for instance, what had determined the choice for plastic as material (possibly for reasons of economy or availability); how severely it would impact the longevity and performance of the projector; and whether the plastic should actually be replaced by a metal flywheel again to bring the projector closer to its original state. The example furthermore demonstrates how the practices of repair and maintenance are not only necessary steps in the preparation of media archaeological experiments, but also integrally part of the object's histories (and futures) of use.

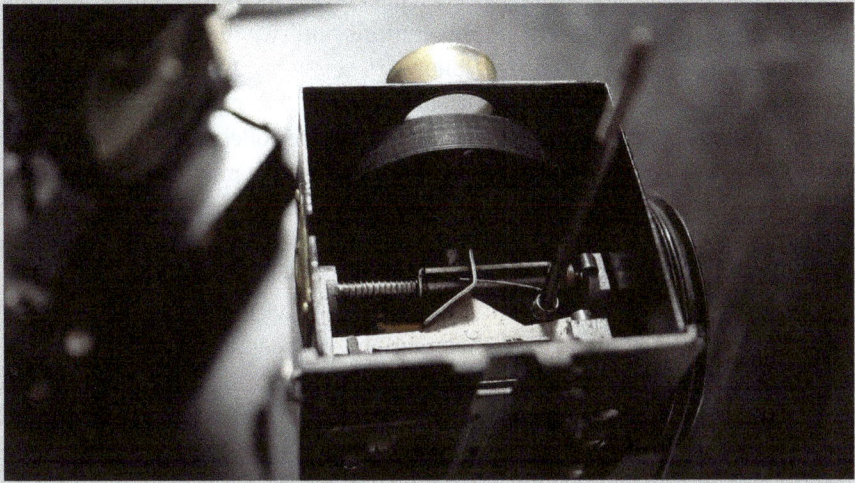

Fig. 29: The modernised Pathé-Baby film projector and flywheel mechanism. Photo by Tim van der Heijden. Courtesy of the C²DH / University of Luxembourg.

Examining an object for signs of wear can also reveal its history of use. Markings on the fascia or erased lettering around controls and switches of an electrical device might reveal user preferences, while worn screw heads will indicate that the device had previously been opened up and is likely to have been serviced internally or repaired.[84] Particular magic lanterns from the collection of media archaeologist Erkki Huhtamo, for example, appear to have been modified, with handles and extensions added to them in order to improve stability and portability. Only referring to an object in its first genuine form misses the fact that many objects in use become modified or improved over time.[85]

Maintenance involves the regular upkeep and servicing of the media archaeological object. It may involve the cleaning and lubrication of a mechanical device, replacing batteries or leaking capacitors and repairing faulty contacts and connections in an electrical one, or the replacement of worn-out parts in general. An unmaintained device is likely to develop faults, so that its performance becomes hindered or fails altogether. There is a common acceptance and even delight in past media technologies malfunctioning and they are often demonstrated in an unrestored or defective state. For example, the authors have witnessed historical gramophones being demonstrated with faulty soundboxes, and using worn out needles and records, with the subsequent distorted sound reproduction being regarded as "part of its charm". Although technological malfunction is an integral part of the historical experience, such demonstrations give a largely incorrect impression of the device's efficacy. Regular inspection and maintenance will therefore ensure the integrity of the object and should be considered as part and parcel of the "re-enacted" user experience.[86]

---

84 Sean Williams discusses physical interactions with electronic sound-making equipment in his study of the stepped filter. See Sean Williams, "Stockhausen Meets King Tubby's: The Stepped Filter and Its Influence as a Musical Instrument on Two Different Styles of Music," in *Material Culture and Electronic Sound*. Series Artefacts: Studies in the History of Science and Technology 8, ed. Frode Weium and Tim Boon (Washington, D.C.: Smithsonian Institution Scholarly Press, 2013), 163–188, http://oro.open.ac.uk/48770/ [last accessed 26.07.2022].

85 Kolkowski and Van der Heijden, "Performing Media Archaeological Experiments." In this context, see also Guy Edmonds, *Vibrating Existence: Early Cinema and Cognitive Creativity* (Plymouth: University of Plymouth, 2020), http://hdl.handle.net/10026.1/16096 [last accessed 26.07.2022].

86 See A. C. Harper, *Lo-Fi Aesthetics in Popular Music Discourse* (Oxford: Oxford University, UK, 2016), https://ora.ox.ac.uk/objects/uuid:cc84039c-3d30-484e-84b4-8535ba4a54f8 [last accessed 26.07.2022].

2.3 Hands-on Exploration and Experimentation

Once the historical object is deemed operational and is safe to operate, it can be used for further hands-on exploration and experimentation. The following preliminaries for setting up an experiment may seem obvious, but are worth noting:

Note Taking/Lab Diary

The experimenter should keep notes that are made before, during and after the experiment. Methods of documentation are discussed in Chapter 3, which gives detailed instructions for creating and keeping a lab diary. The method of note-taking is up to the individual and may depend on the conditions and type of experiment. It may involve making hand-written notes on paper, notating via a touch-screen device, dictating a voice recording onto a device, or any mixture of these.

Preparing the Location

Make sure the location of the experiment has sufficient room to work in and is sufficiently lit to give a clear sight of the object in operation, and to illuminate any aspects of it that you wish to focus on. Additional lighting may also be necessary for the documentation (see Chapter 3). Check that the space is sufficiently ventilated, especially if using equipment that gets hot, or if using heat for your experiment. Organise the worktop or table space and seating, providing ample space for the principal activity and additional space or tables for placing auxiliary objects and for secondary works, such as minor repairs or adjustments, or for storage purposes. Be mindful of your safety and that of any participants, and also of accidental damage that might be caused to your object(s). Make sure there are no trip hazards, such as trailing cables, or bare electrical circuits or wiring, and that the object is securely and safely positioned. Making a risk assessment is a routine part of scientific and engineering lab practice. For the experimental media archaeologist, detailed risk assessments will be required when organising public performances and demonstrations, especially if there are hands-on elements involving participant audiences.[87]

---

87 Numerous templates and guidelines for conducting risk assessments may be found online. Many are specifically designed, for example, for laboratory work, arts performances, public installations, or general work environments.

Tools and Equipment

Make a list of all the tools and auxiliary objects that you might need when conducting the experiment, and lay them out or keep them in a container so that they are easily accessible. If applicable, have small trays available on your work surface for keeping small items such as screws or components that need to be removed during the experiment. Have cloths and cleaning materials at hand and a waste bin nearby in case of accidental spillage or if your experiment will produce substances such as waste material.

Preparing the Documentation

Set up any cameras or sound equipment used for documentation purposes in advance of your experiment. Make sure that the camera tripods and microphone stands do not obstruct the experiment (see Chapter 3). Preparing the documentation well in advance and making decisions on camera and microphone placement and shots you wish to capture will save time during the experiment and avoid interrupting its flow. If working with a videographer, discuss the experiment beforehand and the activity and views you wish to capture for the purposes of documentation.

Setting the Duration and Timings of your Experiment

Setting the duration and timings for your experiments can be a useful way of investigating past practices – rehearsing the time it takes to perform an activity, for instance, to evaluate the skill of the users, who, as they become more proficient, may complete the activity and tasks more quickly. Noting down the timing when actions occur during an experiment borrows from scientific lab diaries. It can help to identify patterns of activity and to map gestures.

Cutting a Record with the HMV 2300H Portable Disc Recorder

After a level of proficiency had been achieved in cutting discs using the HMV recorder, the experimenter's skills were put to the test in a live session, recording speech with an actor. Here the "liveness" of the situation accelerated the decision-making and disc-recording activities, and the process of cutting a record, from sound check to the playback of the finished record, could be timed. The duration of a typical direct-to-disc recording session would depend on the number and size of the discs being recorded (a 10-inch disc holds 3.5 minutes while a 12-inch disc holds 4.5 minutes, both recording at 78rpm). The recording of such live sessions made it possible for the experimenter to experience the timescales under which a small recording studio using the device might operate.

2.3.1 Thinkering and Basic Experiments

As described in Chapter 1.2.2, basic experiments focus on the functionality of the object, measure its performance and indicate the need for repair, restoration and maintenance, and the physical conditions under which it can operate. Basic experiments study the media historical objects as epistemic objects. Included in this category of experimentation is the exploratory mode of "thinkering", where the media historical object undergoes an investigation of its "unique material characteristics, qualities/affordances and functionality". This affords "recreating the experience of past media" (▶ Theory, Chapter 4.2).

Thinkering with the Ciné-Kodak 16mm Film Camera
Making the first 16mm film with the Ciné-Kodak camera could be seen as an example of using the method of thinkering, because an exploratory mode functioned to discover some of the medium's characteristics and functionality. The basic experiment furthermore aimed to test the Ciné-Kodak 16mm film camera as a media historical object by recording both indoors and outdoors.

Doing Basic Experiments with the HMV 2300H Portable Disc Recorder
The first, basic experiment in disc recording using the HMV 2300H took place directly after its cutting head had been restored at repairer Liz Tuddenham's home workshop. The recording served both as a test of functionality and as a process of discovery for the experimenter. The playback of this first disc, cut only minutes before in the repairer's kitchen that had served as an impromptu recording studio, sounded unexpectedly good, given the age of the device and the improvisatory nature of the recording. The elation and delight felt by the experimenter on listening to the successful result was made all the sweeter because the repair process had been so long and difficult. Such experiences are particularly rewarding for the experimental media archaeologist, who gains satisfaction in bringing a past technology back to life and creating an emotional connection with past users and their interactions with the technology.

2.3.2 Simulation, Replication and Media-Technological Experiments

In simulated media archaeological experiments, the relationships between users and objects are reconstructed and the tacit knowledge is demonstrated (see Chapter 1.2.1). The process of replicating media historical objects "provides insights into the resilience of the epistemic object under scrutiny" (▶ Theory, Chapter 4.2). In general, media-technological experiments focus on the technological affordances of the object and the object-user interaction. In the same spirit as "thinkering", they allow for an exploratory examination of the objects and develop the tacit knowledge required to operate them.

3D Simulation in the Kinora Replica Project

The Kinora replica project focused on the replication of several distinguishing features of the viewer and reel, including the image curvature and top, the lenses and their magnification, the worm gear and worm shaft. Replicating – not authentically recreating – these core elements of the Kinora mechanism led to the simulation of their functionality within the 3D model. The making of the replica sometimes required adaptation and use of non-original materials that came with different qualities. For simulating the curvature of the Kinora reel, for instance, tools were used to additionally curve the photographic cards as a way to manually enhance the visual effect for the viewer. When replicating the worm gear and worm shaft, the material qualities of the PLA plastic used for the 3D printing of these parts in the first prototype turned out not to be strong enough. It caused the worm shaft to bend and disconnect from the worm gear, leading to a failure of function. Printing the worm gear and worm shaft in Onyx nylon, and also implementing extra bearings for additional support to the worm shaft, eventually solved the friction and resulted in a fully functioning replica viewer and reel.[88]

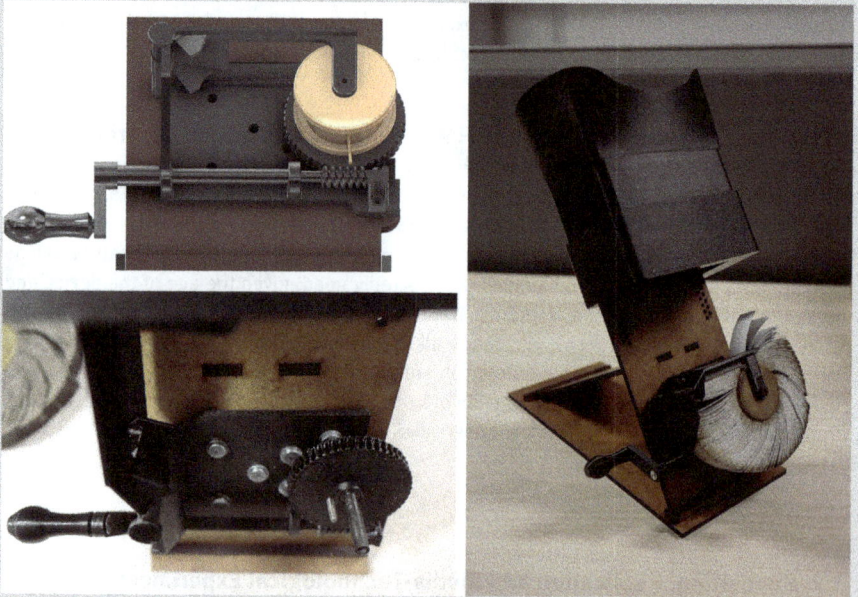

Fig. 30: 3D modelled and printed Kinora replica mechanism. Courtesy of the DoE / C²DH / University of Luxembourg.

---

88 Van der Heijden and Wolf, "Replicating the Kinora."

Cartavox Sound Postcard Recorder: Experiments in Making "Blank Media" and Recording Techniques
With no available "blank" sound postcards to record onto, the experimenter had to create and manufacture his own version of this historical media format. Historically, the front or picture side of the recordable sound postcard would have a lacquered surface that was either brushed on by hand or sprayed using a spray gun, airbrush or another tool.[89] Then, after securing it on a suitable recording lathe or "disc cutter", the postcard could be "cut" in the same way as a conventional blank disc, albeit with adjustments made for a shallower depth-of-cut and reduction in the weight of the cutter-head to allow for the thinner lacquered surface (when compared to a disc). Numerous failed experiments with lacquer led the experimenter to create a picture postcard that was laminated with a layer of plastic rather than the lacquered surface of the original format, and onto which the groove had to be embossed rather than cut (see Chapter 2.5.1). The embossing technique required further experimentation with the purpose of creating a spiral groove on the PVC surface that was deep enough for the playback stylus to track. Small weights were placed on the cutter head and a heated stylus was employed along with chemicals, used in an attempt to soften the surface and emboss a deeper groove. The experiments continued until a satisfactory amount of weight and degree of heat applied to the sapphire embossing stylus was found. A frequency spectrum analysis was also made of test recordings on an embossed laminated card and a lacquer disc cut on the Cartavox recorder. The results showed a lower high frequency response from the embossed laminated card than the cut disc, around 6dB less at its peak, and a signal-to-noise ratio that was audibly worse. However, it is worth noting that a lacquered card may not have performed as well as the disc, and that consistently good voice recordings were made using the embossed cards.[90]

In this project, the making of the recordable sound postcards simulates the original media; it does not recreate it. The recording process had to be changed, but the use of the Cartavox machine remains the same, albeit with some additional technical operations. The media archaeological experimentation into techniques of embossing grooves reconfigured the technical affordances of the Cartavox recorder.

---

89 R. A. J. Roy, "Procédé de Fabrication de Cartes Postales, Photographies et Imprimés Parlants [FR Patent 1.124.915]," 5 August 1955.
90 Aleksander Kolkowski, "The Cartavox Machine: Self-Recordable Sound Postcards. Experimental Report No. 1" (DEMA documentation, January 2021), Appendix 3.

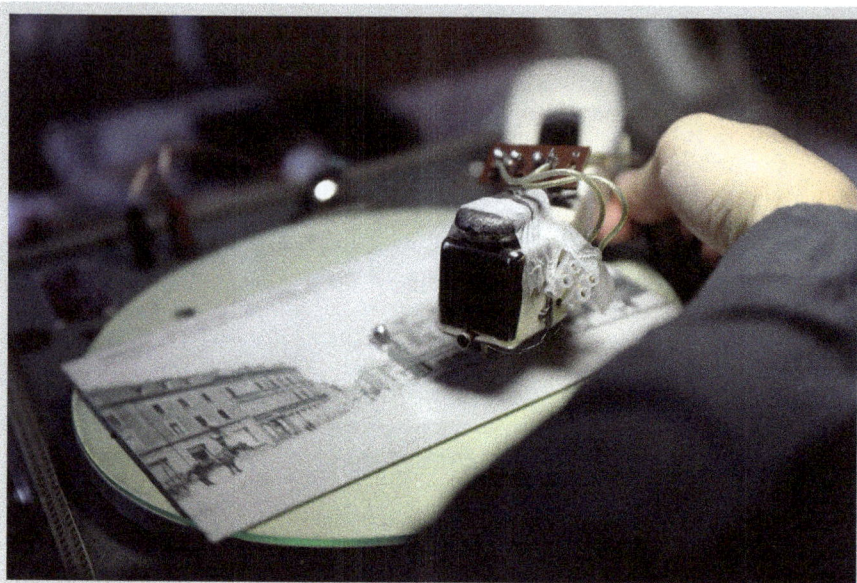

Fig. 31: Cartavox cutter head with weights and self-assembled heated stylus. Courtesy of the C^{2}DH / University of Luxembourg.

Media-Technological Experiments with Improved Phantasmagoria Lanterns

Becoming familiar with the Improved Phantasmagoria Lanterns was a continuous process that began in the basic experiments and continued in the media-technological and performative experiments. After completing the basic experiments, two lanterns seemed to be suitable for the media-technological experiments; however, during the media-technological experiments it turned out that one of the lanterns had a focal length that was much too short for practical use. This was solved by replacing the lens. The testing of the projections and visual effects on the transparent screen confronted the experimenters with viewing habits of images on a screen. The images appeared much darker than contemporary types of projections or even projections with a professional magic lantern from the middle and late nineteenth century. Nevertheless, the images and motion effects were clearly visible on the screen. Especially after almost complete darkness was created in the room, the images gained a kind of "autonomy" as a visual counterpart. Since the screen could not be seen, it sometimes felt as if the images were floating in space. This effect was counteracted when the lantern was directly behind the projection and a "hot spot" became visible in the image and did not dissolve completely. The result of the media-technological experiments in this first series of experiments with Improved Phantasmagoria Lanterns was the creation of a basic understanding of the affordances and aesthetics of this type of projection, which could then become the basis for the performative experiments.

2.3.3 Re-enactment, Creative Re-use and Performative Experiments

A re-enactment of historical practices that examines the technological object as it is being used for its intended purpose is, by its nature, a performative activity. Creative or artistic experimentation in public settings where the historical media technology is "repurposed" and "reimagined" allows us, as modern participants in the performative experiments, to experience the media technologies in new and unexpected ways. We are thus able to experience today's world through the prism of past technologies. Such artistic experiments can go hand in hand with other forms of media archaeological research, such as the staging of historical re-enactments where new artistic work may form part of a larger programme of events (see Chapter 1.4.1).

Artistic work in the field of experimental media archaeology can be said to be characterised by "creative distortion and/or sensorial affection" (▶ Theory, Chapter 4.2). The works of Paul DeMarinis and Toshio Iwai in particular are replete with intentionally distorted sounds and images, and often create surprise and astonishment while at the same time entertaining and evoking curiosity.[91] Historical records, such as patent documents, technical descriptions, schematics and other historical materials, have often become the sources of inspiration for the creation of new media archaeologically informed artworks.[92] Where the historical object or apparatus does not exist or is unobtainable, then models, photographs, sketches and pictorial representations can also provide material for the reimagining and reanimation of past practices, which can stimulate the historical imagination of audiences, participants and researchers.

The Media of Mediumship and The Laboratory of Psychical Research: Encountering the Material Culture of Modern Occultism in Britain's Science, Technology, and Magic Collections (2021)
The Media of Mediumship project aimed to transform understandings of the relationship between science, technology, and unorthodox forms of spiritual belief in modern Britain. In addition to knowledge sharing, lectures and events, a creative performance programme was incorporated to showcase the occultural use-history of artefacts and collections held by the Science Museum Group and the Senate House Library, London. These collections contained cameras, radios, telegraphs and other objects, and the project set out to explore "how these

---

91 Huhtamo, "Art in the Rear-View Mirror," 92–93.
92 Many of Paul DeMarinis' installation works take historical articles, patent documents and writings as a point of departure for sometimes radical reinterpretation. Examples are "The Messenger" (1998–2005), an installation based on early proposals for the telegraph; "Firebirds" (2004), which is drawn from an electrothermal loudspeaker described in a technical journal; and "Raindance" (1998), initially inspired by nineteenth-century experiments conducted by Felix Savart, Chichester Bell and Charles Vernon Boys. See DeMarinis, "Installations 1973–2010," 155, 159, 179.

seemingly secular technological and scientific instruments have been used by spiritual practitioners and sceptics alike to probe the existence of an unseen world."[93]

One such creative event was the *The Laboratory of Psychical Research* – a reimagining of The National Laboratory of Psychical Research (NLPR) established in 1926 by Harry Price, a popular psychical investigator. Visitors explored laboratory equipment and instruments that were used to detect activity of unseen psychic forces. Using a specially developed smartphone app and headphones, visitors could listen to a newly created soundscape inspired by the history of psychical research, overlaid with archival recordings of spiritualist séances and the voices of Harry Price and the physicist and psychical researcher Oliver Lodge.

The installation was inspired by photographs of the original NLPR, original lantern slides and detailed transcriptions of séances that took place in the Laboratory and that are held in the Harry Price collection at Senate House Library. Objects and furnishings similar to those used in the NLPR constituted the physical installation, while the soundscape took its inspiration from the detailed descriptions of sounds found in Price's experimental transcripts. These included rappings and musical instruments, as well as including toys and gramophone records.[94]

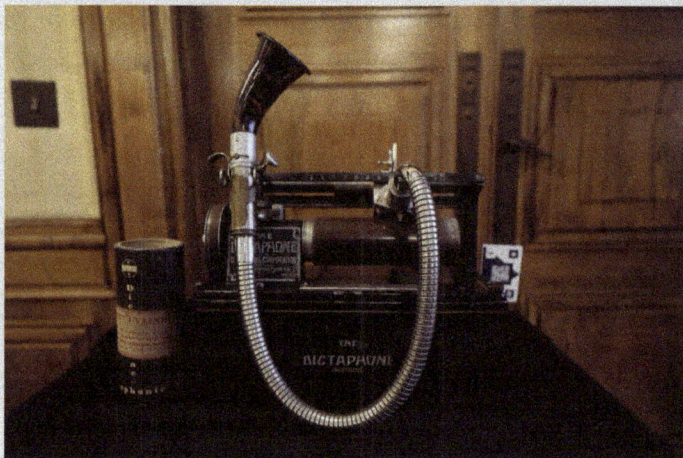

Fig. 32: Cylinder Dictaphone featured in the "Laboratory of Psychical Research". Courtesy of Lloyd Sturdy.

---

93 The Media of Mediumship research project, funded by the Arts and Humanities Research Council, follows on from the Popular Occulture in Britain, 1875–1947, research network. It was produced in collaboration with the Science Museum Group and Senate House Library. For more information, see https://mediaofmediumship.stir.ac.uk [last accessed 26.07.2022].

94 The Laboratory of Psychical Research sound installation was created by Aleksander Kolkowski, kitt price, and Laurence Cliffe. It was produced especially for the Media of Mediumship research project as part of the Being Human Festival 2021, hosted in partnership with Senate House Library. For the video, see https://www.youtube.com/watch?v=5w6FbcnAW4g&t=1s [last accessed 26.07.2022].

HMV 2300 Portable Disc Recorder – "Message from Mukalap" (2020)

Here, the re-enactment of a voice recording session made direct-to-disc, and using early twentieth-century electrical recording apparatus, became part of a wider artistic project. "Message from Mukalap" is the title of a film by the artist Judith Westerveld, which is based on a unique disc recording made in 1936 in Johannesburg by the titular Mukulap, a member of the Khoisan people of Southern Africa, who spoke in the now extinct !Ora language. The film is a response to his recording and Westerveld's newly made disc recordings, which are a way of reaching back in time and communicating with Mukalap, using the same technology of an early twentieth-century disc recorder and the medium of an "instantaneous" lacquer disc. The discs were played back on a 1930s EMG gramophone, digitally transferred and featured in the soundtrack of the film.[95]

The filmed disc recording sessions served as a performative media archaeological experiment. The HMV 2300H disc recorder used in the film was put into service, making recordings to a professional broadcast standard (of the period) destined for artistic or utilitarian use, in this case a film soundtrack. The complete cycle of recording, reproduction and the publication/distribution of it (as in film screenings) was re-enacted within this project.

Fig. 33: Judith Westerveld making a recording on the HMV 2300H. Courtesy of Tijs de Bie.

---

95 For more information, see https://iffr.com/nl/iffr/2021/films/message-from-mukalap [last accessed 26.07.2022].

Auxetophony – Auxetophone-Gramophone Concert with Live Musicians, Science Museum, London (2012)

This re-enacted performance of an early 1900s Auxetophone-Gramophone concert featured early recordings of famous opera singers on gramophone records that were reproduced through a pneumatically driven gramophone and accompanied by live musicians. The concert took place at the Science Museum, London, and used the Museum's prototype "Parson's Auxetophone-Gramophone" from 1905,[96] together with original Victor company "Red Seal" gramophone records from 1906, and contemporary scores published by Victor especially for the live accompaniment to these records. The live music was performed by an ensemble of musicians from the Royal College of Music, following contemporary practices in terms of the required instrumentation and stylistic interpretation. This re-enacted concert, the first of its kind staged since the early twentieth century, investigated the earliest phenomenon of recorded music combined with live musicians in a concert setting – a synthesis that had been made possible through the new technology of air-powered sound amplification. This concert was devised and staged by the Science Museum's first sound artist-in-residence, Aleksander Kolkowski, in 2012.

In addition to the performative re-enactment of a historical concert, the programme included a pianola and Auxetophone-Gramophone recital with pianist Rex Lawson, and two new experimental works. The first of the new experiments combined the Auxetophone gramophone with mechanically amplified Stroh stringed instruments (which were contemporaneous with the Auxetophone technology); the second was an electro-acoustic work for gramophone and vocalist Loré Lixenberg, where live electronic sounds and historical recordings of sound effects on discs were both played through the Auxetophone horn, thus combining air-assisted, electronic sound amplification and the live vocalisations.

Fig. 34: Kolkowski with the Parsons' Auxetophone and live musicians. Courtesy of Aleksander Kolkowski.

---

96 For more information, see https://collection.sciencemuseumgroup.org.uk/objects/co117340/parsons-motor-driven-auxetophone-auxetophone [last accessed 26.07.2022].

2.3.4 Art of Failure

Hands-on experiments will sometimes result in failure – for instance, interruptions to the experimental process through breakages or other accidents.[97] Even if some amount of failure might be expected during an experiment, this might be unforeseen. Unexpected failures and accidental missteps that occur because of a lack of experience and skills or preparedness can be seen as being an important part of doing media archaeological experiments. Fickers and Van den Oever describe failure as "probably one of the most important learning experiences in this heuristic practice".[98] Failures and mistakes then become learning opportunities, as they will produce new insights into actual user practices and experiences of the past (▶ Theory, Chapters 2.7 and 5.4).[99] The act of failure can thus be used as a heuristic tool that brings us closer to historical user practices and their multi-sensorial experiences. Taking into consideration errors that are made by the user and/or are caused by technical malfunction, helps to shift attention away from technological innovation to the actual experience of past media usage. However, it should be stressed that failures can equally be extremely disruptive and damaging – to the physical objects being experimented on, to the experimenter, and to the overall project. While coping with and overcoming the fear of failure are valuable steps in the learning curve, one should strive to undertake an experiment successfully and try to avoid failure through meticulous preparation.

One area that specifically deals with possible failure in a media-archaeological experiment is the risk assessment, especially when dealing with potentially dangerous practices and techniques. The provision, for example, of fire extinguishers when handling open fires, was used by *illuminago* in their experiments with the Improved Phantasmagoria Lanterns. They also had to cope with the extremely high temperature of the glass and tin chimneys of their lanterns. Learning from previous (and painful) experience, they paid a great deal of attention to avoiding contact with these materials. Risk prevention not only served to ensure work safety

---

97 It should be noted that the meaning of "failure" is different for experiments in the sciences, for instance, in a physics lab. In that context, an experiment fails when it is not able to test a certain hypothesis. In both the humanities and sciences, however, failure is generally recognized as an important learning experience. See further ▶ Theory, Chapter 5.4.
98 Fickers and Van den Oever, "(De)Habituation Histories" 70.
99 See also Steven J. Jackson, "Rethinking Repair," in *Media Technologies*, ed. Tarleton Gillespie, Pablo J. Boczkowski, and Kirsten A. Foot (Cambridge, MA: MIT Press, 2014), 221–240, https://doi.org/10.7551/mitpress/9780262525374.003.0011.

when conducting the experiments, but at the same time imparted practical (tacit) knowledge in handling the equipment and learning how to use it. The risk of interrupting or aborting the experiment in the experimental *dispositif* corresponds to the risk in the historical *dispositif* – a risk of having to interrupt or even end a performance event after it had already begun.

The Art of Failure in 16mm Filming Experiments

The hands-on experiments with the Ciné-Kodak 16mm film camera from ca. 1930 serve as examples of how failures can function as heuristic tools in doing media archaeological experiments. In making the 16mm films, many things failed, either due to incorrect usage of the camera or because of a malfunction of the camera itself. As an example, for the second 16mm film, a mistake was made in loading the film camera by accidentally failing to follow a white line marked inside the camera that is meant to guide users in the process of loading the film. Because of this mistake, the film was placed too tightly in the camera's spool mechanism. The result was that the pull-down claw, whose function is to draw the film intermittently past the gate aperture, could barely perform the circular movement of pulling down the film directly before and after the exposure. Fortunately, the film did not break during the recording process, yet it did not contain any of the expected imagery after it was developed. Instead, it showed abstract lines and figures, which moreover appeared to be overexposed. Apparently, this mistake was common in the past.[100] In fact, it was one of the reasons why the white line indicator existed in the first place. In that sense, the experiment was a historically accurate re-enactment (and not really a failure from a methodological perspective). Re-doing these past media practices enables the reliving or experiencing again of such mistakes, thereby revealing not only the process of how past users of media technologies learnt from their mistakes but also the complexity of the innovation process. This information is often difficult to retrieve or find in the written historical sources.

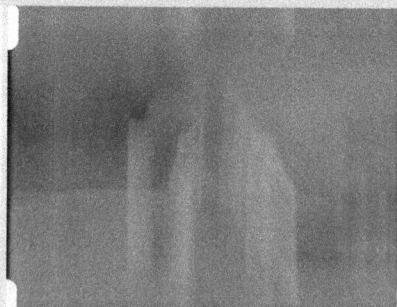

Fig. 35: White line indicator in the 16mm film camera and still from the distorted film. Photo by Tim van der Heijden. Courtesy of the C²DH / University of Luxembourg.

---

100 Onno Petersen, personal correspondence with Tim van der Heijden, 30 May 2020.

Another failure occurred during the experimenter's attempt to make an outdoor recording with the Ciné-Kodak 16mm film camera. The light conditions outdoors required a smaller aperture. However, the diaphragm of the camera did not close well enough, possibly due to issues of wear. As a result, too much light was captured by the lens during the recording process, which resulted in highly overexposed images. After development, the film came out almost completely blank. After scanning, it was possible to bring back some of the imagery in post-production. However, this resulted in some rather abstract and extremely grainy footage – which brought to mind results of some of the pioneering experiments with animated photography in the late nineteenth century.

Fig. 36: Overexposed 16mm film, compensated in post-production by Onno Petersen and reproduced by Tim van der Heijden. Courtesy of the C^{2}DH / University of Luxembourg.

Object Lesson in Avoiding Failures

The experimenter, Aleksander Kolkowski, possesses a good few years of experience in "cutting" records on a number of historical disc recording lathes, and in doing demonstrations and hands-on workshops in the techniques of analogue disc recording. Nevertheless, while attempting to make a direct-to-disc recording during a test of the apparatus, elementary mistakes can still be made, such as forgetting to plug in a cable, adjusting the depth of cut, or properly securing the blank disc onto the platter. Such mistakes can result in a poor or non-existent recording and are a waste of the recordable media, which is costly and hard to replace. It can also leave the experimenter exasperated and dismayed. Having past experience and attaining a level of proficiency at a task, which would include making mistakes and learning from them along the way, should guarantee that such basic errors are beyond the bounds of possibility when, after repeated practice, the operations inherent to the task can be carried out intuitively and the activity becomes second nature. However, mistakes still commonly occur and can be attributed to various reasons, including distractions, such as having conversations or giving a talk during the activity, or multi-tasking. In the latter case, while conducting an experiment, the experimenter might be documenting the activity and having to operate one or more devices simultaneously. The experimenter may also not be able to fully focus on the operation of a device while attempting to think objectively about the activity and writing or dictating lab notes. Avoiding distractions becoming a hindrance and ruining an experiment comes down to meticulous preparation, having sufficient assistance and clearly defining and designating the tasks at hand.

Other failures can, of course, occur due to faults in the media or equipment being used. In the case of lacquer discs, unwanted noise on the recording may be caused by imperfections on the disc surface or because of a worn or damaged cutting stylus. In the latter case, an experienced user will be able to recognise the inferior sound quality, especially in the higher frequency range, and the noise that is typically produced by a worn stylus tip. Such material and technological errors and failures are part and parcel of the disc recording process and of other technologies in general. As such, they contribute significantly to the explication of past usages (see also Chapter 4.3.1).

2.4 Involvement of Experts and the Public in Media Archaeological Experiments

Inviting experts, such as researchers in the given field, specialists, practitioners or professionals (be they active or retired), to participate in experiments is a highly expedient means of reinforcing and developing practical research. Their involvement may take one or more of the following forms: collaboration, participation, supervision and training, observation of experiments, and public events.

Collaboration

By working together, teams and individuals can share knowledge, expertise and skills. Close collaboration when doing experiments can also help in many practical ways, such as through observation, or assistance with documentation and note taking. Institutional collaboration can help in providing resources such as workspaces, equipment, specialist departments, skilled technicians, student assistance and educational projects.

Kinora Viewer and Stentorphone Soundboxes Replica Projects
Both projects were made in collaboration with the University of Luxembourg's Department of Engineering (DoE) on a separate campus. The DEMA project provided the historical objects for study and replication, and historical and technical background research, including patent applications and other sources. The DoE provided students who adopted the replication projects as part of their Bachelor and Master's studies, culminating in the CAD modelling and 3D printing of working replicas of the historic objects.

Participation

The participation in experiments and workshops of researchers in other fields, non-academic laypersons, and members of the public, is useful in gaining reflections and feedback that can inform and enrich the research undertaken by the experimenter. The participation of experts such as active or retired practitioners in simulations or re-enactments is a vital form of experimental media archaeology per se. In one of his lessons learnt from the ADAPT project, John Ellis argued that one of the most valuable contributions of doing media archaeological experiments that involve past users is that they can excavate memories, as in an oral history project (see Chapter 1.2.1). The encounter they have with the material in the historical re-enactments can bring new memories to the fore, including bad memories (e.g., when something went wrong). Re-enactments involve a different form of remembering, which can even dislocate established memories.[101]

---

101 In this context, see also Roger Kneebone's reflections on how re-enactments can foster memories and make explicit unconscious practices. Kneebone's project on keyhole surgery through simulation-based re-enactment – mentioned in Chapter 1 – reunited a distinguished team of (retired) professionals to re-enact a surgical procedure, performed in public at the London Science Museum. Using physical simulation, they aimed to get a sense and insight into the landscape of surgery of the kind Kneebone himself experienced as a junior surgeon, and of the instruments used. See Kneebone and Woods, "Recapturing the History of Surgical Practice."

Recreating an Eighteenth-Century Scientific Experiment: the (Re)production of Lichtenberg Figures

Led by historians of science Falk Rieß and Wolfgang Engels from the University of Oldenburg, the workshop "Images of invisible traces: The repetition of historical experiments producing (and reproducing) Lichtenberg figures" invited participating researchers to recreate a historic scientific experiment on the uncovering of electric discharge patterns and attempts to preserve the results by means of different methods, both ancient and modern. Participants were invited to a hands-on exercise in which they recreated the electric discharge experiments and made their own Lichtenberg figures at their working tables. They were also asked to document the process in detail and to reflect on how performing the experiment might be similar and/or different from the time when Lichtenberg conducted it, more than two centuries ago. Comparing the different reports prompted reflections on the role of documentation and the importance of capturing the verbalisation of thought processes during experiments on video and note form as well as those experiences and physical actions that are not easy to describe spontaneously.[102]

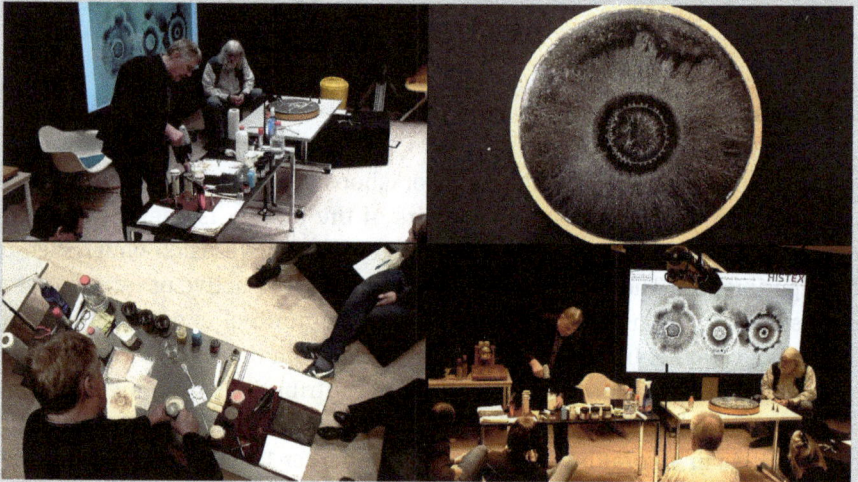

Fig. 37: Illustration of a Lichtenberg figure on a resin plate and its production, demonstrated by historians of science Falk Rieß and Wolfgang Engels. Courtesy of the C²DH / University of Luxembourg.

---

102 Tim van der Heijden et al., "Images of Invisible Traces: Documenting and Re-enacting an 18th Century Experiment," *C²DH | Luxembourg Centre for Contemporary and Digital History* (blog), 16 July 2020, https://www.c2dh.uni.lu/thinkering/images-invisible-traces-documenting-and-re-enacting-18th-century-experiment [last accessed 26.07.2022].

Supervision and Training

Having an expert in the field or an experienced practitioner instructor train the experimenter will, of course, enable the experimenter to learn or acquire knowledge and necessary skills. They can also supervise an experiment, demonstration or workshop, giving information and advice, while allowing the proceedings to be conducted by the principal experimenter(s) and intervening only when necessary or in an instructional capacity.

His Master's Vintage Voice – Experiments in Instantaneous Disc-Recording
This hands-on workshop and demonstration in the techniques of disc-recording on lacquer discs, using the HMV 2300H Portable Disc-Recorder, was supervised by Sean Davies, a world-renowned expert in the field of studio recording, mastering and in the use and restoration of historic disc recording lathes. In addition to giving a talk on the technical aspects of sound recording on disc, he was able to answer questions on the practical aspects of sound recording and reproduction, while providing valuable advice and oversight during the recording sessions.[103]

Observation of Experiments

Here, the role of invited experts is situated outside the experiment, looking in. They cast a critical eye on the experiment, offer advice and ask questions on what they have witnessed and the methods used by the experimenter. Such observation can take place in a laboratory setting or during a public demonstration, in much the same way as a researcher presents a conference paper to an audience, except that in this case the audience is expert and witnesses a practical experiment or the demonstration of a media technology. This may be viewed as a type of performative experiment and is undoubtedly enriching for both parties. The experimenter gains valuable feedback and may receive insightful questions from the audience, while the experts get an opportunity to observe the historical objects in use.

---

103 For more information, see https://dema.uni.lu/his-masters-vintage-voice-experiments-in-instantaneous-disc-recording/ [last accessed 26.07.2022].

Netherlands Institute for Sound & Vision, Hilversum, IASA Conference, Cylinder Phonograph Recording Demonstration (2019)

This was a live acoustic recording on wax cylinders of a choir, made in public by Aleksander Kolkowski, using an original Edison phonograph. The audience consisted of sound archivists, museum curators, sound technicians, conservators and specialists in audio restoration. For the assembled audience it was an enlightening experience, as most had never witnessed a recording being made in this way, even though they may have been actively involved in the archiving and digital transfer of historic cylinders. The demonstrator gained valuable experience in recording a choir using the phonograph and under the difficult circumstances of an unsuitable acoustic environment, while at the same time being able to share his knowledge of the technique of cylinder recording in a gathering of experts in the field of audio conservation. Their feedback included observations on the limitations of the acoustic recording process, such as how only those who sang directly in front of or tangentially across the mouth of the horn were adequately recorded and heard in the subsequent playback, and on the importance of the room, its size and acoustic properties in achieving a successful recording.

Fig. 38: A. Kolkowski records a choir on an Edison phonograph during a demonstration at the IASA Conference, Hilversum. Courtesy of Melanie Lemahieu.

Public Events

Involvement of the public in media archaeological experiments takes place in public demonstrations, workshops and re-enactments to which audiences are invited. In many forms of re-enactment, especially where the historical media technology is being used to entertain or operates as a service (i.e., to make a personal recording, photograph or such), the public role is integral to the experiment which, more often than not, will be a performative one. Where an audience, whether public or comprising expert witnesses, is considered an essential part of the experiment's *dispositif*, then it is important to conduct interviews with them (or as many as is practical) and collect their thoughts and reflections as part of the research undertaken on the event. This type of contextual enquiry is discussed in Chapter 3.4.

Documenting the Early Days of Keyhole Surgery Through Simulation-based Re-enactment
This project, conducted by Roger Kneebone and his team, was carried out in an operating theatre exhibit that provided necessary contextual ties, including original surgical equipment, surgical gowns, etc. The performance mode was heightened by the fact that the simulations took place inside a museum gallery under the gaze of the public, and these layers of performance served to make the experience more authentic for the team of (retired) professionals.[104]

Bandpass Filters in Stockhausen's "Sternklang" – Sean Williams
In his video presentation, musician and researcher Sean Williams stressed the value of doing research projects in live public performances, pointing out that the pressure of a performance situation can illuminate certain questions, in this case around performance practices in electronic music. (See further Chapter 4.2.5 on media archaeological performances.)[105]

2.5 Artistic Research

Artists who are embedded in academic or scientific institutions, museums and archives are able to inform media archaeological research through creative output that allows us to experience past technologies and apparatuses in new and unexpected ways (see Chapter 2.3.3). A creative reinterpretation or reimagining can inspire the historical imagination of researchers in contrasting ways to a historical re-enactment. Through the creative use of past media, the old becomes new. The novelty of using antiquated or obsolete formats can delight

---

104 Kolkowski and Van der Heijden, "Performing Media Archaeological Experiments."
105 Kolkowski and Van der Heijden, "Performing Media Archaeological Experiments."

and stimulate. The act of reviving "dead media" serves to reinvigorate our perception not only of the past but also the present.[106]

2.5.1 Recreating or Substituting Past Media Formats

Some historical media formats used for recording sound or making films are extremely rare and can be extremely expensive if produced today as a specialist product, such as newly manufactured lacquer discs for mastering or 16mm film. Short-lived formats such as recordable sound postcards, for example, may be non-existent, or are so rare that they have historical value as examples of blank media and should be left unused. Finding and using aged NOS (new, old stock) – unprocessed negative films and blank recordable discs and cylinders, for example – is very often a workable solution. Some types of media such as brown wax phonograph cylinders, magnetic tape, video and miniDV allow for erasure and re-use, although the erasure of historical brown wax cylinders that carry old recordings is in no way advocated here. Most likely, the old medium will have deteriorated over time as chemicals lose their potency, materials harden and varnishes craze. This will result in imperfections and distress according to the age and condition of the media. It will not be possible to get the same result as when the medium was fresh off the production line. Instead, it will likely lead to some degree of distortion, and this should be taken into account when assessing performance and other factors from the experiments.

Where no media exists at all, you can attempt to make it yourself by studying methods and formulae in patent descriptions, historical sources, such as workshop journals and handbooks, and by searching online forums devoted to a particular field of interest.[107] There are collectors, artists and enthusiasts who remake old media such as 8mm film or wax cylinders, and many will share their knowledge (see Chapter 1.4.2). Another way around the problem of missing media is to substitute the original medium with one made from different and more easily available

---

106 Aleksander Kolkowski, *The Wax Cylinder Phonograph in the Age of Digital Reproduction: Music-Making, Music Technology and the Aura of Obsolescence* (London: Brunel University, 2011). See also Tom Gunning, "Re-Newing Old Technologies: Astonishment, Second Nature, and the Uncanny in Technology from the Previous Turn-of-the-Century," in *Rethinking Media Change: The Aesthetics of Transition*, ed. David Thorburn and Henry Jenkins (Cambridge, MA: MIT Press, 2003), 39–59; ▶ Theory, Chapter 3.
107 An example is "The Secret Society of Lathe Trolls," an on-line forum that discusses numerous topics to do with disc recording, repairs and maintenance of vintage disc recording lathes. For more information, see https://www.lathetrolls.com/ [last accessed 26.07.2022].

ingredients or materials. An example is the use of discs made from vinyl or soft plastics instead of lacquer in instantaneous disc recording. However, it must be remembered that using different materials might require different techniques and skills and/or a modification of the media technology, and give different results.

How to Cut a Faulty Record from a Plastic Picnic Plate (2021)

This is a video by the sound and visual artist Paul DeMarinis. It gives an illustrated account of an artistic project where he combines past disc-cutting techniques and technology with state-of-the-art digital automation and DIY handicrafts, using glitches and malfunctioning media as the basis for creating music recordings. The title is self-explanatory; however, DeMarinis' use of disposable plastic dinner plates for this work came out of necessity as a recent and devastating industrial fire at the world's largest manufacturer of lacquer masters had resulted in an acute shortage of recordable discs. Hobby or DIY recordists have been using cheap plastic picnic plates as a substitute for lacquer discs for many years. The plate has to be trimmed with a circle cutter, and a centre spindle hole is made with an 8mm hole punch – and, presto, the thin 7" flexible disc is ready to record onto. The plastic disc was "cut" in the same way as lacquer, using a sapphire cutting stylus on DeMarinis' own modified 1948 *Rek-O-Kut* recording lathe. The plastic records are somewhat noisier than lacquer, but surprisingly durable. For this project, DeMarinis developed an automated CNC (Computer Numerical Control) system on his disc recording lathe that could cut grooves on a record that randomly skip, depending on the ballistics of the turntable that they are played on, giving the aural impression of a "faulty record". The plastic records were played in a performance at the Experimental Sound Studio Online Gala event, Chicago, July 2020.[108]

The Making of a New Kinora Reel

Part of the Kinora replica project was the making of a Kinora reel replica that would be compatible with the original Kinora viewer. For recreating the Kinora reel, the image sequence of the 16mm film – an outcome from the basic media archaeological experiments with the Ciné-Kodak camera (see Chapter 1.2.1) – was used to replicate the 640 photographic images of the original Kinora reel. The digitised film recordings of this sequence were first converted into 640 successive frames. For producing the images, the same dimensions as an original Kinora image card were used: 24mm x 19mm, giving an aspect ratio of 1:1.26. A number was added on the left side of the image card, corresponding to the frame number on the reel. Several tools were used to export the image sequence. In a video editing program, the correct speed of the original 16mm film sequence was set in order to export the 640 frames. By means of a photo editing program, the images were subsequently batch cropped and exported. After placing the images on seven A3 sheets of 160 grams paper, each holding 98 images, the images were cut with a laser cutting machine in the University's Engineering 3D Lab. After the printing and laser-cutting processes, the 640 image cards were mounted on a replica Kinora reel. First, the images were

---

108 Kolkowski and Van der Heijden, "Performing Media Archaeological Experiments."

compressed with a clamp and glued onto a piece of canvas, after which the canvas was glued to the core of the reel by means of double-sided adhesive tape. After attaching the top and bottom, the replica Kinora reel was then complete.[109]

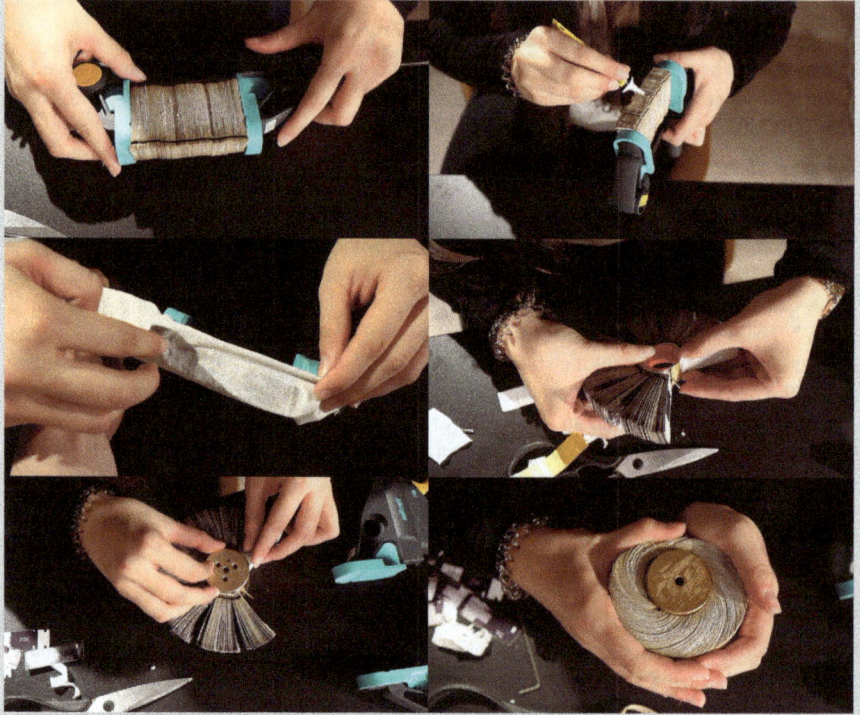

Fig. 39: The making of a Kinora replica reel. Courtesy of the C^{2}DH / University of Luxembourg.

---

109 Van der Heijden and Wolf, "Replicating the Kinora."

Cartavox Sound Postcard Recorder – Temporary History Lab, Esch-sur-Alzette (2020)
More than 50 individual picture postcards, displaying historical images dating from the 1900s to the 1970s, were especially made by the experimenter for this project. The images were mostly related to the industrial and social histories of the Minette Region in southern Luxembourg and digital copies were obtained from the archives of the cities of Esch-sur-Alzette and Dudelange. The postcards were individually hand-made: an image was printed on photographic paper and laminated with a glass clear PVC sheet, 240 microns thick, as a surface on which to record the sound groove. The size of the postcard depended on the original picture format, but they were mostly around 20cm (width) x 14.5cm (height). The reverse side, printed in a typical postcard format for writing and sending a message, together with information on the image, credits and sponsorship logos, was then pasted onto the back. Finally, a centre hole for the spindle was made using a 7mm hole punch. A typical card made this way weighs approximately 50g. The process involved cold lamination, cutting and trimming of paper, card and the PVC laminate.[110]

This recordable postcard-making process is entirely self-designed and does not reflect historical practices. The recordable postcards that were originally used were commercially manufactured and sprayed with a specially formulated nitrocellulose-based lacquer suitable for recording or "cutting". The use of a laminate in this case was borne out of necessity as no commercially manufactured or privately made recording lacquer exists that could be used as a coating for the cards. Experiments with different types of art varnishes had been tried without success. Moreover, the process of applying multiple coats of nitrocellulose lacquer on a large quantity of cards requires a spacious and well-ventilated workplace with a centrifugal fume extractor fan, which would have been beyond the scope of this project.

Recording the spiral sound-carrying groove onto a PVC material requires a technique known as "embossing", where the groove is indented onto the surface, as opposed to "cutting" where a thread of the material is literally cut away in creating the sound groove.

---

110 As a material, PVC was used to make discs for office dictation machines in the 1940s, such as the *Grey Audograph* and the *SoundScriber* (USA, 1945). It was also the base material for the German *Decelith* discs, which were widely used for recording and archiving radio programmes, as well as for private or personal recordings (1936–1951).

Fig. 40: Sound Postcard recorded at the Temporary History Lab.
Courtesy of the C²DH / University of Luxembourg.

2.6 Investigating Sensorial Perception

Media archaeological experiments provide opportunities for examining the role of the senses in performing tasks, operations and other aspects of the "re-enacted" user experience (▶ Theory, Chapters 2.3, 2.5 and 3.3). Determining the primary and secondary modes of sense in performing an activity is a step towards constructing a map of sensory fields in order to show how they are arranged and intertwined in practical, experiential actions.

Cartavox Sound Postcard Recorder – Mapping Sensory Modalities

This study examined the recording process, the operation and evaluation of the Cartavox apparatuses through sensory perception – the visual, aural and tactile or somatosensory modalities – and the multiple attention or multi-layered perception that played a role in carrying out a performative experiment that simulated the Cartavox recorder in use as a means of personal voice messaging. The study was taken from the perspective of both the operator of the Cartavox recorder and the person who records their voice directly onto the sound postcard. A series of visual representations were created to show the technical apparatuses and their physical arrangement in the space where the recordings took place, with lines that connect and map the principal sensory fields or modes. These modes were subsequently codified into lists of individual actions and the corresponding sensory experiences.

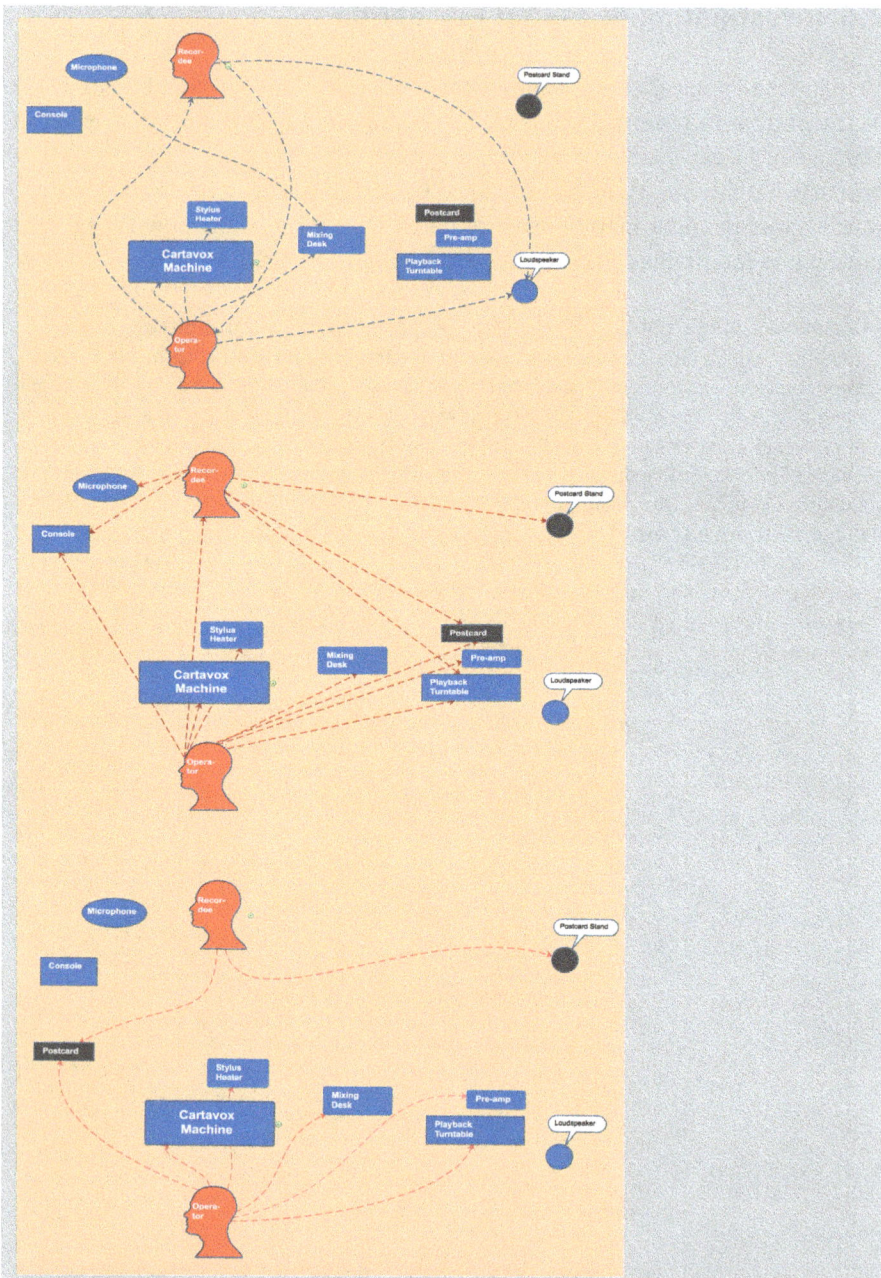

Fig. 41: Mapping Sensory Modalities: the aural (top); visual (middle); and haptic (bottom) sensory modes in relation to the Cartavox sound postcard recording activity. Illustration from Kolkowski, "The Cartavox Machine: Self-Recordable Sound Postcards. Experimental Report No. 1," 8.

An Anthropological Perspective – Using Re-enactment as Methodological Probe in Ethnographic Fieldwork

Anthropologist Anna Harris has examined how doctors learn sensory skills of diagnosis and how materials and artefacts can afford and assist in teaching such skills. Her "Making Clinical Sense" project involved a team of three anthropologists, who did fieldwork in medical schools located in Ghana, Hungary and the Netherlands at the same time. Harris' own field site was a classroom in a "skills laboratory" where medical students learn skills of physical examination, such as listening to heart sounds and learning how to palpate – a simulated clinical environment in an educational setting. In their simultaneous fieldwork, the three researchers performed the same ethnographic experiments or "re-enactment probes" that they had observed in their individual locations, and those were shared with each other in place of written reports. In this way, the anthropologists were able to probe and access unexpected entry points into their field sites. One such "probe" was to re-enact a scene from a photograph of a physical examination technique on how to test visual fields in patients. This test requires both patient and doctor to cover one eye through a series of complicated mirror exercises, and medical students often struggled to accomplish the technique. Harris sought to examine how doctors learn these skills and what media and teaching materials they use, then, through re-enactment, to get a sense of how the skills were documented within the material. These types of ethnographic experiments are atypical in that they re-enact something observed that day, or only a few days ago. The importance of the re-enactments was not only to assess the complexities of learning these skills, but also to try to embody the observed skills and help to archive bodily experiences in their field of science. Importantly for team ethnography, and unexpectedly, it gave an insight into the ethnographic imagination of others, by being given the "probes" to enact and by observing each other's materials.[111]

2.7 Evaluating Acquired Skills and Performance

An investigation into the histories of use of a media historical object takes into account the tacit skills and knowledge necessary to accomplish tasks and operations. The re-enacted user will acquire such skills through a combination of practical experimentation or learning by doing, receiving instruction and advice from experts in the field, and through archival resources. Over time, as users become familiar with an apparatus and gain increasing experience, they will usually move through different stages or levels of proficiency until they themselves attain expertise. The human skills and other aspects of embodied knowledge that are accumulated throughout the course of this media archaeological experimentation can be documented and analysed.

---

111 For the project website, see http://www.makingclinicalsense.com/ [last accessed 26.07.2022]. See further Harris, *A Sensory Education*.

Video and photographic documentation are means with which to capture movement, physical activity and focus on physical and material details, but they cannot adequately represent other fields of sense. The experimenter must find other ways of expressing sensorial experiences, e.g., through textual description, visual representation, voice and sound recording or through analogy and comparison. Where an object or media archaeological apparatus emits sound, a way to represent the auditory experience is through acoustemology: "a portmanteau word combining 'acoustic' and 'epistemology' – to foreground sonic experience as a way of knowing".[112] In its purest form, an acoustemological representation exists only as sound, a field recording or soundscape composition as an edited montage of sounds.[113]

Cartavox Sound Postcard Recorder: Human Performance – Evaluating Skills
The purpose of this study was to survey and codify the practice of tacit skills and the technical knowledge employed whilst operating the Cartavox recorder and auxiliary equipment in a performative mode. The manual dexterity involved may be minimal but high levels of attention and precision are required. As discussed in Chapter 2.6, the entire recording process, from the set-up to the playback, is a multi-modal affair, involving visual, auditory and somatosensory sense organs, and the principal modes of sensory perception in each activity were included in this study. The skills in this study are ascribed to the "re-enacted user" (▸Theory, Chapter 2.3), and, in conclusion, are related and compared to those that it is imagined would have been employed by historical or "configured" users of the Cartavox recorder in the past.

In evaluating the skills employed in the operation of the Cartavox machine and the recording and playback of the sound postcards, the study used the model proposed by Stuart Dreyfus, where the stages of skill acquisition are placed into five categories that are ranked accordingly: novice, advanced beginner, competent, proficient and expert. These can be summarised as follows. Novices need clear instructions on how to accomplish a task and have no intuitive understanding of the skill. Their activity may be free of any contextual understanding. An advanced beginner acquires some contextual understanding and is able to follow maxims. The competent user has gained the experience to recognise appropriate elements and procedures, devise plans and make decisions. With proficient users, experience is assimilated and embodied and they become more emotionally involved in a task. They can call upon a large repertoire of situational discriminations. The expert user, however, is able to call from a much greater repertoire of situational discriminations, and sees immediately and intuitively how to achieve the goal.[114]

112 Tom Rice, "Acoustemology," in *The International Encyclopedia of Anthropology*, ed. Hilary Callan (Hoboken, NJ: Wiley-Blackwell, 2018), https://doi.org/10.1002/9781118924396.
113 See John Levack Drever, "Soundscape Composition: The Convergence of Ethnography and Acousmatic Music," *Organised Sound* 7, no. 1 (2002): 21–27, https://doi.org/10.1017/S1355771802001048.
114 Stuart E. Dreyfus, "The Five-Stage Model of Adult Skill Acquisition," *Bulletin of Science, Technology & Society* 24, no. 3 (2004): 177–181, https://doi.org/10.1177/0270467604264992.

Cartavox Recorder - Activity	Visual Perception	Auditory Perception	Tactile & Haptic Perception	Olfactory Perception	Skills and Skill Level	
Preparation of postcards for recording: checking surface	Yes - primary field of sense	No	Yes	No	To recognise defects on surface. Some experience needed.	
Preparation of postcards for recording: cleaning surface	Yes	No	Yes	Yes	Methodical cleaning, use of chemicals. Some experience needed.	
Gauging distance between stylus tip and edge of card; making adjustments	Yes - co-primary f.o.s. with tactile perception.	No	Yes - co-primary f.o.s. with visual perception.	No	Measuring with calliper; adjustment of cutter-arm base. Experience & high proficiency needed.	
Sound check	Yes	Yes - primary field of sense	Yes	No	Listening for distortion; checking levels on VU meter and LEDs on mixer; adjusting controls.	High proficiency necessary.
Monitoring audio signal at cutter-head	Yes	Yes	Yes - primary field of sense.	No	Feeling for vibrations; using card resonator for hearing signal. Care needed not to damage stylus.	Competent to proficient level necessary.
Starting the machine, observing recording in operation	Yes - primary field of sense.	Yes	Yes	Yes	Recognising possible faults in cutting/embossing, control over signal level.	High level of proficiency.
Stylus heater: setting and operation	Yes - co-primary f.o.s. with tactile perception.	Yes	Yes - co-primary f.o.s. with visual perception.	Yes	Setting correct temperature, avoid overheating.	Competent level.
Examination of stylus tip for wear and damage	Yes - primary field of sense	No	Yes	No	To recognise stylus ware and damage, use of magnifier.	High level of proficiency necessary.
Mixing desk: operation before and during recording	Yes	Yes	Yes	No	Experience of audio mixing, control over input and output signals, familiarity with device.	Competent to proficient level necessary.
Cartavox console	Yes - primary field of sense.	No	No	No	Visual check on VU meter; start/end of recording and lapsed time through cueing light system.	No skill required.
Examination of postcard after recording	Yes - primary field of sense.	No	Yes	No	Recognise defects in grooves, gauge depth of cut or embossed groove using magnifier	High level of proficiency necessary.
Playback of sound postcard on external turntable	Yes	Yes - primary field of sense.	Yes	No	Operation of turntable, phono-preamp controls, placing of stylus on postcard record	Competent level.
Communicating with the "recordee"	Yes	Yes	Yes	No	Communications skills (see p.16).	Competent level.

Fig. 42: A digested "Senses & Skills" table. Illustration from Kolkowski, "The Cartavox Machine: Self-Recordable Sound Postcards. Experimental Report No. 1," appendix.

HMV 2300: Recording the Recorder – an Acoustemological Study

Here, the sounds recorded were not by the HMV disc recorder per se, but of it, namely those sounds and noises produced during its running and operation. Each facet of operational sound was individually recorded, including those made by the switches and controls, the platter motor and overhead lathe, the positioning of the cutter-head, the placing and removal of the recordable disc, and the hum and crackle produced by the amplifier and its vacuum tubes as they heated up or cooled down. These numerous elements were combined in a montage that delivered a sonic representation of the HMV 2300 recorder in action, from the perspective of the listening user.

2.8 Analysis, Interpretation and Reflection

How should we assess, analyse, interpret and reflect on the experimental process and its outcomes? The use of lab diaries, which describe the steps taken within the experiment, together with audio-visual documentation, form the basis for analysing the experimental process and its results in experimental reports. These experimental reports can also include examinations of historical sources and literature, and thus provide insightful perspectives on the media historical object and histories of its use. The conclusions drawn from an experiment can prompt further actions and improvements that could be carried out in experiments that follow, or as a guide to other users (see also Chapter 4). They may contain observations about the behaviour of the object, reflections on the success or failure of the experiment, or a phenomenological analysis aimed at understanding the user experience. The examples given in this section show how we have analysed and interpreted the results of various experiments and reflected on the experimental process and its outcomes. They demonstrate how media archaeological experiments can function as a heuristic tool for multidimensional analysis, for conducting reception/audience studies through performative research methods, for explicating (and excavating) the materiality, functionality and (hidden) infrastructures of historical media objects, and – on a methodological level – how experimental reports enable reflection on the experimental process itself.

2.8.1 Multidimensional Analysis

Hands-on experimentation facilitates processes of learning and understanding in embodied and sensorial ways. Through media archaeological experiments, Fickers and Van den Oever argue, the historian is consequently enabled to grasp "a new degree of complexity" when interpreting the traditional source materials (▶ Theory, Chapter 2.7). One may become more attentive to, for instance, the role of the sensorial, material, performative, social, spatial and tacit dimensions of past media technologies and their user practices.

Multidimensional Analysis of Ciné-Kodak 16mm Film Experiments

The experiments with the Ciné-Kodak 16mm film camera made explicit various dimensions that often remain implicit in written historical accounts. The sensorial dimensions of past media usages become apparent: feeling the weight and size of the 16mm film camera; hearing the rattling sound of the camera during the recording process; or experiencing the limited recording time of the film camera, for instance (▶ Theory, Chapter 1.6). Furthermore, the reenactments with the Ciné-Kodak 16mm film camera made explicit the social dynamics involved in home movie recording practices, such as the social interactions between the person behind the camera and the family members participating in the filmmaking process. This role play or "Ensemblespiel", as discussed by the German scholar of amateur film Martina Roepke, is an important characteristic of home movie making.[115]

In addition to the sensorial and social dimensions, the media archaeological experiments made explicit the user-technology relationship. Unlike semi-automatized film cameras, such as Super 8 film cameras from the late 1960s and 1970s, the Ciné-Kodak 16mm film camera needed to be operated completely manually. The spring-motor had to be manually wound, the light to be measured, and the focus and aperture to be set and controlled for each new recording. The experiment explicated these technological constraints, which, in combination with the high cost of celluloid film, required the user to be selective in what to record. Ultimately, such a multidimensional analysis of the Ciné-Kodak 16mm film experiments contributes to a better understanding of the "constructivist nature" of home movies as media products, namely as the outcome of a complex social, cultural and technological process (▶ Theory, Chapter 2.8).

Fig. 43: Making-of and still from Ciné-Kodak 16mm film experiment. Image by Tim van der Heijden. Courtesy of the C²DH / University of Luxembourg.

---

115 Martina Roepke, *Privat-Vorstellung: Heimkino in Deutschland vor 1945* (Hildesheim: G. Olms, 2006). See also Roger Odin, *Le film de famille: usage privé, usage public* (Paris: Méridiens Klincksieck, 1995); ▶ Theory, Chapters 1.6 and 2.7.

2.8.2 Reception, Participation and Tacit Knowledge in Practice-Led Research

Media archaeological experiments can make explicit experiential dimensions in practice-led research that involves the participation of audiences, which allows for studying their reception and interpretations of the activities they have experienced.

Report on the "Cartavox" Sound Postcard Recording Apparatus (1958)

This report gives a detailed account of a performative experiment staged at the C²DH pop-up Temporary History Lab in the city of Esch-sur-Alzette in October 2020. Here, the Cartavox recording device from 1958 was installed in a simulated sound postcard recording station where guests and members of the public were invited to make voice recordings directly onto bespoke picture postcards. As well as containing a complete description of the recording activity, the technical operation of the machine and the making of the sound postcards, the report discusses possible reasons for the Cartavox's commercial failure. A theory put forward by the manufacturer of the machine was "Microphon-Angst" (fear of the microphone): it was suggested that members of the public were reluctant to talk freely or recite personal messages in the presence of a recordist, in contrast to the privacy of an enclosed fully automatic coin-operated and enclosed recording booth. Those visitors who recorded at the sound postcard recording station at the History Lab were questioned and their answers were revealing; some found the presence of the recordist reassuring – a guarantee of a successful recording, while others stated that this arrangement would not have been suitable for recording very personal messages. None of the recordees were intimidated by the experience; it seemed the nervousness felt at recording a message for posterity would have been the same if the recording took place in an enclosed booth. The report concluded that the more likely reason for the Cartavox's failure was the cost of having to employ somebody to operate the machine.

In reflecting on the performative experiment, the report also examined the multi-sensory nature of the activity in detail and the level of skills necessary to successfully operate the Cartavox. The apparatus may be semi-automatic, but there are basic skills that are a prerequisite for making sound recordings, such as adjusting sound levels to avoid distortion and maintain an optimum signal-to-noise ratio. The operator should also ensure that the recordee maintains a suitable distance from the microphone, depending on the loudness of their vocal delivery. Added to these are more specific skills pertaining to disc-cutting and embossing grooves on lacquer or other surfaces. The operator has to learn how to adjust the weight of the cutter-head to regulate the depth of cut, which has a bearing on the success and quality of the recording, and to brush away swarf while the groove is being cut, carefully pushing or guiding the thread of swarf towards the centre of the platter where it coils around the spindle. Individual skills were evaluated and assessed (see Chapter 2.7) and it was found that a strong level of competency would have been necessary to ensure satisfactory results and satisfied customers using the sound postcard service. A competent user soon becomes proficient after practice and experience, which involves the making of errors and gaining an awareness and better understanding of the recording process. Operators would, therefore, have had to familiarise themselves with the apparatus and make several test recordings prior to offering a paid service to the public. In identifying and practising these skills in a live situation with members of the public, the experimenter was able to make a tangible connection with past users of the Cartavox recorder.

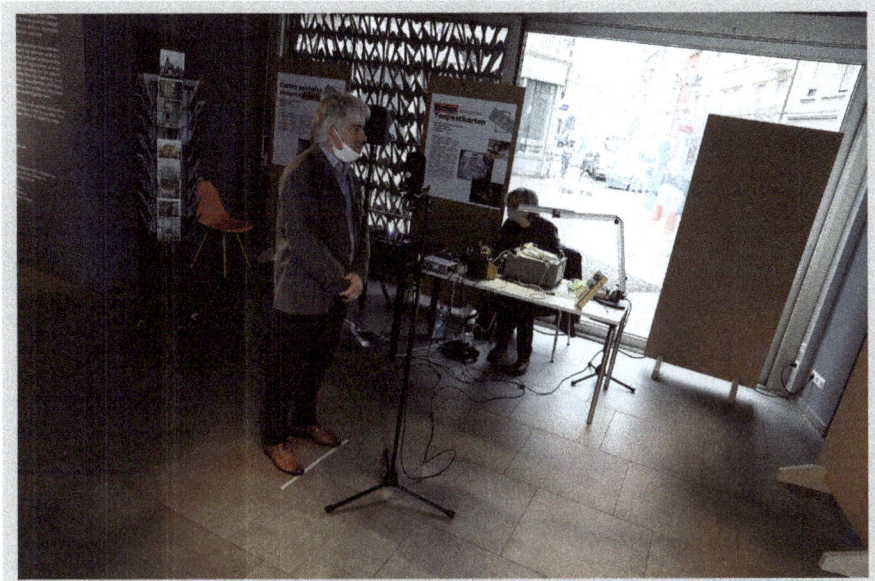

Fig. 44: Making a sound postcard voice recording with the Cartavox machine. Photo by Noëlle Schon. Courtesy of the C^{2}DH / University of Luxembourg.

Wilcox-Gay 1C10 Recordio (1952) – a Use of Audio and Video Documentation to Understand Tacit Knowledge

An examination of video footage taken during the creation of the signal-to-noise composition (see Chapter 1.2.1) reveals the high level of physical engagement with the Recordio device and the patterns of physical actions performed during the recording and playback operations. As with most analogue electronic audio devices, the Recordio relies on the physical handling of switches, levers and knobs for the control elements, while the magnetic tape has to be threaded and spooled, the disc placed on the platter, needles exchanged, and microphones and instruments plugged in. Moreover, there is a typical order in which these actions are carried out, with minor variations, during the recording process. Only the most basic operating instructions are outlined in a technical schematic obtained for this model, and the tacit knowledge necessary to obtain seamless control over the device was acquired through practical experience and experimentation. Audio-visual documentation not only captures the activity but allows for an analysis of the elements of this tacit knowledge. The analysis may then be used to construct a graphical representation, such as an activity diagram that, as well as providing an overview of the activity, will help familiarise inexperienced users of the device with its controls and operations.

2.8.3 Materiality, Functionality and Infrastructures

A study of the materiality, the physical properties of the media historical object, can be a valuable part of the experimental investigations. This can take into account the role of the different raw materials and component parts that make up the whole. These entities are never chosen arbitrarily and discovering the reasons why they were used over other materials can be illuminating. For instance, in his investigation on the construction of historical resonator boxes for tuning forks, Kolkowski noted the use of tone wood for the upper surface of the resonator, similar to the sound boards of guitars and violins, which demonstrated the link between musical and scientific instrument-making during the nineteenth century.[116]

During the process of restoration and repair, it sometimes becomes necessary to replace parts in order to bring the historical object into a working condition. With electronic equipment, components such as capacitors and resistors have a limited shelf life and will become ineffective over time, thus needing replacement. There is a trade-off between keeping the object in its original condition and substituting old for new parts to allow it to function as it once did. When such components have been exchanged, the status of the historical object changes too; it is no longer in its original condition as at the time it was made. In most cases, the substitution of parts or elements with modern equivalents will affect the efficacy of the experiment, giving false or unsatisfactory results, or none at all if they are not fit for purpose. In Paolo Brenni, Anna Giatti and Roland Wittje's "The Speaking Arc and Singing Arc" experiments, modern alternatives were tried but found to be unsatisfactory and even dangerous: a substituted capacitor exploded, the new voltage transformer caused interference, and a modern microphone would have overheated. It thus becomes necessary to go back as closely as possible to the original ways and means of doing such experiments (see Chapter 4.2.5).

The study of materiality can also challenge assumptions about the superiority of modern technology over past developments (▶ Theory, Chapter 3.1). The triple-spring motors and complex gearing of enduring phonographs and gramophones from the early 1900s are often described as being "bomb-proof" or "over-engineered", but they bring into stark contrast the built-in obsolescence of modern mass-produced consumer products. Examining the materiality of historical media objects can also give us information as to their longevity and the

---

116 See for more information: https://www.mpiwg-berlin.mpg.de/users/akolkowski [last accessed 26.07.2022].

conditions they were kept in. Brown wax cylinders from the late nineteenth and early twentieth centuries may have developed mildew; Blue Amberol cylinders may have become warped and deformed; and the surface of nitrocellulose/lacquer discs may have become cloudy and brittle. The causes may have to do with humidity (or lack of it), temperature and other factors and, while such considerations are traditionally in the province of conservators and archivists, it is nevertheless in the interest of the experimental media archaeologist to gain an understanding of the care and handling of media objects. As with technological objects, upon inspection the media objects too will reveal their own histories of use. Furthermore, the machines are not isolated as historical objects, but their user practices involve hidden or disappeared infrastructures.[117]

The Materiality of Swarf

Swarf is a byproduct of the process of physical inscription when recording sounds onto discs and cylinders. It is the term for the threads of material that are "cut" away from the wax cylinder or lacquer disc as the recording stylus ploughs through the surface forming a spiral groove. Its name refers to the metal filings and stone chips produced when operating a lathe machine (disc recording machines with overhead lead screw systems are also called lathes). Swarf or "chip" (U.S.A.) has to be removed during the recording by brushing, suction or blowing as, if not done, it will ruin the recording by clogging up the stylus and interfering with the cutting of the groove. Swarf problems will cause noise and distortion on playback, and it can be made worse by atmospheric conditions and electrical static. Nitrocellulose swarf from lacquer discs is also highly inflammable and has to be carefully managed and disposed of. Despite these negative aspects, swarf is a fascinating substance: it is the material negative of the inscription and, when the swarf is magnified, the cut-out groove formations can be seen in 3 dimensions. The rustling, squealing and other "unwanted" noises caused by the swarf are recognisable, and the user will learn to identify these sounds as part of their learning and development of skills in disc recording. The connotative nature of swarf has inspired artists to make work using the material.[118]

---

117 This point was made by John Ellis as part of his lessons learnt from the ADAPT project. See Van der Heijden and Kolkowski, "Documenting Media Archaeological Experiments."

118 Artist Cornelia Parker's "The Negative of Sound" (1996) is a framed relief containing clumps of swarf threads from a master disc record that was cut at Abbey Road Studios, London. The work is part of her collection of "avoided objects" that speak of their role in a process which has made them seem redundant, " . . . things that have lost their life or not yet got a life." [. . .] "The idea of the negative of sound, for me, is fantastic. How can you listen to it? What does it sound like? What kind of instrument would you have to have to play them on?" (David Gale, "Cornelia Parker," *Strength Weekly* (blog), 1997, https://strengthweekly.com/cornelia-parker/ [last accessed 26.07.2022]).

Fig. 45: Swarf from cutting records on the HMV 2300H. Photo by Aleksander Kolkowski. Courtesy of the C^{2}DH / University of Luxembourg.

Paul Morris Music and the Vulcan Cylinder Record Company – Manufacturers of Blank Cylinders and Hardwearing Cylinder and Disc Records

While the traditional infrastructure for the manufacture and supply of cylinder records has long disappeared, today's aspiring cylinder phonographer is fortunately able to order blank "wax" cylinders for recording and to also have limited editions of duplicated cylinder records produced with either two- or four-minute duration times. This is thanks to Paul Morris and Duncan Miller in the U.K. who have both devoted a large part of their careers to the making of cylinder records. Morris' new blank cylinders are made to original formulae obtained through many years of practical research and inspection of historic sources, including Workshop documents from the Edison Record Company. Some ingredients that are now unobtainable, such as aluminium oleate, have had to be substituted, but the mixture of metallic salts, fatty acids and waxes, which make up what is essentially a metallic soap, is largely the same as was used for the production of recordable cylinders, employed in sound studios, for office dictation, and for home use. Miller's process for the duplication of hardwearing cylinders and discs involves electroplating and moulding, and is also based on the study of historical sources, aided too by his own knowledge of chemistry. Both these experts share their knowledge widely and have collaborated with researchers and archives in addition to supplying cylinders for collectors and hobbyists. Whereas in the past the relationship between the phonograph user and the supplier of machines and blank and pre-recorded cylinders may have been more direct and transactional, these examples of modern cottage industries supplying a particular demand represents an infrastructure network where relationships are formed between the manufacturer, various types of users and the media object itself.[119]

Kinora Replication Informing the Reading of its Original Patents and Functionality

The hands-on experimentation and replication processes of the Kinora replica project informed the analysis and interpretation of the historical sources, such as the Kinora patents from 1896 and 1912. They shifted the focus towards some of the media historical object's distinguishing characteristics, for instance, the curvature of the Kinora image cards. During the replication process, we experienced problems with disassociating the images well enough. This made us re-evaluate the importance of the reel's curvature for establishing the effect of the illusion of moving images in the viewer. The process of making the Kinora replica was thus not only informed by studying the patents and other historical sources, as described in Chapter 1.3, but also by their re-reading and re-interpretation based on replication practices.

2.8.4 Reflecting on the Experimental Process

The experimental reports are a valuable place to reflect upon the experimental process itself, not just the results it brought. What things went as expected, what things failed, and what things could be improved for the next experiment?

Stentorphone Replica Soundbox Test Report

A report on a basic experiment, where a 3D-printed replica model of the Stentorphone soundbox was used for the first time on a gramophone, contained conclusions on its performance and practical recommendations for the improvement of the replica model. The following aspects were identified:

Air Pressure and Flow
The air compressor employed for the experiment was found to be significantly underpowered in terms of delivering the required amount of air pressure. It did, however, successfully provide high and continuous airflow that enabled the experiment to be carried out. An air compressor or blower that met the correct specifications was to be sought. In the meantime, higher air pressure would be used for subsequent experiments.

Control of the Valve
The action of the torsional spindle controls the action of the moving valve by applying pressure on a fulcrum, which increases or alleviates the resistance of a steel spring at the base of the valve. This action was shown to be fundamentally crucial to the operation of the Stentorphone and its performance. Some aspects of the replica spindle's design needed modification and improvement.

---

119 See http://www.paulmorrismusic.co.uk and https://www.vulcanrecords.com [last accessed 26.07.2022].

Escape of Air

Factors contributing to the lack of power and relatively poor sound quality were, in part, due to the poor sealing and high leakage of air from the front of the valve. The importance of sealing leaks and improving the closure of the valve to prevent excessive escape of air when in closed position was noted.

Weight

The 3D-printed polymer replica soundbox is much lighter than the original, which was made of brass. For the mechanical reproduction of shellac 78 rpm records, the weight for a gramophone soundbox should be no less than 140g and usually not exceed 225g.[120] If too light, the sound-box will start to vibrate or resonate along with the needle. This was apparent during the experiment on playback, when no air passed through the replica Stentorphone soundbox, but sound was heard emanating from it. Another problem with insufficient weight is that the needle has a tendency to ride up the walls of the record groove if there isn't enough weight to keep it down. Adding weight to the replica or 3D printing of the component parts in metal was suggested as a solution.

The detail in the report, which identified the above and other key areas of improvements to be made to the Stentorphone replica, proved to be crucial in the design of subsequent models.

2.9 Recommendations and Reflections

Within this chapter, we have discussed various aspects related to the practice of researching media archaeological experiments. Based on the examples discussed, we can summarise the following recommendations and reflections:

- Media historical objects should be assessed, tested and repaired before commencing any hands-on experimentation (2.1 and 2.2).
- Failures, mistakes and unexpected problems can become learning opportunities as they can offer new insights into actual user practices and experiences of the past (2.3).
- Involving experts from the field of practice and participation of the public in media archaeological experiments can be helpful for sharing knowledge, expertise and skills (2.4).
- Artistic research can inform media archaeological research by means of presenting and experiencing past technologies and apparatuses in new and unexpected ways (2.5).
- Media archaeological experiments provide opportunities for examining the role of the senses in performing tasks, operations and other aspects of the "re-enacted" user experience (2.6).

---

120 H. A. Gaydon, *The Art and Science of the Gramophone* (London: Dunlop, 1928).

– An investigation into the histories of use of a media historical object takes into account the tacit skills and knowledge necessary to accomplish certain tasks and operations. The re-enacted user will acquire such skills through a combination of practical experimentation or learning by doing, receiving instruction and advice from experts in the field, and consulting archival resources (2.7).
– Media archaeological experiments are both informed by and can inform the reading of traditional historical sources, such as handbooks, magazines and advertisements (2.8).

Chapter 3
Documentation

Documentation is essential to an experiment and therefore forms an integral part of the experimental system. But how can we document our experiments in such a way that they can be useful for others in both research and teaching environments? This chapter looks at different documentation methods and tools; ways to create a documentation set-up and formulate the aims, strategies and protocols of documentation; the use of contextual inquiry at public events; and the opportunities and challenges of documentation. It makes use of lab diaries and technical reports, as well as the use of audio and video tools for the documentation of experiments.

3.1 Documentation Methods and Tools

Different means can be used for documenting media archaeological experiments. It is recommended that you carefully choose your documentation methods and tools, as each comes with different affordances and limitations. We distinguish between the following documentation tools: lab diary, photo and video camera, smartphone, sound recorder, live action camera, 360-degree camera, and multicam technologies. In the sub-sections below, we elaborate on how these tools can be used for documenting media archaeological experiments, as well as their affordances and limitations.

3.1.1 Lab Diary

The lab diary – also known as "lab manual", "logbook" or simply "notebook" – is a standard method of documenting the results of scientific experimentation as done, for instance, in the fields of physics and chemistry. In humanities disciplines, lab diaries and documentation protocols have also been implemented more and more, along with the emergence of so-called "humanities labs".[121] The main objective of a lab diary is to describe the objectives of the experiments

---

[121] Darren Wershler, Lori Emerson, and Jussi Parikka, *The Lab Book: Situated Practices in Media Studies* (Minneapolis, MN: University of Minnesota Press, 2022).

∂ Open Access. © 2023 the author(s), published by De Gruyter. [(cc) BY] This work is licensed under the Creative Commons Attribution 4.0 International License.
https://doi.org/10.1515/9783110799767-004

and systematically write down the experimental process and its results. Lab diaries can be in either paper or digital form.

Kinora Replica Project
In the Kinora replica project, lab diaries were used to document the process of making the 3D replica. An online note-taking platform was initially used for sharing resources and documentation materials within the project team. Since the lab diaries often included images and videos, which required additional storage space, it was decided to use a cloud-based server hosted by the University of Luxembourg for sharing the lab diaries, together with the audio-visual documentation materials and AutoCAD files. Hosting a combination of textual and audio-visual sources on one location accessible to all team members worked very well for documenting the project's development.

Thick Description Versus Summary
In terms of content, the lab diary usually provides a step-by-step description of the experimental process and its results. Keywords noted down during the experiment can subsequently be transformed into a more detailed description of the media archaeological experiment. The cultural anthropologist Clifford Geertz coined the term "thick description" to describe this interpretative methodology used in anthropological and ethnographic studies.[122] A thick description of the media archaeological experiment provides a way to verbalise and "translate" the embodied and sensorial experiences of the experiment into a written and linear account. Thick descriptions may be a suitable method for capturing such details, yet the question remains of how detailed the descriptions need to be and in what form. An alternative approach is to make the descriptions rather short, by means of short statements or even only keywords, for instance. The experimental report (see Chapter 4.2.1) can then serve as a space to summarise or synthesise the gathered information, and to reflect on the most important aspects of the experimental process and lessons learnt from the media archaeological experiment.

Thick Description in the ADAPT Project
A good example of a thick description is presented by John Ellis in his article "Filming for Television: How a 16mm Film Crew Worked Together". It explores the complex process of analogue television production in the 1960s and 1970s by re-uniting a former BBC television crew and simulating their collaborative practices. Supported by a multicam video recording of this simulation, Ellis aims to provide a detailed description of all the actions and interactions involved

---

122 Clifford Geertz, "Thick Description: Towards an Interpretive Theory of Culture," in *The Interpretation of Cultures*, ed. Clifford Geertz (New York: Basic Books, 1973), 3–30. See also ▶ Theory, Chapter 4.3.

in the simulation in the part of the article entitled "24 Minutes in the Life of a Film Crew": "After 18 minutes of preparation, and prompted by the simulation director, the electrician checks his final light with the director, and declares 'that's all the lamps'. He is indicating that his preparations are over. As the assistant returns the loaded magazine back to the camera, they engage in an exchange about an anonymous unit manager who insisted that all lights sent on a job should be used, followed by a story about camera tape and the BBC's influence on the film manufacturer Kodak. The cameraman, however, has realised that the sound record-ist has a problem and begins to help out by checking cables. The director is trying to move things along, and thinking that everything will be ready once the magazine is back on the cam-era, asks whether he should bring the 'professor' in and 'light him for real'. The sound record-ist declares that 'we'll have to sort out my little problem first'. The camera assistant appears not to have noticed this and continues the process of putting the loading bag away, an impor-tant procedure as it has to remain clean and dust free inside."[123]

3.1.2 Photo and Video Camera

The lab diary, as a documentation of the experimental process in written form, can be supported by photos and videos. In general, photo and video cameras have become essential tools for researchers.[124] Researchers can choose to use, for instance, a digital single-lens mirror reflex camera (DSLR) or a mirrorless camera. DSLRs are often heavier than mirrorless cameras, but usually provide better battery life and a greater selection of lenses – although these differences have been increasingly diminishing over time. Since DSLR cameras are usually heavier, they provide more stable recording practices compared to mirrorless cameras. To compensate for any motion blur, a gimbal can be used for extra stability. Alternatively, the photo/video camera can be placed stationary on a tripod at a 90-degrees angle, for instance, so that the experiment is documented from a third-person perspective.

Video Documentation of Small-Gauge Experiments
A mirrorless camera was used for documenting the experiments with the Ciné-Kodak 16mm and 8mm film camera technologies. The camera was placed on a tripod at a 45-degree position behind the experimenter, establishing an "over the shoulder" point of view. This position

---

123 John Ellis, "Filming for Television: How a 16mm Film Crew Worked Together," *VIEW Jour-nal of European Television History and Culture* 8, no. 15 (27 October 2019): 9–10, https://doi. org/10.18146/2213-0969.2019.jethc167.
124 Jane Anderson et al., "Using Video in Research and Documentation: Ethical and Intellec-tual Property Issues to Consider – Fact Sheet," 2013, https://summit.sfu.ca/item/16151 [last ac-cessed 26.07.2022].

enabled the capture of the historical object in use from a third-person perspective. The mirror-less camera provided stable and high quality video recordings, so it was often used as the main digital recording device, sometimes in combination with live-action and 360-degree video cameras. The recorded footage was used to present the results of the experiment as a split screen video montage, including the 16mm and 8mm film recordings (see Chapter 4.2.4).

Fig. 46: Documentation of the Ciné-Kodak Eight film experiment. Image by Tim van der Heijden. Courtesy of the C²DH / University of Luxembourg.

One of the advantages of video documentation is that it enables you to catch certain physical and tacit techniques that are often difficult to verbalise (▶ Theory, Chapters 4.1 and 4.4). As John Ellis argued: "The use of audio-visual documentation of hands-on practices makes visible much that has escaped analysis in the past. Viewing filmed footage opens up the world to a fresh process of seeing. The viewer is enabled to see actions, attitudes and exchanges that would have been overlooked even by alert observers during the actual filming."[125] At the same time, the use of video in documenting media archaeological experiments comes with various challenges, as we will discuss later in this chapter.

Fondazione Scienza e Tecnica Video Demonstrations

The Science and Technics Foundation, founded in 1987, produced a series of videos by historians of science, Paolo Brenni and Anna Giatti, that serve to document the functioning of several original instruments from the collection of the Fondazione Scienza e Tecnica in Florence. In the numerous videos, Brenni and his team re-enact a number of historical scientific experiments using original historic instruments from the museum. The experimental process and the handling of objects are very clearly shown, and videos are presented without commentary. The project description on the YouTube channel states that the videos aim "to offer a source for didactic activities and historical research".[126]

Use of Video Documentation in illuminago's Experiments

In *illuminago's* experiments with the Improved Phantasmagoria Lanterns, video was used to document the set-up of the temporary laboratory and the processes of the experiments. The experimenters used the photo and video recordings to recapitulate the experiments and to explain them to partners, as well as to prepare further experiments. In the experimental report, these visual records illustrate the written accounts, which would otherwise often not be comprehensible. There was uncertainty initially about the recorded sound in video recordings; however, the sounds made during the experiments are an indispensable part of the documentation and therefore cannot be omitted. At first, after listening to the informal oral communication in the videos, the question arose as to whether the experiments should be conducted in silence. In the end, it was decided to include team communication. Another important note is that the projections, like many other historical projection apparatuses, require darkened rooms. This meant that the experimenters had to set up spotlights, which could be turned on during the preparation stage and dimmed during the actual recording. This led to limitations in the recording quality, but did not necessarily have a negative effect on the documentation as a whole.

---

125 John Ellis, "Why Hands on History Matters," in *Hands on Media History: A New Methodology in the Humanities and Social Sciences*, ed. Nick Hall and John Ellis (London: Routledge, 2019), 13.

126 For more information about the Fondazione Scienza e Tecnica video demonstrations, see https://www.youtube.com/user/florencefst/about [last accessed 26.07.2022].

Fig. 47: Experimenter Ludwig Vogl-Bienek testing the lamp of the Improved Phantasmagoria Lantern. Courtesy of Bienek / illuminago.

3.1.3 Smartphone

The smartphone can be a useful additional documentation tool. An advantage of the smartphone is that it is generally more portable than regular DSLR and mirrorless cameras. It may also be experienced as less visible, intrusive and impactful on the experimental process compared to other documentation tools. On the other hand, smartphones usually provide less control over the recording process. In recent years, various accessories have been made available that optimise the smartphone as a recording medium, which can benefit documentation purposes. These include auxiliary lenses for enhancing image quality, smartphone-adapted gimbals, and LED ring lights.

3.1.4 Sound Recorder

A stand-alone sound recording device is an essential documentation tool. A solid-state recorder can be used for field recordings, to record interviews and, especially when equipped with external microphones, can provide a vastly improved sound quality compared to what is obtainable from the inbuilt audio facility on cameras and video recorders. A sound recorder could also be used as a tool for making a *spoken* lab diary, an audio fragment that contains verbal descriptions during the experimental process, recording reflections on its results. Additionally, having a single audio track of the whole duration of the experiment can provide a useful reference point for the video montage. Such an inbuilt synchronisation feature facilitates the editing process when dealing with multiple audio-visual sources.

It is recommended to use a sound recording device that allows for the connection of external microphones in order to extend the possibilities of audio recording in media archaeological experiments. The type of microphone(s) used will depend on the use case/situation, as well as the sounds that are to be captured in the hands-on experiments. A brief summary is given below of common microphone types and their applications.[127]

Omnidirectional

One or two omnidirectional microphones will record at a full 360 degrees, and this type of microphone will deliver a natural, "open" sound that captures a wide sound field. However, it will record more ambient sound than other types of microphone, and therefore requires careful placement so as to obtain a good balance of direct and ambient sound. The microphones should be placed far away from extraneous noise sources, such as heating units, fans, buzzing strip lights, etc. The recording from an omni microphone can, if desired, be mixed with that of a more directional type, in order to provide additional ambience.

Unidirectional

The most common unidirectional (*uni* as in single) microphone has cardioid (heart-shaped) response; it is most sensitive to sound arriving directly in front of the microphone's diaphragm and is least sensitive at 180 degrees off-axis. A cardioid microphone will therefore record much less ambient sound than its omnidirectional counterpart when it is placed directly in front of the sound source or human speaker(s). This type of microphone is most commonly used for recording interviews, musical instruments and in situations where the focus

---

127 The website of the Shure audio products corporation provides a number of educational publications, downloadable as PDFs, with many informative guides on microphone types, techniques of recording, and film and video production: https://www.shure.com/en-US/sup port/downloads/documents?document=educational-publications [last accessed 26.07.2022].

is placed on the subject of the recording, in much the same way as in using a camera. Stereo recordings can be made using a coincident pair of cardioid microphone and a X-Y technique, where they are placed closely together or criss-crossed at an angle between 90 degrees and 130 degrees from each other.[128]

Hypercardioid

Videographers will commonly use an external microphone with a hypercardioid polar pattern connected to the camera. While this highly directional type of microphone is useful in focusing on speech or to pin-point a sound with increased isolation from surrounding noises, there is a danger that the audio source can go off-axis due to movement of the camera or the subject, to the detriment of the recording. It is therefore wiser to use this type of microphone only for stationary sound sources. Hypercardioid microphones are also more likely to produce a strong proximity effect when placed too close to a subject, making the sound "muddy" or "boomy" due to an increase in low frequency response. They are therefore generally unsuitable for close-miking purposes.

Binaural

The simulation of immersive and life-like sound in 3D is achievable through binaural and ambisonic recording. Once the province of *Dummy Head* recording in professional studios and concert halls, binaural recording has become more common with the advent of affordable in-ear binaural microphones that are worn by the recordist. Having the appearance of playback earphones makes them discreet and they can be a useful means of fully capturing a sound environment, for recording sound walks, and for creating an immersive listening experience. However, they are designed only for sound reproduction through headphones and not loudspeakers, where the 3D effect will be lost. When using wearable binaural microphones, the recordist must take great care not to touch the cables as this will result in unwanted noise. Monitoring the recording and sound levels can only be done visually through the display on the recording device. Care must also be taken with sudden or fast head movements as the sound field will, of course, be audibly affected. In the context of a media archaeological experiment, these microphones could be employed to capture a particular "point of listening" – capturing the sound from an experiment or apparatus as it would be heard by the users/experimenters themselves.

---

128 For stereo recording techniques, see https://www.dpamicrophones.com/mic-university/stereo-recording-techniques-and-setups [last accessed 26.07.2022].

Ambisonic

As with binaural recording, ambisonic microphones and devices have now become available as "consumer electronics", marketed mainly for Virtual and Mixed Reality applications. The 360-degree recording is made with an array of up to eight individual microphone capsules, each of which has a dedicated channel that can be controlled. A stand-alone ambisonic microphone will require software or a compatible DAW. However, portable ambisonic recorders are widely available and have an inbuilt decoder, which enables different editing and playback modes, and they can, for example, be configured for creating 5.1 and 7.1 surround sound as well as standard stereo sound. Ambisonic recording would therefore seem to be an ideal method for capturing the entire soundscape of a performative experiment. However, faithfully reproducing the multichannel recording will require an audio playback system with a surround sound facility and multiple loudspeakers.[129]

Recording the Recording Process: HMV 2300H and Wilcox-Gay IC10 Recordio
For recording the sounds of the above recording apparatuses in action, three different types of small diaphragm condenser microphones were used: a hypercardioid type directed at the specific moving parts we wished to record with more isolation; a cardioid type to cover a larger area or when directed at the device's playback loudspeaker; and two omnidirectional microphones hung overhead to capture the natural sound of the apparatuses at work.[130] When making recordings for analytical purposes, such as for spectral analysis when analysing the performance of the Stentorphone soundbox in comparison with conventional diaphragm soundboxes, a measurement microphone was used (See Chapter 1.2.2). This type of microphone is an omnidirectional condenser with a flat frequency response across the spectrum.

3.1.5 Live Action Camera

A live action camera can be used to document media archaeological experiments from a first-person perspective. Live action cameras are increasingly used for documenting scientific experiments and as a pedagogical tool in scientific lab

---

129 An excellent training guide for recording spatial audio for 360-degree video is found on the NPR (National Public Radio) website; see https://training.npr.org/2018/11/27/360-audio/ [last accessed 26.07.2022].
130 Condenser microphones require external power, see https://www.neumann.com/home studio/en/what-is-a-condenser-microphone [last accessed 26.07.2022].

settings.[131] One of the advantages of the live action camera is its flexibility, due to its small size and light weight. It can be attached to different surfaces. Generally, there are two main positions for placing the camera: on the head ("headset") and on the body ("body set"). It is recommended to test the camera position in advance of the experiment to guarantee it will document the right information in the preferred way. It is possible to check and adjust the angle and frame either manually in the menu settings accessible via the small LCD display or in the smartphone app that controls the camera via Bluetooth.

Various accessories can be purchased to enhance the live action camera's recording possibilities, for instance, an additional lens modification to maximise image stabilisation, extra ports for additional light sources, secondary microphones, or an external monitor. Live action cameras can also be used in combination with a tripod as a stationary recording device. Their light weight and small size make them easy to attach to any object, so they can be used as "overhead" cameras, for example. Due to the relatively small sensor, the image resolution of the video recordings made by live action cameras is often relatively low compared to regular video cameras. This limits, for instance, their use for extracting stills from the raw video footage. Furthermore, live action cameras usually provide a macro or fish-eye perspective, which may or may not be desirable. Nevertheless, some recent live action cameras can record in "standard" recording mode as well. On the GoPro Hero 8, the type of live-action camera used in the DEMA experiments, one could choose between four different fields of view (FOV): "super view", "wide", "linear" and "narrow". The super view FOV provides an extreme wide-angle view, whereas the (cropped) linear view provides a normal view comparable to a regular video camera.

131 F. M. Fung, "Seeing through My Lenses: A GoPro Approach to Teach a Laboratory Module," *Asian Journal of the Scholarship of Teaching and Learning* 6, no. 1 (2016): 99–115; Sara McCaslin, Marilyn Young, and Adarsh Kesireddy, "Using GoPro Hero Cameras in a Laboratory Setting," in *Proceedings of the 2014 ASEE Gulf-Southwest Conference* (Tulane University, New Orleans, LA: American Society for Engineering Education, 2014), http://asee-gsw.tulane.edu/pdf/using-gopro-hero-cameras-in-a-laboratory-setting.pdf [last accessed 26.07.2022].

Use of a GoPro in Recording the Wilcox-Gay 1C10 Recordio

The light weight and small size of the live action camera makes it easy to set up an overhead shot of the recording device by mounting the camera on a tripod and fully extending the height. An overhead GoPro camera was used, for instance, in the case of documenting the experiments with the Wilcox-Gay Recordio in order to capture the manual operation of the controls. A conventional camera at a 90-degree angle could have been used as well, but would be more difficult to balance on the tripod, and weights would need to be added to the feet to prevent the camera and tripod from tipping over.

Fig. 48: Documenting experiments with the Wilcox-Gay Recordio using an overhead GoPro camera and condenser microphone. Photo by Aleksander Kolkowski. Courtesy of the C^{2}DH / University of Luxembourg.

Cartavox Sound Postcard Recorder

The live action camera was placed on the top works of the recording device to capture footage of the recording process from the user's perspective. When recording, the operator will often look closely at the stylus embossing the groove from this angle.

Fig. 49: Live action camera attached to the Cartavox Sound Postcard Recorder. Photo by Tim van der Heijden. Courtesy of the C^{2}DH / University of Luxembourg.

Use of GoPro in Small-Gauge Experiments
In the small-gauge experiments with the 16mm and 8mm Ciné-Kodak film cameras, the live action camera was used to complement the third-person perspective of the regular photo and video camera by providing a first-person perspective. One of the advantages of the light weight and small size of the GoPro is that it can be attached, for instance, on top of the film camera. In one of the Super 8 film experiments, the live-action camera was used to capture the subject digitally in this way. Instead of waiting for the film to be developed and digitised, this made it possible to watch and reflect on the recordings right after the experiment.

3.1.6 360-Degree Camera

As with the live action camera, the 360-degree camera was recently introduced as a consumer media technology and may be used as a documentation tool. A 360-degree camera can record still and moving images in a 360-degrees all-round view. Such a complete angle extends the limited angles provided by regular photo and video cameras, as well as live action cameras. On the Insta360 company's website, the camera was promoted as "a camera crew in your hand", which allows for capturing images without "leaving the moment" – suggesting an unobstructed process of recording the event.[132] Moreover, the footage potentially allows for interesting Augmented Reality and Virtual Reality applications yet to be explored in experimental media archaeology.[133]

As a tool for documentation, a 360-degree camera can be useful when documenting the interaction between the experimenter and the audience in a performative experiment, for instance. Similar to some of the other documentation tools, the use of 360-degree cameras can be enhanced with various accessories. The back bar accessory, for instance, allows for placing the 360-degree camera on the back of the experimenter and extending the camera's perspective so that it provides a bird's-eye view.

---

132 Insta360, "Insta360 ONE – A Camera Crew in Your Hand," 2022, https://www.insta360.com/product/insta360-one/ [last accessed 26.07.2022].
133 Gert Jan Harkema and André Rosendaal, "From Cinematograph to 3D Model: How Can Virtual Reality Support Film Education Hands-On?" *Early Popular Visual Culture* 18, no. 1 (2 January 2020): 70–81, https://doi.org/10.1080/17460654.2020.1761598.

Use of 360-Degree Camera in 16mm and 8mm Filming Experiments
A 360-degree camera was used as a tool to capture the actions involved from multiple perspectives in a filming experiment with the Ciné-Kodak 16mm film camera. The indoor setting
allowed for staging the setting, with the film camera positioned on one side, the subject of
recording on the other side, and the 360-degree camera positioned in between the experi-
menter/camera and the subject. That way, the 360-degree camera could capture both perspectives at once. In this case, it allowed for capturing the experimenter making the film as
well as the subject approaching the camera during the re-enactment. For documenting the
first experiment with the Ciné-Kodak Eight 8mm film camera, it was tested whether the back
bar accessory could provide added value, in presenting a bird's-eye perspective to the experimental setting.

A disadvantage of 360-degree footage is that it takes up a lot of space on the
hard drive. For the DEMA experiments, a 128 GB micro-SD card was used that
can record up to 130 minutes when recording in 5.7K 30fps resolution. Another
disadvantage, at least at the moment of writing this guide, is that the 360-degree
footage is difficult to view back without a dedicated app or 360-degree viewer installed on the computer. The 360-degree angle of the footage is suitable for virtual reality purposes but, when making a regular two-dimensional video out of
the footage, it may be cumbersome to select fragments and edit the footage.

3.1.7 Multicam

The last documentation tool that we would like to focus upon is the multicam – an
installation of multiple cameras which synchronously document the hands-on experiment or demonstration in sound and image. Multicam documentation can be
particularly useful in "in situ" lab environments, in which the experimental process can be documented from multiple perspectives, without the need to reposition
the cameras during this process. In the ADAPT project, multicam was used for
both documentation and dissemination purposes.[134] In the case of the DEMA
project, the professional studio of the Media Lab of the University of Luxembourg
generously facilitated the recording and documentation of our experiments and
demonstrations by means of multicam equipment. The multicam videos usually
featured video input from four different cameras, which were merged together into
one multicam clip. Each video was recorded in Full HD resolution (1920 x 1080 pixels), exporting a multicam clip of 4K video resolution (3840 x 2160 pixels).

---

134 See, for example, ADAPT Television History, *16mm Film Crew Prepares to Shoot: Multi-Angle
Version*, 2016, https://www.youtube.com/watch?v=BDlKVGtxXpo [last accessed 26.07.2022].

Pathé-Baby Demonstration with the Multicam

The media-technological experiments with and demonstration of the hand-cranked Pathé-Baby 9.5mm film projector were documented by means of the multicam facilities of the University of Luxembourg's Media Lab.

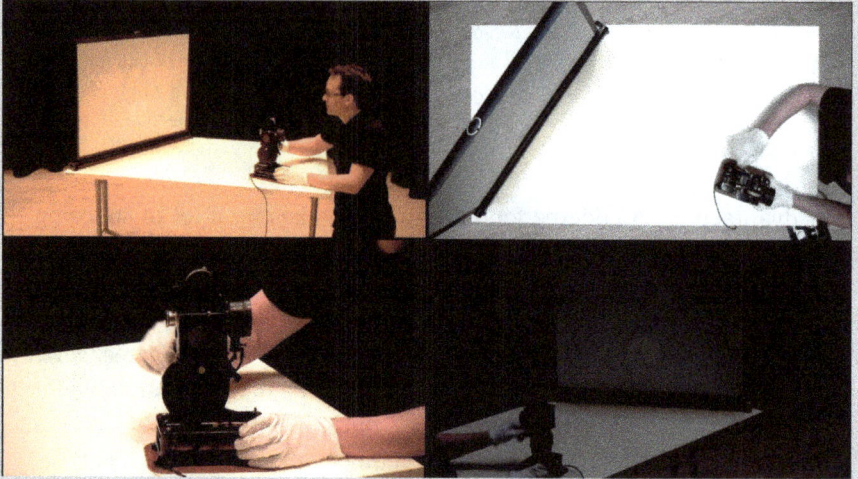

Fig. 50: Multicam recording of a demonstration of the Pathé-Baby 9.5mm film projector at the Media Lab of the University of Luxembourg. Courtesy of the C^{2}DH / University of Luxembourg.

"His Master's Vintage Voice: Experiments in Instantaneous Disc Recording" Public Workshop (2020)

The multicam setup was used in this workshop not only to document the activities from four different angles, but because it also enabled the participants to gain a close overhead view of the disc recorder in action while other information was displayed simultaneously on adjoining screens.[135] Further experiments took place in the Media Lab and were captured using the multicam system. The video footage allows for a close examination of the techniques of analogue disc recording.

---

135 For more information about the event, see https://www.c2dh.uni.lu/events/his-masters-vintage-voice-experiments-instantaneous-disc-recording [last accessed 26.07.2022].

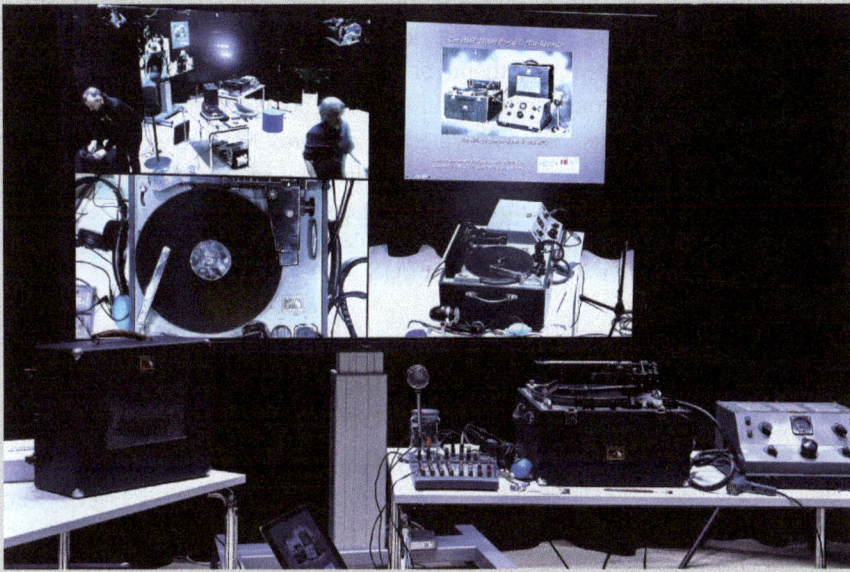

Fig. 51: His Master's Vintage Voice workshop: multicam view on monitor screen. Courtesy of the C²DH / University of Luxembourg.

3.2 Documentation Set-up

3.2.1 Data Storage, Management and Organisation

Documenting media archaeological experiments usually requires a high level of file organisation and data management. In the case of the ADAPT project, for instance, more than 16TB of audio-visual footage was generated, including the editing of more than 160 videos.[136] Before starting the experiment and its documentation, it is therefore important to think about where and how to store, manage and organise your data. Needless to say, it is important to regularly back-up your data and drives and store the files in different physical and virtual locations. It is recommended to use at least two external hard drives and one cloud-based drive. The latter is useful especially in case of team collaboration.

---

136 For all video documentation from the ADAPT project, including links to the original videos uploaded to the Figshare depository, see https://www.adapttvhistory.org.uk/ [last accessed 26.07.2022].

Depending on the project's needs and requirements, data storage can be organised in various ways – per type of documentation medium, chronologically (per date of the experiment), per theme or topic, or per media historical object itself, for instance. It is recommended to differentiate between the unprocessed data (i.e., unedited photo, video, sound, live-action camera, 360-degree and multicam recordings) and the processed data (i.e., experimental reports, edited videos and any other edited footage based on the unprocessed data), so that one can always go back to the source. Using folders, tags, labels and categories is useful to organise the data.

Use of Folders, Tags and Categories for Data Management

For storing data of the media archaeological experiments with early twentieth-century home cinema technologies, two external hard drives were used: one main drive and one back-up drive. On these drives, the experiments are organised chronologically. Folders are titled by the date of the experiment (yyyy-mm-dd) and name of the experiment including the media historical object at stake. For example, the folder "2020–02–06 – Ciné-Kodak 16mm film camera, experiment 1" includes all the documentation material of the first basic media archaeological experiment with the Ciné-Kodak 16mm film camera, which took place on 6 February 2020. Within this main folder, a sub-folder titled "Media" includes all unprocessed documentation material, stored and organised per media type (e.g., footage from Canon mirrorless camera; footage from the GoPro live action camera). The unprocessed data captured on these media are stored in their own respective sub-folders. Organising the documentation files this way – chronologically and per experiment – makes it relatively easy to locate and import the files in a video editing programme, such as Final Cut Pro X. The chronological organisation of the unprocessed documentation material also works well in corresponding to the lab diaries, which are also organised by date (see Chapter 3.3.3). In the experimental reports, on the other hand, multiple days and types of experiments can be combined. Clustering the experiments per type of media historical object, instead of chronologically, can therefore be another useful approach to data management. This approach was chosen for the media archaeological experiments with twentieth-century sound recording and amplification technologies.

3.2.2 Data Ethics and GDPR

Data ethics and the consideration and application of the General Data Protection Regulation (GDPR) is another important aspect of the documentation set-up. This is applicable in cases where other participants or an audience are involved in media archaeological experiments. In their report "Using Video in Research and Documentation", Anderson et al. argue that video "makes it easy to share cultural material with larger audiences", yet at the same time it is important to "be aware of considerations regarding the sharing of knowledge and intellectual property represented in video and film."[137] Topics such as data authorship, ownership and copyright, permission for the publication of online videos, and informed consent of participants should be addressed. In general, it is recommended to verify these topics with the participants involved in the media archaeological experiment and to respect the latest rules and regulations on copyright and data protection applicable in the country where the experiment takes place. Every participant of the experiment should be informed about the objectives of the experiment and the requirements for participation at the outset. Interviewees also need to be asked to give their written consent before project members can make oral history recordings.

Within the DEMA project, our post-doc research projects were submitted and approved by the Ethics Review Panel of the University of Luxembourg before the start of the project. In our ethical review applications, we addressed the following ethical principles of the university's policy on ethics in research that were identified as relevant for the project:[138]

Ethical principles	Measures
Research integrity	– All direct and indirect contributions of colleagues, collaborators and others will be acknowledged. – Participating researchers are accountable to society.
Involvement of human participants	– Project researchers will be aware of the active involvement of human participants (e.g., for oral history interviews) in research and dissemination of findings. – The project will consider the impact that publication of research findings may have on participants and on the groups they represent.

---

137 Anderson et al., "Using Video in Research and Documentation."
138 For more information about the ethics policies and committees of the University of Luxembourg, including the Ethics Review Panel, see https://wwwen.uni.lu/research/researchers_research/ethics_policies_and_committees [last accessed 26.07.2022].

(continued)

Ethical principles	Measures
Informed consent and respect of confidentiality	– Participation of external stakeholders shall be voluntary. – Informed, competent and understanding consent by participants will be respected. This involves the full and careful explanation in language understandable by lay persons. – The purpose of the research, the procedures, and the possible risks involved will be carefully explained to the participants and participants' rights will be clearly communicated. – Participants are free to withdraw from the project at any time. – The confidentiality of information provided by participants will be respected. – Collected data will be anonymised if required or requested by participants. – Access to the source material will be limited to the project team.
Consideration of vulnerable people	– Enhanced ethical consideration will be given to those who may be less competent or able to offer or refuse consent.
Consideration of risks	– The project will implement a continuous evaluation of risks and opportunities. – Risks will be minimised by using the safest procedures consistent with UL's ethical policies. – The PI will be responsible to ensure that all ethical policies and procedures concerning the involvement of human participants are adhered to in the research project and the publication and dissemination of research findings.
Independent ethics review	– The Commission Nationale pour la Protection des Données will be consulted if required. – The UL's Data Protection officer will be contacted concerning the implementation of the new data protection regulations if required.
Dissemination and publication of results	– Results will be published and disseminated responsibly and with awareness of the consequences of dissemination through media outlets. – Every effort will be made to inform all sponsors of any publications or dissemination of project's research findings.
Other considerations	– All researchers in the DEMA project should be aware of the ethics policies of research sponsors and publishers and check for compliance with university regulations, national laws and EU regulations.

3.2.3 Practical Set-Up

In terms of the practical set-up of the media archaeological experiment, it is useful to think about whether the space and location of the experiment is large enough for the experiment to take place and whether additional lightning is possibly required to be able to conduct and document the hands-on practices, and also to think about which tools you will be using to document the experiment (see also Chapter 2.3). Using many documentation tools can become a distraction to the experimental process, especially when the experimenter is also responsible for the documentation. In terms of setting-up the documentation equipment, it is recommended to position the documentation tools towards the historical object, instead of the other way around.

Cartavox Sound Postcard Recorder, Temporary History Lab, Esch-sur-Alzette (2020)
The location provided ample space for the live recordings of the sound postcards and for other activities to take place simultaneously alongside them. The multiple recordings made by visitors to the sound postcard installation also allowed for the stationary camera to be repositioned after each voice recording and a new perspective captured.

Fig. 52: Cartavox sound postcard recordings were captured from multiple perspectives at the Temporary History Lab. Courtesy of the C²DH / University of Luxembourg.

3.3 Documentation Aims, Strategies and Protocols

3.3.1 Aims

Documenting media archaeological experiments may serve different aims, namely: (1) to document the material object itself, (2) to document the tacit knowledge involved in the use of past media technologies, (3) to facilitate the possible replication and reproducibility of the experiment itself, and (4) for the purpose of dissemination and communication.

Material Object

When documenting the material object, the documentation focuses on the materiality, shape and size of the object itself. The documentation may also capture visible traces of use and wear, indicating how the object may have been used in the past.

HMV 2300H Portable Disc Recorder and Wilcox-Gay 1C10 Recordio Tape & Disc Recorder

Both appliances had visible signs of wear. The HMV recorder showed slight damage to the slotted screw heads on the amplifier unit casing, indicating that the unit had been opened by a previous owner to access the internal workings for servicing, repair or modification. Further inspection showed that modifications had been carried out in order to increase the frequency response of ribbon microphones (as recommended in the accompanying service notes, see Chapter 2.2). The damage to the screw heads, due to an improperly selected screwdriver, together with the poor soldering job, indicate that the work was not done by a professional electrician. Opening the recorder unit and inspecting the electrical circuitry revealed that a resistor had been exchanged with one of an "incorrect" value (according to the accompanying service sheets). This may have been carried out to increase the level of signal to the cutterhead, which had lost sensitivity due to the strength of its internal magnets diminishing over time. The user manual also revealed traces of use as a previous owner had made pencil notes and lines on one page that lists possible faults and their effects on the recording.

The Wilcox-Gay Recordio had been acquired in a very used condition showing considerable wear and tear, especially on the exterior of the casing. One obvious fault with the unit was the stability of the platter, which was loose on the spindle and wobbled badly during playback. A feature of the machine is that a single motor drives the running of both the magnetic tape recorder and the disc platter, and the unit has been designed so that the magnetic tape passes around and underneath the platter and is wound onto the spool or reel without necessitating its removal. However, in practice, the tape often becomes stuck and the platter needs to be taken off to untangle and realign the tape. The repeated removal and replacing of the platter had, over many years of use, resulted in considerable wear of the platter's centre hole, so that it no longer fitted snugly onto the spindle. This particular example of wear and tear showed the extent to which the unit had been used in the past, as well as an obvious fault in the design of the machine.

Tacit Knowledge

One of the main objectives of doing media archaeological experiments is to inform us about and document the tacit knowledge that is involved in the use of media technologies. As mentioned in the Introduction, this guide uses the term "tacit knowledge" to refer to all implicit forms of knowledge invested in past media usages, including "embodied" and "gestural" knowledge. Fickers and Van den Oever argue that it is through hands-on practice and the acts of capturing and documenting that such "embodied forms of implicit or tacit knowledge" can be made explicit, thereby making visible also the "limitations of speech and written language as primary modes of knowledge production" (▶ Theory, Chapter 3.6; see also Chapters 4.1 and 4.4). In *Hands-on Media History*, John Ellis similarly emphasises the gains of the hands-on approach for capturing and learning from tacit knowledge through audio-visual documentation:

> Multiple camera points of view can capture interactions of people with people, people with machines, and machines with machines that are simply too complex or too fleeting to be apprehended in the flow of events. [. . .] Researchers will at last be able to perceive that which is not easily articulated in words alone. The "hands on" method combines audio-visual recording [. . .] with the direct sensory experiences of researchers. Researchers deploy a combination of audio-visual recording of skilled users with the immersion of the researcher into similar or analogous physical interactions with those machines. They would both experience for themselves and observe the experiences of others. This would enable researchers to perceive the physicality of human/machine interactions; to grasp the processes that are not verbalised by the human participants in those activities; and, importantly, to observe the activities of teams of humans working with arrays of machinery.[139]

Documenting media archaeological experiments thus not only helps to capture and analyse the tacit knowledge that includes complex technical and social interactions involved in hands-on practices. It can also explicate and evaluate the acquired skills and performance of the experimenter (see Chapter 2.7).

"Closely Observed Lathes" – The Cartavox Sound Postcard Recorder and HMV 2300H Portable Disc Recorder

In documenting the operation of both of these recording devices, it was possible to closely observe from it the patterns of physical actions and gestures that are used when engaged in the process of cutting and embossing sound grooves; the position of hands on the controls and the lowering of the cutter-head onto the disc to gauge the depth of cut; the sensing of the strength of sound vibrations by placing a finger on the stylus tip; the scrolling movements and positioning of the cutter arm on the overhead lathe; the brushing away of swarf towards the centre spindle; the close inspection of the freshly cut sound grooves with a loupe after recording; and so

---

139 Ellis, "Why Hands on History Matters," 13–14.

on. Beyond the tacit knowledge required to cut a disc, there is a choreography of user actions that is put into play once the recording commences.

Fig. 53: Cartavox: sensing temperature and signal from audio input by touching the tip of the embossing stylus. The postcard surface is heated with a hairdryer prior to recording. Photo by Aleksander Kolkowski. Courtesy of the C^{2}DH / University of Luxembourg.

While the documentation footage aims to make the tacit knowledge of working with the media historical object visible and explicit, it should be noted that tacit knowledge is by definition implicit and personal knowledge.[140] Documenting demonstrations is therefore sometimes not enough to explicate the tacit

---

140 Philosopher Michael Polanyi defines tacit knowledge as "personal knowledge", which is opposed to the idea of "objective knowledge" as propagated in modern science. See Michael Polanyi, *The Tacit Dimension* [1966] (Chicago, London: University of Chicago Press, 2009). See also Véronique

knowledge involved in using a media historical object. The presence of tacit knowledge should also be verbalised and reflected upon. In addition to documenting the historical re-enactment and hands-on experiences through audiovisual means, it is therefore recommended to conduct oral history interviews with the participants prior to or right after the experiment or demonstration. This gives participants the opportunity to reflect on their practices and verbalise to what extent tacit knowledge is involved.

Roger Kneebone's Simulation-Based Re-enactments

In his simulation-based re-enactments of historical surgical practices, Roger Kneebone made use of "post-enactment video review sessions", in which participants viewed and commented on the freshly made video documentation. This helped to identify some of the non-verbal communication and non-explicit forms of behaviours involved in the practices, and enabled Kneebone to "derive insights into the social and technical nature of surgical expertise, its distribution throughout the surgical team, and the members' tacit and frequently subconscious ways of working".[141] "In post-enactment video review sessions, they repeatedly identified aspects of their behaviour of which they had been wholly unaware at the time, and which they had not mentioned during pre-enactment interviews. Such behaviours included anticipating the needs of other team members; passing instruments unprompted; assisting with surgical techniques; communicating in a variety of verbal and non-verbal ways; and using banter, humour and challenge for educational purposes while operating. Our recordings from multiple perspectives have created a record of these behaviours, and of multiple other aspects of routine surgical and pedagogic practice, which can be readily viewed by those not present during the 'operation' itself".[142] Kneebone and Woods' example indicates how simulation-based re-enactments and video documentation can function as tools for memory retrieval and the reconstruction of both technical and social aspects involved in past user practices.

Replication and Reproducibility

The documentation of the experiment can further serve a methodological aim: the possible replication or reproduction of the experiment, so results can be validated or compared – a standard practice in the context of scientific experimentation. The documentation of the experimental process can also be an opportunity for the researcher to recreate certain steps in a case where something goes wrong. The practices of recording and documenting mistakes provide valuable opportunities for learning, as discussed in Chapter 2.3.4. Although replication and reproducibility are worthwhile objectives, it should be noted that each media

---

Ambrosini and Cliff Bowman, "Tacit Knowledge: Some Suggestions for Operationalization," *Journal of Management Studies* 38, no. 6 (2001): 811–829, https://doi.org/10.1111/1467-6486.00260.
141 Kneebone and Woods, "Recapturing the History of Surgical Practice," 107–108.
142 Kneebone and Woods, "Recapturing the History of Surgical Practice," 120.

archaeological experiment is a unique experience and may therefore have different outcomes – even if the conditions and people involved are the same. The focus of the documentation should not dwell excessively on the outcomes, but rather focus on the experimental process itself. After all, it is within this process that the actual learning takes place.

Documentation of Measurements and Parameters in the Kinora Replica Project
In the Kinora replica project, various measurements were taken of the original Kinora viewer and reel in order to design and 3D model their parts in AutoCAD. These measurements were documented, as well as the user tests conducted for testing the four parameters formulated in advance (see Chapter 1.1.1). For testing the first parameter – the optimal distance between the lens and the image – it was found that the sharpness of the image is hardly affected when the lens changes its position from the bottom of the lens hood (so at the closest position to the image), to approximately half-way up the lens hood. Even when the low lens is in the highest position all the way up the lens hood, the image is still in focus. For the second parameter – the optimal magnification of the lenses and distance between them in the viewer – it was found that the combination of a 6x magnifier (high lens) and 5x magnifier (low lens), with a space between the lenses of 4.8cm, gives the most optimal presentation. It was found that the third parameter – the optimal thickness of the paper of the Kinora image cards for smooth rotation – is between 120 and 200 grams. For the fourth parameter – the optimal relation between the recorded frame rate and the viewer's speed of rotation – we found a frame rate of 14.6 fps with a rotation speed of 60 revolutions per minute was best. These practices of measurement and calculation were documented by means of a mirrorless camera and a live action camera, so other researchers would be able to replicate or reproduce them.

Dissemination

Finally, the documentation can serve processes of knowledge dissemination, for example, the recording of a demonstration of the media historical object in use for educational purposes. However, the dissemination of the media archaeological experiment usually requires some form of "translation" of the documented footage and data into a processed form. As Kneebone and Woods argue in relation to their simulation-based re-enactments:

> The novelty of this methodological approach brings challenges. For example, how can we make this rich data accessible to other scholars, and how should data analysis be approached? Since social practices in the operating theatre are complex, layered and mediated through multiple modes, written transcripts alone are inadequate. At this stage we do no more than highlight the issue and open it for debate. Our own view is that video recordings could be mapped against a written summary, chronicling the key steps of the operation and providing time codes for specific events and transition points. Further analysis at

a micro level could be conducted at a later date, perhaps drawing on the growing body of work around ethnomethodological approaches within the operating theatre.[143]

Within the DEMA project, we similarly faced this challenge of translating the documentation material into forms suitable for dissemination. One strategy is to combine the lab diary or experimental report, as processed written reflections of the experimental process, with either the raw or edited audio-visual documentation of the experimental process. By combining textual and audio-visual sources, it is possible to document and reflect on the experimental process at the same time. In Chapter 4, we will further elaborate on the challenges of making the documentation of media archaeological experiments useful for both research and educational purposes.

EMA-Journey: Exploring the Roots of Transnational Television in Europe
The article "On the road again", written by Andreas Fickers, Andy O'Dwyer, and Alexandre Germain, exemplifies how video documentation can be used for the dissemination of media archaeological experiments. It "documents the authors' journey back to the origins of transnational television in Europe. Inspired by the idea of experimental media archaeology (EMA), the trip to original locations of the transnational media event known as 'Paris-week' in 1952 illustrates a new approach to media historiography, which aims to sensitise television historians for the material remains, topography and physical spaces of early television transmissions. Readers/viewers are invited to watch the different episodes of the author's journey by clicking on the figures."[144]

Documentation as Representation of the Experiment
Instead of capturing the experiment objectively, each and every means of documentation necessarily comes with certain affordances and limitations that shape how the experimental process is documented. One important reflection is therefore to think about documentation as a representation of the experiment, as an imaginary of the technological re-enactment. This has consequences for how we analyse the documentation, namely as a *representation* of how we think a media archaeological experiment should be performed (▶ Theory, Chapter 4.4). The way in which the documentation is edited, or the way the handling and operation of

---

143 Kneebone and Woods, "Recapturing the History of Surgical Practice," 121. For more reflections on this topic from the field of ethnography, see, for instance, Tim Ingold, *Making: Anthropology, Archaeology, Art and Architecture* (London, New York: Routledge, 2013).
144 Andreas Fickers, Andy O'Dwyer, and Alexandre Germain, "'On the Road Again': An Experimental Media Archaeology Journey to the Origins of Transnational Television in Europe," *VIEW Journal of European Television History and Culture* 7, no. 13 (16 May 2018): 1, https://doi.org/10.18146/2213-0969.2018.jethc148. See also ▶ Theory, Chapter 4.5.

objects is shown, should be considered. The question of reception is also important: should the documentation be edited with a certain type of viewer in mind? Ideally, multiple versions are produced for different purposes and types of audiences; for instance, a short 90-second videoclip that could be used in a lecture, a longer one of mid-length for use in a seminar or online, and a full-length source that is made available for researchers.[145]

In addition to the documentation tools presented in this chapter, one may consider using alternative forms and techniques, such as drawing. This can help to select, guide and prioritise what the viewer should look at.[146] By contrast, video documentation material usually gives a lot of information, which makes it difficult to focus on what may be important. Serious thought needs to go into the editing of the documentation materials and thinking about the story one wants to tell. Documentation in the form of 360-degree video recordings as well as 3D scans of objects give an illusion that all the information is there, but may not actually tell you very much about the object itself. Objects belong not only to the experiment being recorded, but to a wider performative context in which the object can be handled. While 3D scans are arguably very much like museum objects in a glass case, they can provide some degree of interactivity in certain contexts. In that sense, it is important to think carefully about which documentation tools are the most appropriate for presentation purposes.[147]

3.3.2 Strategies

Various strategies of how to prepare and conduct the documentation of the experiment can be discussed, for instance: (1) whether or not to divide roles between the experimenter and documentalist, and (2) whether or not to document the experiment during the experimental process itself or rather afterwards.

Role Division Versus No Role Division
Depending on the aims of the experiment, it may be a useful strategy to divide roles within the experimental system, to separate the roles of experimenter,

---

145 This was argued by John Ellis during the DEMA workshop in 2019. For the report, see Van der Heijden and Kolkowski, "Documenting Media Archaeological Experiments."
146 See Harris, *A Sensory Education*; Ruxandra Lupu, *The Home Movie 4.0: (Co)Creative Strategies for a Tacit, Embodied and Affective Reading of the Sicilian Home Movie Archive* (Leeds: University of Leeds, 2020), https://etheses.whiterose.ac.uk/27966/ [last accessed 26.07.2022].
147 Van der Heijden and Kolkowski, "Documenting Media Archaeological Experiments." See also ▶ Theory, Chapter 4.5.

documentalist, observer and assistant, for instance. The advantage of such role division is that the experimenter can focus solely on doing the hands-on experimentation without being hindered or distracted by the documentation practices. Furthermore, each of the participants brings another perspective to the experimental process, which can be helpful when subsequently reflecting on the end results. A disadvantage of such a role division is that the experimenter often discovers what is important to document during the experiment itself, hence some pertinent material may not immediately be captured. Another disadvantage is that a role division comes with an increase in labour and costs, and potentially turns the documentation of the experiment into a media production in its own right.

HMV 2300H Portable Recorder in "Mukalap" – a Collaboration with Artist Film-makers

The independent film project *Mukalap* featured recordings cut onto discs that were made using the HMV recorder. It provided an opportunity to work with film-makers to document the recording apparatus in action using their expertise and equipment. Aside from material that was shot for the production, additional filming was done by the artists at the request of the experimenter, in order to capture the HMV operator's perspective with close-ups of the disc-cutting process. Here, some excellent documentation was achieved through close collaboration, in a setting where two projects were happening simultaneously: the filming of *Mukalap* and a performative media archaeological experiment (see Chapter 2.3.3).

No Clear Role Division in the DEMA Hands-on Workshop "Lichtenberg figures"

Role division requires clear communication in advance of the experiment. During the DEMA workshop in 2019, participants were asked to make their own Lichtenberg figures and to document the process. This exercise showed what can happen when there is no clear role division between the experimenter and documentalist. Instead of dividing their time between roles, as the participants were asked to do, most immediately started the hands-on experiment forgetting to systematically document the process. Consequently, one group was unable to understand the different outcomes between their first and second experiments, when the latter produced more satisfying results. The exercise furthermore made clear how doing the experiments and documentation simultaneously can be a challenge. One participant argued that it keeps you away from a certain "rhythm" because, after you do something for the first time, you then will have to repeat it in order to write down what actually happened. Another participant argued that if the documentation of the experimental process is begun too quickly, there is a danger that the documentation itself becomes the "epistemic object" rather than the object or experiment under scrutiny. Besides role division, a solution to this problem might be to do a "thought experiment" prior to the physical experiment; to imagine first what the salient points should be. By hierarchising the elements of the process beforehand, then to know what and what not to document becomes clearer. On the other hand, such thought experiments can also create certain expectations, which make the researcher less open to "the unexpected".[148]

---

[148] Van der Heijden and Kolkowski, "Documenting Media Archaeological Experiments."

Alternatively, the practices of experimentation and documentation are combined, which affords a more economical mounting of the experiment. The experimenter, as the one who develops (tacit) knowledge about the media historical object in use, knows exactly what is important to document at the time of doing. A disadvantage of combining the roles of experimenter and documentalist, as mentioned previously, is that the documentation could form a distraction to the experimental process.

Wilcox-Gay Recordio 1C10 – Signal to Noise

The documentation of this project was achieved solely by the experimenter. Most of the shots were planned in advance and a storyboard was created that contained all aspects of the experiment that were to be captured, including a timeline of the experimental activities. Documenting alone involved having to review footage during the experiment to ensure that the cameras and microphones were correctly focused on the activity, which meant constant interruptions to the work. This form of multitasking during the experiment often led to errors being made, both in operating the apparatus experimented upon and the equipment used for the documentation. Because, in this case, the experiment was geared towards the production of a video, it also became a performance for the camera. However, this method of working did have its advantages: the repeated takes caused by errors being made while having to oversee the documentation, allowed the experimenter to fully master the operation of the apparatus through the constant repetition! The documentation captured the numerous mistakes made while getting to grips with the apparatus, which are part of the learning process, and this material has been archived. The storyboarding technique also greatly facilitated the final editing. The resultant video documentation showed a flawless operation of the apparatus, which can be used for demonstration and instructional purposes. Documenting experiments without external assistance becomes more manageable and less of a distracting influence when done regularly and repeatedly.

Live Documentation Versus Redoing

Another strategy in practices of documentation concerns the choice of whether the documentation should take place simultaneously with the experimentation, or whether the documentation is done *after* the experimental process and so involves a form of "redoing". When replication or reproducibility are the aims of the experiment, it is recommended to document the experimental process synchronously, as this gives a more authentic account of the experiment. However, in a case where the main objective of the experiment is its dissemination, or when the documentation of the experiment hinders the experimental process too much, the choice for redoing and documenting after the experiment is justified.[149] This way, the object

---

149 Within the history of science, the re-doing of experiments is often "part of the game". See Peter Heering and Roland Wittje, eds., *Learning by Doing: Experiments and Instruments in the History of Science Teaching* (Stuttgart: Franz Steiner Verlag, 2011); H. Otto Sibum, "Science and

and its use can be properly captured. In cases where redoing an experiment will come at a cost, e.g., because of the use of expensive or rare recordable media such as celluloid film or blank lacquer discs, then doing a trial or "dummy run" of the experiment is recommended. Then the experiment is rehearsed, but the precious medium is left untouched.

Stentorphone Soundbox – Testing the Replica Model

The Stentorphone Soundbox project serves as an example of how redoing can be a useful strategy of documentation when testing a replica model. Restrictions in place due to the Covid-19 pandemic meant that the principal experimenter and the student working on the *Stentorphone* soundbox replication project were unable to work together in person. Initial tests of a first 3D printed model were conducted by the experimenter at his home. The experiments were then repeated and documented on video so that they could be simulated by the student in the engineering faculty laboratory. The explanatory video documentation included a spoken commentary that guided the viewer through the stages of the preparation, setting-up and experimental testing of the *Stentorphone* soundbox. This was necessary as the student had no prior experience in operating a gramophone, and the tests to be made required specialist knowledge that went beyond giving a series of instructions. For example, the gramophone's existing soundbox had to be replaced with the Stentorphone, which then had to be correctly aligned and calibrated; the tubing for the external air supply had to be affixed and stabilised in such a way that it did not interfere with the functioning of the soundbox; and other actions too were best illustrated by doing and showing. A series of experimental objectives were established for the tests, which sought to appraise its performance and recommend improvements to be made on further replica models. The student was able to repeat the experiment and corroborate at first hand the initial findings that identified a number of faults and malfunctioning of the replica model. Modifications were then implemented on the next printed model, including work on the *Stentorphone's* torsional spindle and the moveable comb valve, with markedly successful results.

the Knowing Body: Making Sense of Embodied Knowledge in Scientific Experiment," in *Reconstruction, Replication and Re-enactment in the Humanities and Social Sciences*, ed. Sven Dupré et al. (Amsterdam: Amsterdam University Press, 2020), 275–294, https://doi.org/10.1515/9789048543854-012.

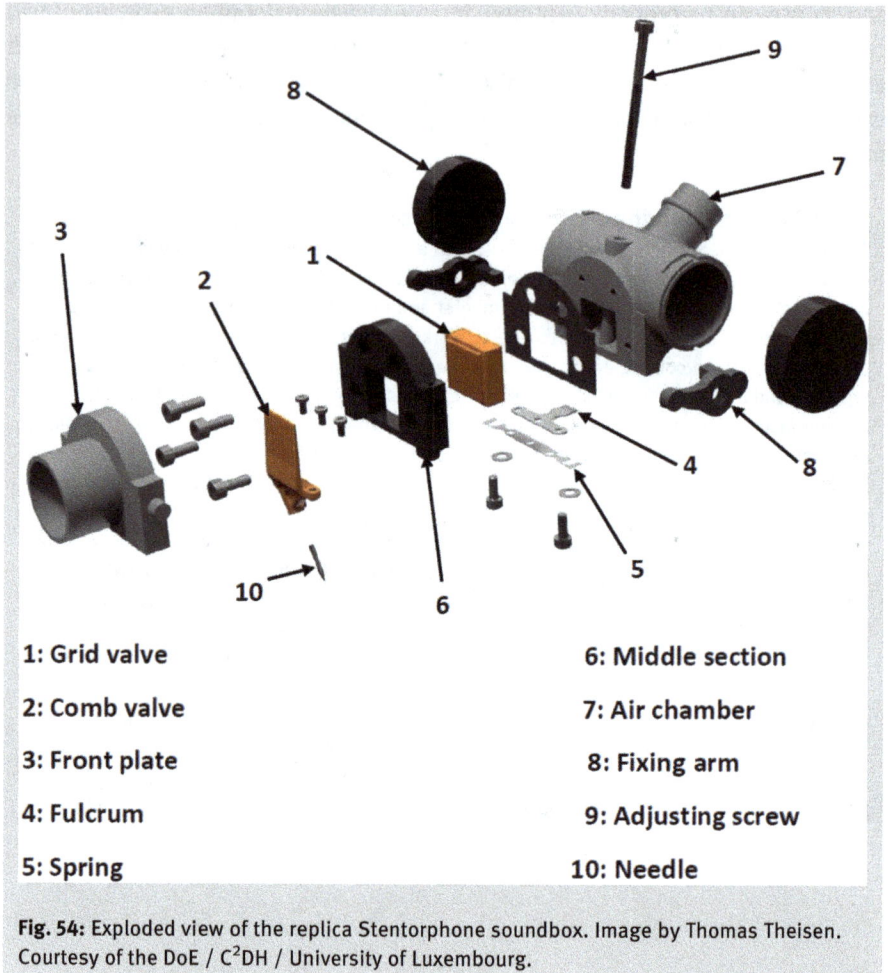

Fig. 54: Exploded view of the replica Stentorphone soundbox. Image by Thomas Theisen. Courtesy of the DoE / C²DH / University of Luxembourg.

1: Grid valve

2: Comb valve

3: Front plate

4: Fulcrum

5: Spring

6: Middle section

7: Air chamber

8: Fixing arm

9: Adjusting screw

10: Needle

3.3.3 Protocols

In making use of protocols for documenting media archaeological experiments, inspiration can be gained from various other disciplines, such as physics, chemistry, ethnography and the history of science, in which protocols have been developed over a considerable time for systematically documenting the experimental process, its objectives and results. From these examples we can extract various elements that a documentation protocol should ideally include, namely:

- General information: date, time, place, experimenter, documentalist and participants
- Information about the object: its materiality, history and context of use
- Information about the experiment: type of experiment, research questions, objectives, methods and approaches, experimental setting
- Results of the experiment: process and findings, lessons learnt, new questions

Two protocols were developed for doing media archaeological experiments for the DEMA project: one for the lab diary and one for the experimental report. Whereas the lab diary protocol aims to support the immediate recording and description of all the actions and steps involved in the experimental process, the experimental report protocol aims to develop the interpretation and reflection of the experimental process and its results. Naturally, there is an overlap between the two protocols. The experimental report can be seen as a more detailed version of the lab diary with additional information and reflection on the outcomes of the experiment. While a lab diary is usually limited to a single day, an experimental report can cover multiple days of experimentation.

Lab Diary Protocol
- Date, time and place: the date, time and place where the experiment takes place
- Object: the media historical object used in the experiment
- Name: names of the experimenter, documentalist and participants
- Project: name of the research project (if applicable)
- Experiment: type of experiment and description of the objective
- Notes on process: step-by-step description of the experimental process, including information on the processes, experiences and mistakes or accidents that take place in the experiment
- Conclusions: short description of the main findings of the experiment, conclusions, surprises, questions, and possible next steps to take

Experimental Report Protocol
- Title
- Date, object and name of the experiment
- General information
    - Date
    - Time
    - Place
- People
    - Experimenter
    - Documentalist
    - Participants

- Objects
  - Description of the objects
  - Historical context and user practices
- Experiment
  - Research question and objective
  - Method and approach
  - Type of experiment and experimental setting
- Process
  - Preparations of the experiment
  - Experimental process
- Results
  - Results of the experiment
  - Reflections on documentation
- Conclusions

3.4 Use of Contextual Inquiry at Public Events, Re-enactments and Workshops

The field study technique known as contextual inquiry is a useful means by which to gain a deeper understanding of user, participant or audience behaviour and to reveal tacit knowledge during a media archaeological experiment. It was developed by Hugh Beyer and Karen Holtzblatt as an initial phase in their contextual design process for collecting field data.[150] Contextual inquiry reveals the "unconscious and tacit aspects of life. It guides researchers in going out into the field and talking with people about their work and life while observing them . . . Contextual inquiry immerses designers in the user's whole life – including those aspects which the user doesn't know how to articulate."[151]

This research method takes place in the location or environment where the experiment is carried out, be it a laboratory, studio, theatre or workplace. The researcher or experimenter observes the user(s), participant(s) and any audience members and elicits information from them to help the researcher understand more deeply how the activity is being conducted (or received) and the experience of the user and of those taking part or spectating. Contextual inquiry can take the form of (recorded) interviews that are done on-site, just before,

---

150 Hugh Beyer and Karen Holtzblatt, *Contextual Design Defining Customer-Centered Systems* (San Francisco, CA: Morgan Kaufmann, 2000).
151 Karen Holtzblatt and Hugh Beyer, *Contextual Design: Evolved*, Synthesis Lectures on Human-Centered Informatics 24 (San Rafael, CA: Morgan and Claypool, 2015), 11–12, https://doi.org/10.2200/S00597ED1V01Y201409HCI024.

during and/or after the experiment, and through written questionnaires that are completed during the experiment or as soon as possible after the activity has ceased. According to Beyer and Holtzblatt, the contextual interview should be based on four guiding principles:[152]

1. Context: The interviewees are asked about the work or research activity and the objects or tools they are using or interacting with.
2. Partnership: The direction of the interview is shared so that the interviewee can take the lead by describing and doing the activity themselves, putting forward ideas and stating their own observations. Preplanned questioning becomes secondary as the interviewer will instead guide the conversation towards the important aspects of the experiment.
3. Interpretation: The interviewers share their interpretation of the activities and what has been expressed by the interviewees and allows them to respond to and correct the interviewers' understanding of the experience where necessary. This form of co-interpretation avoids giving false impressions and misrepresentations.
4. Focus: The interview should concern itself primarily with the experimental activity at hand and not be side-tracked by other matters and subjects.

In a situation where a contextual inquiry is desired, but the principal researcher or experimenter is occupied in, say, operating a device during the experiment involving participants and/or an audience, then the interviewing can be carried out by an associate or by assistants.

The interviewing of a small number of participants can be combined or supplemented with a questionnaire that is given to a larger number of persons involved in the media archaeological experiment. In designing a questionnaire for collecting participant and audience responses, attention should, of course, be given to asking questions that are appropriate to the experimental activity and that address the research questions being asked in the experiment. Guidelines for the formulation of questionnaires can be found in A. N. Oppenheim's book on questionnaire design and attitude measurement, which also gives advice on planning, wording, types of questions and statistical analysis.[153] Before finalising the questionnaire, it is highly recommended that a draft is shared among research colleagues who may suggest new questions, reject others, and help to edit them (especially if there are too many questions).

---

152 Holtzblatt and Beyer, *Contextual Design: Evolved*, 13–14.
153 A. N. Oppenheim, *Questionnaire Design and Attitude Measurement* (London: Heinemann, 1966).

When interviewing and handing-out questionnaires, it is vitally important to get permission from every interviewee for recording the interview before any recording device is activated. Permission must also be sought to use the interview material and the information collected from the questionnaires (see Chapter 3.2.2).

Art and Science of Acoustic Recording: Re-enacting Arthur Nikisch and the Berlin Philharmonic Orchestra's Landmark 1913 Recording of Beethoven's Fifth Symphony (2014)

The aim of this re-enactment was not only to afford insights into how this early twentieth-century acoustic recording was achieved technically, but also to learn about the performance that lies behind such a recording. Here, the attempt to capture an orchestral sound in its entirety, and without the instrumental substitutions and curtailments that were common practice in the recording studios until ca. 1913, puts additional demands on the musicians, who have to play in extraordinary conditions that are hot and cramped, with their normal positions radically rearranged, in stark contrast to a concert performance. The re-enactment sought to assess to what extent the musicians had to adapt or change their playing styles in order to conform to the acoustic recording system, and the overall effect it had on their music-making. Ethnographic techniques were employed by the musicologist/researcher Amy Blier-Carruthers to collect data, involving fieldwork observation and audio-visual documentation of the rehearsal and recording processes, along with individual interviews of a cross-section of the orchestra musicians. These interviews were conducted before, during and after the orchestral recording sessions and documented audio-visually. The data was used, together with an analysis of the orchestral recordings made during the project, to investigate the factors in the acoustic recording process that affect performance, musical style and interpretation. The interviewees volunteered to participate in the study and ethical considerations were observed during its conduct.

The study noted significant changes in musical performance induced by the acoustic recording process, including a more expressive and extroverted playing style, with increased articulation, forcefulness in attack and an overall much louder dynamic level. Such intensity of sound is needed so that the recorded music is made audible and intelligible over the inherent noise produced by the cutting stylus as it ploughs through the wax recording medium. These observations were corroborated by the interviews, which also offered revealing insights into the musicians' experiences of recording in this way, including the enjoyment of the close proximity to each other and the focus and energy of making direct-to-disc recordings in one take with no recourse to editing-out mistakes or rebalancing the sound. Changes in style aside, the immediacy and exigency fostered by this type of recording process was noted to be much closer to the experience of live music-making than when using modern methods.[154]

Cartavox Sound Postcard Recorder – Temporary History Lab, Esch-sur-Alzette, a "Semi-Contextual" Inquiry (2020)

Visitors and invitees who made voice recordings onto sound postcards were asked to fill in a questionnaire after the event to gather their reflections on the recording activity. The event

---

154 Kolkowski, Miller, and Blier-Carruthers, "The Art and Science of Acoustic Recording."

occurred during the Covid-19 pandemic and restrictions on indoor activities that were in place limited the amount of time allowed for each visitor in the space. They were, therefore, not able to complete the questionnaires or be interviewed directly after the recording and writing of messages on the postcards. Instead, they took away the printed questionnaire, a copy of which was subsequently sent to them via email. A list of ten questions asked the respondents to reflect on their experiences of recording on analogue media; of hearing their recordings played back on a turntable; on the conditions under which the recording was made; and on participating in an historical re-enactment. Not all of those who recorded returned a completed questionnaire. Nevertheless, the responses of those who did were illuminating, if possibly not entirely representative of all who took part in the activity. Some respondents likened the experience to being in a professional recording studio and found the presence of the Cartavox operator to be reassuring in terms of the efficacy of the recording, while others remarked that the close proximity to the operator was not conducive to recording a private message.

A reading of the data obtained from the questionnaires surmised that comments about the anxiety of making a recording, whether live or in private, would have applied had the technology been entirely digital. It was much the same as the "Mikrophon-Angst" encountered by the manufacturer of the Cartavox recorder when attempting to market the device during the 1950s, although today we are far more accustomed to recording voice messages on telephone answering machines and on portable devices. Perhaps then, the shyness felt in making a recording with an operator present was not as significant factor in the demise of the Cartavox as had been suggested by the manufacturer, although it would have been unsuitable or unattractive for those wishing to record very personal messages. There would, however, have been the possibility to erect a screen next to the Cartavox console, as the long cable length connecting it to the recorder allows for this, thus giving those recording more privacy.

3.5 Challenges of Documentation

As mentioned above, documenting media archaeological experiments entails various challenges. In our media archaeological experiments, we encountered conflicts between the modes of experimentation and documentation, as well as challenges concerning the historical authenticity of the re-enactments and hands-on practices.

3.5.1 Conflicting Modes of Experimentation and Documentation

Documentation is an intrinsic part of the experimental system. As John Ellis has argued: "An experiment without documentation is not an experiment [. . .] experimentation and documentation are not separate processes, but rather 'two sides of a sheet of paper'".[155] On the other hand, the practices of documentation might

---

155 John Ellis, personal correspondence with Tim van der Heijden, 17 September 2020.

form an obstacle or source of distraction to the experimental process. In such cases, the modes of experimentation and documentation may conflict rather than support each other. From ethnographic studies and media theory, we know that documentation practices involve both observation and participation. Documentation, in other words, involves some kind of "intervention" in the media archaeological experiment.[156]

Challenges in Documenting Small-Gauge Film Experiments

In the small-gauge film experiments, which aimed to explore and re-enact early twentieth-century home movie recording practices by using original Ciné-Kodak 16mm and 8mm film cameras (see Chapter 1.2.1), no role division between experimenter and documentalist was foreseen. The documentation tools therefore had to be set and activated by the experimenter prior to the experiment. To make the documentation operate relatively independently, the cameras' automatic recording mode was selected for setting the focus, aperture, ISO and shutter speed. Most of the time, this worked well for determining the right focus and exposure. However, sometimes the subject would suddenly go out of focus or become under- or overexposed due to light changes in the "in situ" experimental setting. Often during the outdoor re-enactments, the dynamics of the recording caused the experimenter and participants to move outside the frame of the video camera. This necessitated the repositioning of the camera, causing an interruption in the experimental process. Other interruptions were caused by overheating issues leading to camera malfunction, by empty batteries, or when the SD-card became full. In all such cases, the modes of experimentation and documentation conflicted with each other, shifting the attention of the experimenter away from the experimental process to the documentation equipment and its workings. To limit the risk of potential interventions, it is recommended to have spare batteries and SD-cards in reserve, and to regularly check – either by looking at the LCD-display of the camera or via the mobile app – whether the documentation apparatuses are still recording.

Conflicting Modes of Experimentation and Documentation in the Improved Phantasmagoria Lanterns Experiments

The workload of the experimental series with the Improved Phantasmagoria Lanterns was considerably increased by the visual documentation. It also had a great influence on the set-up of the experimental arrangements. A reciprocal influence between the conduct of the experiments and their documentation could also be observed. Experiments with historical projection apparatuses require dark rooms. Therefore, spotlights had to be set up for the recordings, which could be turned down when necessary. All in all, the degree of brightness still acceptable for the experiments led to limitations in the recording quality, but without a marked negative influence on the documentation. The documentation also had a significant influence on the experimenter. The documentation demands attention and creates tension. This has a negative effect on the concentrated execution of the experiments (e.g., small technical errors, inattention). In the planning of experiments, this aspect should be seriously considered in order to achieve a balanced ratio of attention for the media documentation and the execution of the experiments.

---

156 Ellis, "Why Hands on History Matters," 13. See also John Ellis, *Visible Fictions: Cinema, Television, Video* (London; New York: Routledge, 1992); see also ▶ Theory, Chapter 4.

While documentation practices may influence the experimental process, conversely each type of experiment and epistemic object will afford and limit different documentation practices. The experiments with the Improved Phantasmagoria Lanterns in the theatre, for instance, required a dark setting, which had an impact on the documentation practice. The same applied for the small-gauge film experiments, which cannot easily be redone and so require documentation synchronous to the experiment. Some of the experiments with sound recording technologies, on the other hand, afforded the possibility of (re)doing the documentation after the experiment. Each media archaeological experiment thus faces different challenges of documentation and ways of dealing with them.

3.5.2 Historical Authenticity of the Experiment

Another challenge of documentation pertains to the historical authenticity of the media archaeological experiment, as when the experimental setting has to be adjusted for documentation purposes. This happened in the historical re-enactments of the eighteenth-century phantasmagoria and twentieth-century small-gauge film projection practices, which required low-light conditions. Consequently, the experimental setting needed to be adjusted in order to meet the documentation requirements.[157] While many media archaeological experiments aim to recreate or reconstruct something of the "original" experience of past media usages, it is by definition impossible to make the media archaeological experiments completely historically authentic. The experimental setting is manifestly different from the original historical setting. In the case of the small-gauge experiments, for instance, the Ciné-Kodak film camera may be the original technology, but the "fresh" emulsion and the laboratory practices used to produce the film are based on modern industry standards, practices, techniques and infrastructures. Instead of a goal in itself, historical authenticity may therefore rather serve as a reflexive means and heuristic instrument within the experimental system. As Fickers and Van den Oever argue: "Experimental media archaeology is not about the reconstruction of authentic historical experiences", but "it is geared to raising the awareness of participants in the experiment . . . " (▶ Theory, Chapter 2.8). In other words, instead of providing a historically authentic reconstruction, the media archaeological experiment focuses on the process of making

---

157 The use of Improved Phantasmagoria Lanterns requires darkness. On the operator's side, the projections appear much dimmer than on the audience's side. Visual documentation of this aspect was not possible. For more reflections, see Van der Heijden and Kolkowski, "Documenting Media Archaeological Experiments."

the reconstruction and the new questions this leads us to ask.[158] To what degree these reconstructions are historically authentic, in the sense that they represent past media constellations and usages, should be reflected upon and made explicit in both the documentation and the dissemination of the media archaeological experiment.

The Art and Science of Acoustic Recording (2014)

This project did not set out to faithfully recreate the historic recording session from 1913 in its entirety, which, for true authenticity, would have involved using, among other things, period instruments, accessories such as gut strings, and a distinct stylistic interpretation of the music, let alone an all-male orchestra. Instead, the re-enactment focused on replicating the acoustic recording technology and practical recording techniques; using the blank recording medium of wax discs; discovering how the orchestra musicians would have been arranged in front of the recording horn; and inquiring to what extent the unusual conditions and the requirements of recording acoustically affected the music-making. Much effort went into creating a recording wax that performed similarly to the original medium and the re-enactment could be described as being historically accurate in the way it was achieved technically. This was vital in the making of recordings that could be analysed and compared to the originals from 1913.

16mm Film Re-enactment and Authenticity of Film Stock

In the media-technological experiments with the Ciné-Kodak 16mm film camera from ca. 1930, the question of historical authenticity was addressed in relation to the use of film material. The "fresh" 16mm film available in film shops today, which was used for this experiment, comes with slightly different aesthetic and technological affordances compared to historical film material. Differences pertain, for instance, to the light sensitivity of the film material. The Fomapan black-and-white reversal film has a light sensitivity of 100 ISO, whereas 16mm reversal film of the 1920s and 1930s used to be approximately 10–25 ISO.[159] During presentations of the first 16mm film to expert audiences, the aesthetic of the re-enacted film was discussed in terms of whether the film had been digitally "enhanced" or even manipulated to look like a historical film.

---

158 illuminago, "Improved Phantasmagoria Lanterns [Experimental Report]," 2022.
159 Kattelle, *Home Movies*, 333. See also https://www.britannica.com/technology/motion-picture-technology/Film#ref508443 [last accessed 26.07.2022].

Fig. 55: Roll of 16mm film on the drying rack after development. Photo by Tim van der Heijden. Courtesy of the C²DH / University of Luxembourg.

For Fickers and Van den Oever, re-enactment is always about a combination of the old and the new. In the words of Tilmans, Van Vree, and Winter: "Re-enactment is both affirmation and renewal. It entails addressing the old, but it also engenders something new, something we have never seen before. Herein lies the excitement of performance, as well as its surprises and its distortions."[160] Although we agree that the notion of historical re-enactment is problematic and striving for historical authenticity should not be the end goal of media archaeological experiments, we see value in using the notion as a heuristic instrument and reflexive means. For instance, one could address and specify the relationship between the "old" (e.g., the media historical object, its materiality and past user practices) and the "new" (e.g., the replicated object, any added, reconstructed or modified parts, and the re-enacted practice). In doing so, we draw on the framework provided by art historian Leslie Carlyle.

---

160 Karin Tilmans, Frank van Vree, and Jay Winter, *Performing the Past: Memory, History, and Identity in Modern Europe* (Amsterdam: Amsterdam University Press, 2010), 7. See also ▶ Theory, Chapter 3.6.

Instead of "historical authenticity", Carlyle refers to "historical accuracy" and considers it a continuum, which we believe is a useful framework to think about when doing media archaeological experiments. Her work in the restoration of paintings led to a publication and the database "Historically Accurate Reconstructions of Artist's Oil Painting", which includes recipes for artists' materials from ca. 1750–1900. Instead of relying on more traditional reconstructions or copying techniques when reconstructing these recipes, Carlyle employed what she terms "historically accurate reconstructions".[161] In formulating her terminology, Carlyle used the International Organization for Standardization (ISO) definition, where accuracy equals the closeness of a measurement to the true value. The analogy of a circular target is employed, in which the bullseye represents true value and the closer the "hits" or black dots are to the bullseye, the more accurate they are.[162] The bullseye represents historical accuracy, but as it is nigh on impossible to reproduce the past usages to reach this "true value", it can only be aspirational. Instead, what is important is the position in relation to the bullseye, or closeness to the impossible goal. Applied to the study of historical artists' materials, the visual analogy demonstrates that using modern artists' paint does not go anywhere near the bullseye, whereas using traditional oil and pigment-based paint starts to get us somewhere within the circle. For doing media archaeological experiments, one can take inspiration from Carlyle's approach of historical accuracy as a relative concept in order to think about how certain elements of media archaeological experiments, such as the technology, materiality, aesthetics, design, functionality and usages of the media historical object, are more or less historically authentic compared to others.

Historical Authenticity in Making the Kinora 3D Replica

In the process of making the Kinora 3D replica, it was frequently discussed to what extent the replica should be authentic in relation to the original viewer in terms of its materiality, functionality and use. While striving to make the replica appear as authentic as possible, choices had to be made due to constraints in time, materials and equipment available for 3D printing. For instance, instead of steel we used PLA plastic and Onyx Nylon as the main materials for the 3D-printed parts, while we matched some of the original materials of the Kinora viewer by using wood (for the base) and glass (for the lenses) for the replica. Because the 3D printer could not print objects with dimensions smaller than 0.4mm, we had to increase the dimensions of the worm gear. We also had to move away from the original dimensions of the lenses. Instead of recreating the glass ourselves, prefabricated magnifiers with standard dimensions

---

161 Leslie Carlyle, "Reconstructions of Oil Painting Materials and Techniques: The HART Model for Approaching Historical Accuracy," in *Reconstruction, Replication and Re-enactment in the Humanities and Social Sciences*, ed. Sven Dupré et al. (Amsterdam: Amsterdam University Press, 2020), 141–168.
162 Van der Heijden and Kolkowski, "Documenting Media Archaeological Experiments."

(50mm x 100mm) were chosen as a cost-efficient solution. As a consequence, the size of the lens hood had to be adapted to these dimensions so that the magnifiers would fit. While the flexibility of the design made the replica less historically authentic, it enabled the testing of the predefined research parameters (see Chapter 1.1.1) that would have been impossible to test with the original object.[163] As such, the process of making and using the replica served as a heuristic instrument for understanding the functionality of the Kinora and its histories of use.

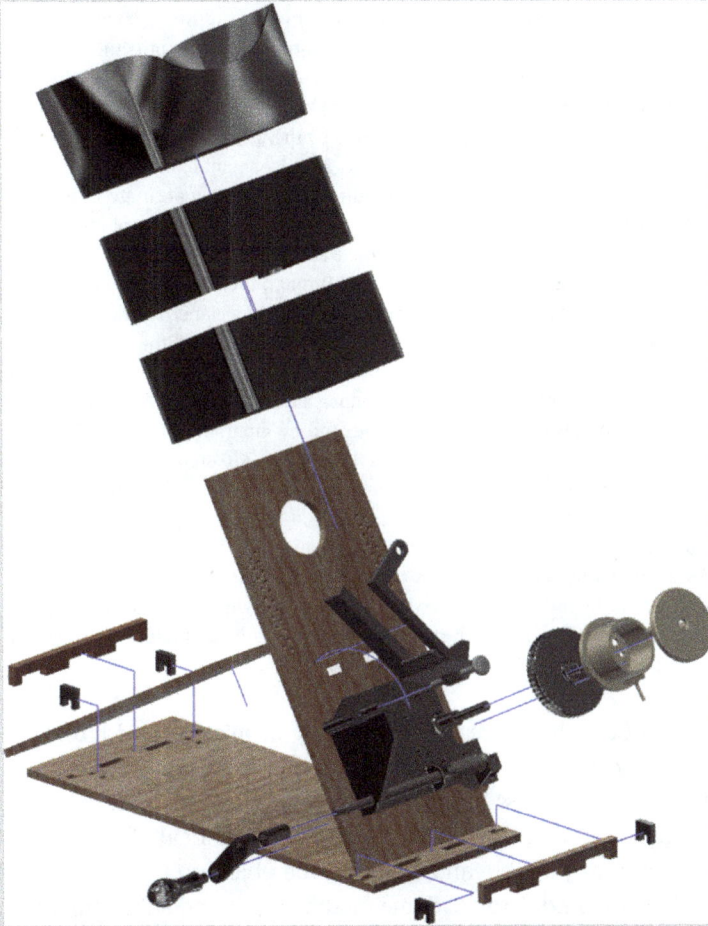

Fig. 56: Exploded view of the Kinora replica 3D model. Image produced by Claude Wolf. Courtesy of the DoE / C²DH / University of Luxembourg.

---

163 Van der Heijden and Wolf, "Replicating the Kinora."

Auxetophony, Science Museum, London (2012)

Auxetophony is the title of a re-enacted Auxetophone-gramophone concert from ca. 1907. Such concerts used an air-powered gramophone for increased loudness of sound reproduction and were able to successfully combine live musicians with recorded music for the first time in musical history. Considerable preparation went into making the re-enacted performance as historically accurate as possible, which it managed to achieve in many and unforeseen ways. The Science Museum's own prototype Auxetophone-Gramophone (1905), equipped with a giant horn, was used for the performance. The instrument was in working order, aside from its blower/air compressor, which had to be replaced by a modern equivalent substitute. Original Victor company records from the "Red Seal" label, ca. 1905–07, were used, featuring operatic arias sung by famous opera singers of the period that were known to have been played in Auxetophone concerts, along with historical scores published by the Victor record company specifically for accompanying the very same disc records. A full ensemble was employed as specified by the musical scores, and their playing had to be stylistically accurate in order to match the musical phrasing and tempi of the singers reproduced in the historical recordings. The re-enacted concert provided the audience with a near authentic historical experience; they listened to the very same sounds and music reproduced through the same technology as the original audience over a hundred years ago. The participating musicians had to struggle in much the same way as their predecessors in playing to a recording, with all the idiosyncrasies of the operatic voices and a lack of familiarity with the technology. For their part, the audience was presented with a totally unfamiliar kind of performance and, like their predecessors, experienced something new. The awestruck feeling expressed by members of the audience in 2012, in hearing a recorded voice "brought back to life" by the Auxetophone-Gramophone twinned with the live musicians, could be compared to the astonishment experienced by contemporary audiences according to published accounts.[164] This brings questions to the fore about the historicity of perception or spectatorship, and the effects on modern users, participants and audiences by their *closeness* to functioning media historical objects. In keeping with the theme of historicity and showing the risks involved in demonstrating new technologies for the first time in public, the concert also entertained a "historically accurate failure" when the air supply was cut off mid-performance!

Often, certain parts of an object are malfunctioning or missing and have to be repaired or replaced by modern equivalents. Repairs such as the replacement of worn or faulty parts will doubtless have an impact on the authenticity of the historical object. There is a trade-off between keeping the historical object as close to its original condition as possible and restoring the object so that it can function as it was originally intended to do. Some modifications and substitutions are necessary because of safety reasons, or the scarcity of materials or affiliated

---

164 For example, the live organ accompaniment to a recording of De Gogorza's baritone voice played on an Auxetophone at the Royal Albert Hall, London, was considered "miraculous" by a correspondent to *The Gramophone* magazine: N. N., "Direct Comparison (Letter to the Editor)" (*The Gramophone*, London, April 1933), 40.

media, and these will affect the outcome of the experiment as well. The quality of a film or a sound recording may differ from what would have been expected in the past; the light sources of a projector or magic lantern, for instance, may be radically different to what was originally used, and other techniques may need to be employed to achieve meaningful results. Here the objectives of the media archaeological investigations are not directed towards an authentic reconstruction of past practices, but rather a redoing and explication of past usage.

Exponential Horn: In Search of Perfect Sound, Science Museum, London (2013–2014)

The main task in reconstructing this historic loudspeaker horn was to replicate the missing sections as only the initial 9-foot (2.74m) section survived. The original measurements were followed in order to accurately replicate the entire exponential shape of the original horn, which measured 27 feet (8.23m) in length with a cross-section that curved exponentially from $1^{1/16}$ inches (27mm) to 7-foot-1-inch sq. (2.16m sq.) at the horn mouth. The original material was terne plate (a tin and lead alloy that is no longer manufactured), coated with a thick layer of pitch, onto which wooden battens were added to dampen resonance. Instead, a fibreglass construction was chosen for the missing sections, as members of the Science Museum Workshops had experience in working with this material. An aim of the project was to replicate the quality of the original sound reproduction as closely as possible. Using different materials, in this case, did not affect the sound adversely or otherwise, and the 12mm thickness of the fibreglass proved to be effective against resonance. More crucial to the sound reproduction was the use of the very same model of loudspeaker driver that was connected to the horn – a Western Electric 555W moving coil driver from ca. 1930. It was fortunate that the Museum had two working examples of this historic driver that were made available for the project. To follow the path of true historical accuracy would also have involved reconstructing the original valve amplifier and radio receiver that were matched to the driver and horn (which did not survive), but this was beyond the scope of the project. Instead, a custom-built amplifier was commissioned that included protection circuitry to ensure that the Museum's driver was not damaged through exposure to extended high or low frequency sounds.

This was an artist-led project and the intention was not primarily to achieve historical authenticity, but to create an art and science exhibit *informed* by an object from the museum's collection. However, there was a desire to reconstruct the horn to its exact original form, to reproduce its fabled 3D sound quality, and to create an authentic listening experience akin to the 1930s as far as was possible under the circumstances. Visitors and audiences listened to live radio broadcasts, live music and events of today through the prism of the historic horn. In addition, archival radio programmes that were broadcast in the 1930s were featured and the practice of listening to BBC lunchtime concerts, a mainstay of the original horn demonstrations throughout the 1930s, were re-enacted daily for a modern audience at the Science Museum during the Exponential Horn exhibition.[165]

---

165 Kolkowski, "In Search of Perfect Sound."

> **Cartavox Sound Postcard Recorder**
> The rarity of blank recordable sound postcards, which are no longer manufactured, meant that the experimenter had to fabricate a substitute medium to record onto for using on the *Carta-vox* apparatus (see Chapter 2.5.1). The chosen surface material of PVC instead of lacquer required a different technique of recording to that originally used, namely embossing the sound groove instead of cutting it, which involved modifying the cutterhead and softening the surface using heat. Here, it was necessary to cede some of the historical accuracy so that experiments with the apparatus could take place at all.

3.6 Recommendations and Reflections

Within this chapter, we have discussed various aspects related to the practice of documenting media archaeological experiments. Based on the examples discussed, we can summarise the following recommendations and reflections:

- Carefully choose your documentation methods and tools, as each comes with different affordances and limitations (3.1).
- Before the experiment takes place, think about the objectives of the documentation practices and ways to store, manage and organise your data, including back-up strategies (3.2).
- Apply data ethics and consider the latest General Data Protection Regulation (GDPR) in cases where participants or audiences are involved in the experiment and ask for their explicit agreement in (audio-visual) documentation practices (3.2).
- Define the aims and purposes of documentation in advance of the experiment and make use of certain documentation strategies and/or protocols accordingly (3.3).
- Make use of contextual inquiry as a method for documenting audience behaviour and responses to media archaeological experiments (3.4).
- In advance of the experiment, think about how the process of documentation may influence the experimental process and vice versa (3.5).
- Re-doing the documentation after the experiment can be a strategy to solve the problem of the documentation practice potentially influencing or distracting the experimentation process. This is particularly useful in cases where there is no role division between experimenter and documentalist foreseen within the experimental process (3.5).

–   Do not strive for historical authenticity, as this is by definition impossible, but use it as a heuristic instrument to reflect on the question to what degree the reconstructions represent past media constellations and usages and so mediate between the "old" and the "new". These reflections can be made explicit in both the documentation and dissemination of the media archaeological experiment (3.5).

Chapter 4
Dissemination

How should one disseminate media archaeological experiments and the (tacit) knowledge produced within these experiments? In this chapter, we will discuss the various modes of dissemination (on location, online, hybrid) and types of dissemination of media archaeological experiments. Some ideas will also be explored for how to embed hands-on experiments and learning by doing in teaching and other contexts of use.

4.1 Modes of Dissemination

4.1.1 On Location

Media archaeological experiments can be disseminated through hands-on demonstration or performance on location. In a performative experiment, for instance, a media historical object is displayed and its use demonstrated on a stage in front of an audience. A more traditional way of disseminating media archaeological experiments on location is through the presentation of the results and the knowledge the experiment has produced. Advantages of performing or presenting media archaeological experiments on location are the elements of liveness, physical presence, proximity to the media historical object, and the possibility of direct interaction between the experimenter and the audience. The on-location mode is therefore preferred over the online and hybrid modes of dissemination, which either lack or limit the sensorial, hands-on form of knowledge production and transmission promoted by experimental media archaeology as a methodological approach.

"His Master's Vintage Voice: Experiments in Instantaneous Disc-Recording" Public Workshop (2020)
This hands-on workshop and demonstration of direct-to-disc recording on lacquer discs was centred upon the HMV 2300H Portable Disc Recorder (1948). It gave an opportunity for its participants to learn first-hand about the disc recording process, to be directly involved in it by making their own recordings and therefore see and experience "instantaneous" disc recording in practice.[166] The workshop sessions were supervised by Sean Davies, a renowned expert in the field of studio

---

166 The instantaneous disc record is the historic term for the recordable blank medium of lacquer or cellulose discs, first used during the 1930s. Such discs could be played immediately after recording. See Samuel Brylawski et al., eds., *ARSC Guide to Audio Preservation* (Eugene,

ⓐ Open Access. © 2023 the author(s), published by De Gruyter. (cc) BY ▪▪▪▪ This work is licensed under the Creative Commons Attribution 4.0 International License.
https://doi.org/10.1515/9783110799767-005

recording and an authority on disc-cutting lathes.[167] Davies also gave talks and answered questions about historical recording techniques and about his vast experience working as a sound engineer in the recording industry. The workshop was documented using a multicam system (see Chapter 3.1.7). Edited versions of this, along with other experiments, can be used for reference and analysis purposes, as well as for further dissemination through the sharing of instructional and demonstration videos.

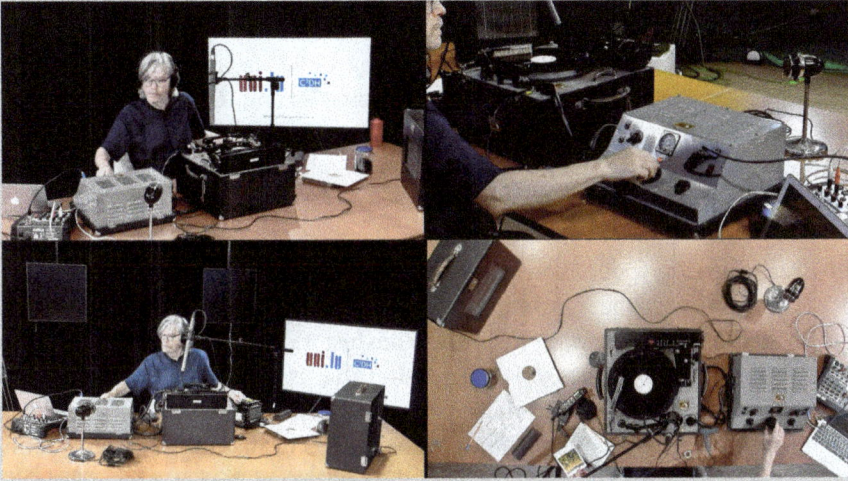

Fig. 57: Experiment in instantaneous disc recording with the HMV 2300H. Courtesy of the C²DH / University of Luxembourg.

Roger Kneebone's Simulated Re-enactments

Roger Kneebone's simulated surgical re-enactments, described in more detail in Chapter 1, serve as an example of how the location and "live" nature of the performance enhanced the authenticity of the re-enacted experience. Kneebone's re-enactments were preceded by interviews with the participants about the work they had done. These interviews were not very revealing. However, once placed in the recreated clinical environment, there were a lot of contextual cues that brought the re-enactment to life. In his case, they were fortunate to be able to use the London Science Museum's 1984 operating theatre exhibit that provided the necessary contextual ties, including even the colour of the drapes and the material of the surgical gowns. The participants went back to the performative ways of their past practices, including the banter among them, and even in the treatment of visiting medical students. The performance mode was heightened

---

Washington: Association for Recorded Sound Collections; Library of Congress, and Council on Library and Information Resources, 2015), Glossary, App. B, 226.
167 For more information, see https://www.discogs.com/artist/872736-Sean-Davies [last accessed 26.07.2022].

by the fact that the re-enactments took place inside a museum gallery and under the gaze of the public. These layers of performance served to make the experience more authentic for them.[168]

4.1.2 Online

Media archaeological experiments can also be disseminated through online platforms. In video demonstrations, for example, the audio-visual documentation footage can be used to present the experimental process and its results. In addition, the documentation of the experiment can stimulate other forms of dissemination and transmedia storytelling, through the combination of textual fragments of experimental reports with audio-visual documentation, in the form of a video essay or virtual exhibition, for example (▶ Theory, Chapter 4.5). While having the advantage of reaching far wider audiences, a disadvantage of virtual demonstrations or performances is that they prevent audiences from having the possibility for live physical access, presence and proximity to the historical object and its user practices, thereby lacking the sensorial dimension that is so crucial to experimental media archaeology as a methodological approach. The online mode of dissemination nevertheless enables new affordances in terms of the digital display of and engagement with media historical objects, through zooming in and out on specific details of the digitised (3D) object, for instance, or by means of adding additional layers of contextual information.

Demonstration Video: Edison 'Fireside' Phonograph (1909)
The purpose of this video was to show how a simple voice recording is made on an Edison cylinder phonograph and then reproduced (played back). The process is shown in its entirety so that the video not only demonstrates usage of the apparatus but serves as an instructional medium, enabling a novice to make a recording by following the same steps.

---

168 Kolkowski and Van der Heijden, "Performing Media Archaeological Experiments."

Fig. 58: Aleksander Kolkowski making a phonograph recording at the Media Lab, University of Luxembourg. Courtesy of the C²DH / University of Luxembourg.

Kinora Replica 3D Model and 360-Degree Pathé-Baby 9.5mm Film Camera

After finishing the last prototype of the Kinora replica 3D model, the exported STL-files were used to upload the model to Sketchfab, a popular platform for sharing and displaying 3D content.[169] For the project "CRAFTED: Enrich and Promote Traditional and Contemporary Crafts", 360-degree photography was used to capture various analogue media technologies from the C²DH media archaeological collection and present them on *Europeana*, the online platform for European cultural heritage.[170] One of the objects included is a 360-degree representation of a Pathé-Baby 9.5mm film camera, which users can interact with virtually.[171]

---

169 Claude Wolf and Tim van der Heijden, *Kinora Replica 3D Model* (Sketchfab, 2022), https://sketchfab.com/3d-models/kinora-replica-3d-model-2a189b74c5c34c0c9918c10644c1e8b8 [last accessed 26.07.2022].

170 "CRAFTED: Enrich and Promote Traditional and Contemporary Crafts" is a project co-financed by the Connecting Europe Facility of the European Commission. For more information, see https://pro.europeana.eu/project/crafted [last accessed 26.07.2022].

171 For a 360-degree representation of a Pathé-Baby 9.5mm film camera, see https://my360viewer.com/view/9.5%20Camera%20Test/4d7425080fc37947 [last accessed 26.07.2022].

Fig. 59: 360-degree documentation of a Pathé-Baby 9.5mm film camera. Courtesy of the C^{2}DH / University of Luxembourg.

4.1.3 Hybrid

Hybrid or blended forms of knowledge dissemination, in which on-location and online modes of dissemination are combined, seem to have become the "new normal" as a response to the COVID-19 pandemic. Within the DEMA project, we have also organised hybrid events as an alternative way of sharing our media archaeological experiments during the pandemic. The greatest advantage of the hybrid mode of dissemination is the enhanced accessibility it provides to participants, giving them the possibility to attend the event either physically or virtually. Organising a hybrid event is complicated to set up technically, because it requires significant preparation to ensure a satisfying experience for audiences.

Virtual Demonstration of the Kinora Replica

In September 2020, a hands-on demonstration of the replica Kinora viewer took place in the Media Lab of the University of Luxembourg as part of the DEMA project, presented by Tim van der Heijden, Claude Wolf and Morgane Piet, who had collaborated in the making of the replica. This hybrid public event was almost entirely attended online due to COVID-19 restrictions in place at that time. The event included hands-on demonstrations of both the original and replica Kinora viewers. Furthermore, a historical background to the Kinora was presented and a detailed account was given of the process of making the replica in the Engineering 3D Lab of the University of Luxembourg. The event was live-streamed through an online platform. Thanks to the multicam facilities of the University's Media Lab, participants attending online were able to follow the demonstrations from four camera angles. Due to its hybrid nature, the event had a large international contingent. Unfortunately, technical difficulties hampered the live demonstration, notably when a camera providing a close-up view was not able to properly focus on pictures displayed in the Kinora viewer, resulting in blurred images on screen. When organising a hybrid event or virtual demonstration, it is highly recommended to take enough preparation time to set up the technical equipment and do a thorough technical run-through in advance. Despite the technical issues, however, the event was favourably received by most participants.[172]

Fig. 60: Still from the multicam video recording of the Kinora virtual demonstration at the Media Lab of the University of Luxembourg. Courtesy of the C²DH / University of Luxembourg.

---

172 For more information, see https://www.c2dh.uni.lu/data/dema-demonstration-kinora-viewer-replica [last accessed 26.07.2022].

4.2 Types of Dissemination

Given their audio-visual nature, media archaeological experiments are particularly suitable for multimodal forms of communication. Complementary to sharing knowledge by means of written texts, such as journal articles, book chapters and other traditional forms of scholarly output, various other types of dissemination – and their corresponding audiences – can be considered. Below we will discuss the experimental report, blog post, video demonstration, video essay, and media archaeological performances. We will not elaborate on online exhibitions or virtual reality installations, which are beyond the scope of this guide.

4.2.1 Experimental Report

Traditionally, the experimental report has been used to share the results from scientific experiments. As indicated in the protocol presented in Chapter 3, an experimental report provides both a description and a reflection on the media archaeological experiment. To make the experimental report useful to future researchers and students as well, it further includes a detailed description of the media historical object and its historical context of use. The experimental reports from the DEMA project can be found on the project website.

Media Archaeology Lab (MAL) Technical Reports

Media archaeologist Lori Emerson, founder of the Media Archaeology Lab (MAL) at the University of Colorado, Boulder, has reflected on the use of documentation in the hands-on teaching and research activities conducted at MAL. One of the barriers to a systematic documentation of these hands-on activities, she argues, is that every technology is different. Good documentation is also labour intensive and time consuming, and currently there is no incentive for students to do this. Instead of writing lengthy white papers, MAL now invites visitors to contribute a short "MALware Technical Report" for the lab's website and newsletter. These reports "document events, research, teaching, and artist residencies taking place in and through the lab."[173] Emerson argues that ". . . nobody wants to document, but if we don't want to engage in black-boxing, documenting hands-on activities is crucial!"[174]

---

[173] For examples of MALware Technical Reports, see the website of the Media Archaeology Lab, https://www.mediaarchaeologylab.com/projects/ [last accessed 26.07.2022]. See also the experimental reports on slow networks experiments, for example, Lori Emerson and libi rose striegl, "Slow Networks Experiment 1: Over-the-Air TV Transmission," loriemerson.net, 14 December 2020, https://loriemerson.net/2020/12/14/slow-networks-experiment-1-over-the-air-tv-transmission/ [last accessed 26.07.2022].

[174] Van der Heijden and Kolkowski, "Documenting Media Archaeological Experiments."

4.2.2 Blog Post

Another way to disseminate media archaeological experiments is by means of a blog post. A blog post can be, for instance, a slightly modified and less detailed version of the experimental report. Depending on the platform, blog posts may include photo and video content as well. Several blog posts of our hands-on experiments and other activities of the DEMA project can be found on the project website.

4.2.3 Video Demonstration

Besides documentation, video can play an important role in the dissemination of media archaeological experiments as well. Video has the potential to engage audiences and provide a rich platform for knowledge transfer and exchange.[175] While the use of moving images in education and other forms of knowledge dissemination goes back to the early twentieth century, video has become a standard educational tool in the twenty-first century, along with the increased accessibility of digital recording technologies and proliferation of audio-visual materials online. For the dissemination of media archaeological experiments, video can be used for the recording of hands-on demonstrations, personal vlogs and "how-to" tutorials online, showcasing, for instance, the media historical objects in use.

Various examples of video demonstrations can be found on social media platforms, such as the popular channel Analog Resurgence run by Toronto-based film enthusiast Noah Henderson, which provides numerous how-to videos on often rare or forgotten analogue film and photography formats and technologies, such as Polavision, 3D film cameras and nitrate film.[176] Besides young enthusiasts discovering old media technologies, experienced filmmakers, media historians and educators have also been using video as a way to demonstrate the workings and repair of media historical objects from their collections (▶ Theory, Chapter 3.4). In his video demonstrations, media historian Stephen Herbert, for instance, presents various motion image technologies from his collection, including a model of Robert Paul's first 35mm film projector and a Kinemacolor projector of the 1890s, and

---

175 Alan D. Greenberg and Jan Zanetis, "The Impact of Broadcast and Streaming Video in Education," Report commissioned by Cisco Systems Inc. to Wainhouse Research, LLC. (San Jose, CA: Cisco Systems, 2012), https://www.cisco.com/c/dam/en_us/solutions/industries/docs/education/ciscovideowp.pdf [last accessed 26.07.2022].
176 Noah Henderson, "Analog Resurgence – YouTube," 2018, https://www.youtube.com/c/AnalogResurgence/about [last accessed 26.07.2022].

demonstrates how they work (or used to work) and how they can be repaired for possible reuse today.[177] In the series "Professor Huhtamo's Cabinet of Media Archaeology", media archaeologist Erkki Huhtamo likewise presents various media archaeological objects from his personal collection, including magic lanterns and other optical media from the nineteenth and early twentieth century.[178]

For the DEMA project, we have recorded various video demonstrations as a way to document and share knowledge about their usages. These videos document, for instance, the internal mechanism of the Kinora camera, the processes of loading a Ciné-Kodak 16mm film camera and screening films with the hand-cranked Pathé-Baby 9.5mm film projector. Additionally, a video showing the comparative testing of the Stentorphone replica and original soundboxes was uploaded to a YouTube channel along with a short animation illustrating how the Stentorphone's soundbox works.

---

177 Stephen Herbert, "Stephen Herbert – YouTube," 2006, https://www.youtube.com/user/horipet/about [last accessed 26.07.2022]. For Herbert's latest writings on nineteenth- and twentieth-century popular visual culture and media technologies, see also his excellent blog *The Optilogue*, https://theoptilogue.wordpress.com/ [last accessed 26.07.2022].

178 UCLA DMA, *The Magic Lantern – Professor Huhtamo's Cabinet of Media Archaeology: Part 1*, 2017, https://www.youtube.com/watch?v=V37S95AE3Pc [last accessed 26.07.2022]; UCLA DMA, *Peep Media – Professor Huhtamo's Cabinet of Media Archaeology: Part 2*, 2018, https://www.youtube.com/watch?v=CRb8IusOe6A [last accessed 26.07.2022].

Video Demonstration and Animation: Testing and Illustrating the Working Function of Original and Replica Stentorphone Soundboxes

This video demonstration includes a test of the original and replica Stentorphone Soundboxes, produced in collaboration with the University of Luxembourg, Department of Engineering. The aim of these tests was to compare the performance of the restored original soundbox (used for the first time in this video) and the polymer replica models.[179] Another video – an animation created by former student and DEMA collaborator Thomas Theisen – shows the working function of a Stentorphone soundbox. The animation illustrates how the balanced comb valve of the Stentorphone operates under air pressure from a compressor and reproduces the sounds from a record groove.[180]

Fig. 61: Working function of a Stentorphone soundbox. Stills from animation by Thomas Theisen. Courtesy of the DoE / C²DH / University of Luxembourg.

---

179 Thomas Theisen, *Testing of Original and Replica Stentorphone Soundboxes*, 2021, https://www.youtube.com/watch?v=CWSubuug5rc [last accessed 26.07.2022].

180 Thomas Theisen, *Working Function of a Stentorphone Soundbox*, 2021, https://www.youtube.com/watch?v=NfNpah8U3Yg [last accessed 26.07.2022].

Video Demonstration: Kinora Camera (ca. 1911)

In this video demonstration, the Amsterdam-based filmmaker and collector Michael Rogge demonstrates the internal mechanism and workings of a Kinora motion picture camera from ca. 1911.[181] The Kinora camera takes 40 feet of 1-inch unperforated light-sensitive paper or celluloid film, corresponding to 640 pictures in total. After exposure, the film was processed by the Bond's Ltd. company in London, which produced the Kinora reel that could be viewed in the Kinora viewer. The Kinora camera is a hand-driven camera, whose intermittent gear worked differently compared to most other film cameras of the times. Instead of a claw pull-down mechanism, which transports the film frame by frame by means of sprocket holes, the Kinora camera makes use of two eccentric rollers.[182] In the video demonstration, Rogge showed the internal workings of the camera's shutter, film gate and focusing mechanism.[183]

Fig. 62: Michael Rogge demonstrating the Kinora camera from his collection. Photo by Tim van der Heijden. Courtesy of the C²DH / University of Luxembourg.

---

181 Rogge's personal website presents an overview of all the film historical objects of his collection, which, besides the Kinora motion picture camera, includes a Lumière Cinématographe, a Biokam, Chrono de Poche, and a Japanese 26mm Recfy paper film projector: https://wichm.home.xs4all.nl/cinimage.html [last accessed 26.07.2022].

182 For a more detailed description of how the Kinora camera worked, see Frederick A. Talbot, *Moving Pictures: How They Are Made and Worked* (Philadelphia, PA: J. B. Lippincott Co., 1914), 302–303. For high resolution scans of the Kinora camera instructions, see https://collection.sciencemuseumgroup.org.uk/objects/co8345945/kinora-camera-instructions-instruction-booklet [last accessed 26.07.2022].

183 For the video demonstration, see https://dema.uni.lu/demonstration-kinora-camera-by-ijsbrand-rogge/ [last accessed 26.07.2022].

4.2.4 Video Essay

The video essay is another popular form for academic research output and knowledge dissemination.[184] Film scholars Estrella Sendra and Bartolomeo Meletti define video essays as "scholarly videos that invite researchers and class members to explore the audiovisual and multimedia language to make an academic argument. When applied to film research and pedagogy, the video essay is thus a recursive text. That is, the object of study, film, is mediated, or rather, performed, through the film medium."[185] Compared to video demonstrations, video essays are characterised by their creative and interpretative form, in which the video material is used in a reflexive way. For making a video essay, one can make use of the audio-visual documentation of the media archaeological experiment and "remix" it with other historical sources to generate new meanings.[186]

> **Split Screen Montage in 16mm Film Re-enactments**
> For presenting the results of the media archaeological experiments with the Ciné-Kodak 16mm film camera, the split screen technique was used to juxtapose the recorded film images with the original film footage the re-enactment was inspired by or based on: fragments of the films *Le Repas de Bébé* (Louis Lumière, 1895) and *Jetty from about two weeks until her first steps* (Schendstok, 1941–1942) (see Chapter 1.3). The split screen montage enabled a visual comparison of the original and re-enacted film sequences. This provided a useful method for analysing and reflecting on their differences and similarities, as well as a way of presenting the outcomes of the experiment in general.[187]

---

184 See, for instance, Christian Keathley and Jason Mittell, *The Videographic Essay: Criticism in Sound & Image*, Kino-Agora 9 (Montreal: Caboose, 2016); Christian Keathley, Jason Mittell, and Catherine Grant, *The Videographic Essay: Practice and Pedagogy*, 2019, http://videographi cessay.org [last accessed 26.07.2022].

185 Estrella Sendra and Bartolomeo Meletti, "Introduction to Video Essays: Studying and Researching Film through Film," *Learning on Screen*, 2022, https://learningonscreen.ac.uk/guid ance/introductory-guide-to-video-essays/introduction-to-video-essays-studying-and-research ing-film-through-film/ [last accessed 26.07.2022]. See also Catherine Grant, "The Audiovisual Essay as Performative Research," *NECSUS. European Journal of Media Studies* 5, no. 2 (2016): 255–265, https://doi.org/10.25969/mediarep/3370.

186 As a technique, the split screen has a longer tradition in film history. See, for instance, Malte Hagener, "Divided, Together, Apart: How Split Screen Became Our Everyday Reality," *Pandemic Media: Preliminary Notes Toward an Inventory*, ed. Philipp Dominik Keidl et al. (Lüneburg, Germany: Meson Press, 2020), 33–40, https://pandemicmedia.meson.press/chapters/time-tem porality/divided-together-apart-how-split-screen-became-our-everyday-reality/ [last accessed 26.07.2022]; and Franziska Heller, *Update!* (Paderborn, Germany: Wilhelm Fink Verlag, 2020), https://doi.org/10.30965/9783846764602.

187 Kolkowski and Van der Heijden, "Performing Media Archaeological Experiments."

Fig. 63: Still from *Jetty from about two weeks until her first steps* (Schendstok, 1941–1942) and still from 16mm film re-enactment (2020). Courtesy of the Netherlands Institute for Sound & Vision / C²DH / University of Luxembourg.

The video essay invites creative forms of digital storytelling. A good example of this is the video essay "560 kHz+", produced by libi rose striegl, an artist, teacher and manager of the Media Archaeology Lab (MAL) of the University of Colorado, Boulder, in collaboration with MAL founder Lori Emerson.

560 kHz+ (MAL)

The video *560 kHz+* presents some of the hands-on experiments performed in the MAL with the lab's collection of over-the-air transmission and reception devices. In their joint presentation, striegl and Emerson "performed" the lab itself as experienced in the frequency ranges of 500–1100 kHz and 30mHz to 3GHz. The video starts with how radio as a medium represents space in the sense of distance and obstruction: buildings and landforms may dictate, for instance, how information can be transmitted over the air. A short-ranged television transmitter, part of the MAL collection, was used for broadcasting VHS tapes to various televisions at the MAL. It was set to broadcast channel 8, which receives a VHS signal between 180–186 mHz, corresponding to a wavelength of 161–166 centimetres. With regard to AM-radio, this means a spectrum of 560–1600 kHz, corresponding to a wavelength of approximately 535 metres. The hands-on experiments with over-the-air transmission and reception devices made striegl and Emerson explore the concept of broadcast strength and the specifics of antenna shape and power, as well as enabling them to experience and conceptualise a new way of measuring space, namely in terms of wavelengths. As a laboratory space, the MAL can be measured, for instance, as 10 x 20 channel 8 wavelengths in size. Navigating the world based on such measurements, and thinking about what it takes for the invisible signals that emanate from every device and connect us to every other device to get through the world, provides a new sensory experience of, and perspective on both our past and current (media) landscapes.[188]

---

[188] The video was presented at the DEMA workshop 2020 and is embedded in the workshop report. See Kolkowski and Van der Heijden, "Performing Media Archaeological Experiments."

4.2.5 Media Archaeological Performances

While the previous types of dissemination are predominantly aimed at online forms of presentation, media archaeological performances require a physical or hybrid setting. In general, we can distinguish between four types of media archaeological performances: (1) the re-enactment as public spectacle, (2) the lecture performance, (3) the recorded simulated or re-enacted practice, and (4) the reflexive performance.

1) Re-enactment as Public Spectacle

A media archaeological performance can take place in the form of a public spectacle and serve as a pedagogical attraction, meant to both entertain and inform an audience. Public historical re-enactments are usually performed by artists and showmen, yet historians can play a part in their preparation, organisation and performance as well.

Re-enacting the Crazy Cinématographe

From 2007 to 2011, the Cinémathèque Municipale de la Ville de Luxembourg organised the "Crazy Cinématographe", a historical re-enactment of early cinema performance at the city of Luxembourg's Schueberfouer. For three weeks in August and September, short 35mm film programmes of roughly 20 minutes each were performed in a tented cinema auditorium called the Crazy Cinématographe. These early fairground cinema revival shows included all the performative elements of live accompaniment that were usual in theatrical film screenings before the First World War: live music, bonimenteurs, and actors attracting patrons into the tent. Crazy Cinématographe was an experiment in media archaeological practice – taking place not in a lab, but in today's cultural context. The project was by far one of the largest experiments on cinema archaeology – attracting nearly 10,000 participants every year.[189] Without employing such a performative approach, the German film historian Martin Loiperdinger argued, the 2011 Crazy Cinématographe performance of Winsor McKay's "Gerti the Dinosaur" (1914) and its reconstructed public reception would be incomprehensible.[190]

---

189 Crazy Cinématographe originated as a project of the Cinémathèque Luxembourg, conducted by director Claude Bertemes and Nicole Dahlen, within the framework of the European Capital of Culture project "Travelling Cinema in Europe" in 2007. For more information, see https://www.uni-trier.de/index.php?id=65359 [last accessed 26.07.2022].
190 Kolkowski and Van der Heijden, "Performing Media Archaeological Experiments."

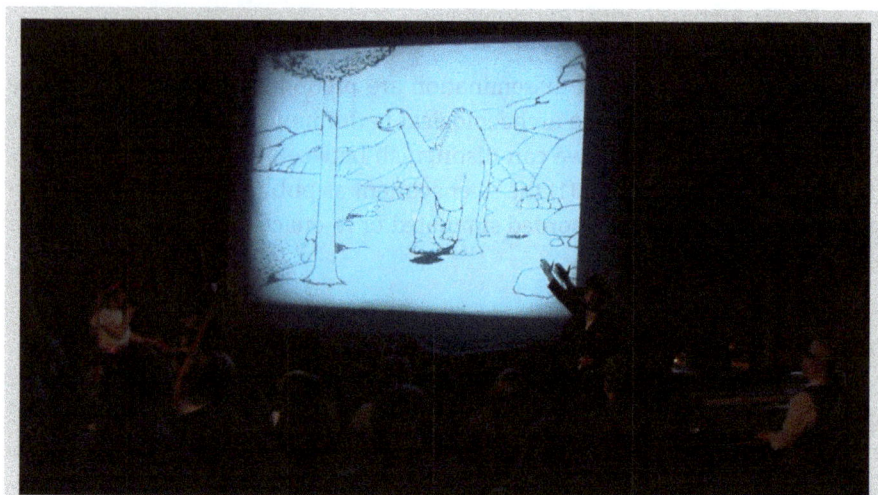

Fig. 64: Still from "Gerti the Dinosaur" (1914), presented at the Crazy Cinématographe performance 2011. Courtesy of the UVA, University of Trier.

2) Lecture Performance

Another type of media archaeological performance is the lecture performance. Contrary to the historical re-enactment as a public spectacle, lecture performances are primarily meant to educate audiences. They are usually performed by educators and experts from the field of inquiry. The virtual demonstrations given by photography historian Mark Osterman, organised at the Eastman Kodak Museum in Rochester, New York, in 2020, serve as a good example. The Museum has a long history of giving on-site demonstrations on various historical photography techniques. During the COVID-19 pandemic, these hands-on demonstrations continued online. In the online lecture performances, Osterman demonstrated various processes and techniques from the history of nineteenth-century photography, while giving verbal explanations at the same time.[191] This combination of demonstration and explanation – "show and tell" – is characteristic of lecture performances.

---

191 For more information about the Eastman Kodak Museum virtual demonstrations, see https://www.eastman.org/demos [last accessed 26.07.2022]. See also Kate Meyers Emery, "A Whole New (Digital) World: Online Experiences at the Eastman Museum during 2020," *George Eastman Museum* (blog), 20 May 2021, https://medium.com/george-eastman-museum/a-whole-new-digital-world-online-experiences-at-the-eastman-museum-during-2020-8c352494bba2 [last accessed 26.07.2022].

Staging the Amateur Film Dispositif

The lecture performance and media archaeological experiment *Staging the Amateur Film Dispositif*, conducted by the members of the NWO-funded research project "Changing Platforms of Ritualised Memory Practices: The Cultural Dynamics of Home Movies", explored in three *tableaux* how past media usages of film, video and digital media altered the practices of home movie staging. The lecture performance addressed the problem that screening practices "[. . .] belong to the more ephemeral moments of family life. They are about watching recorded moments, but they are usually not recorded themselves."[192] A theatre play was developed in which a small family re-enacts the familial screening practices of the 1950s, 1980s and into the twenty-first century. This re-enactment, done in a staged domestic setting, explored what it meant to watch home movies, videos and digital videos, and sought to capture some of those bygone experiences.[193]

Fig. 65: Still from video documentation of the lecture performance *Staging the Amateur Film Dispositif*. Courtesy of Maastricht University.

---

192 Susan Aasman, "Report 'Staging the Amateur Dispositif,'" 27 June 2014, https://homemo viesproject.wordpress.com/report-staging-the-amateur-dispositif/ [last accessed 26.07.2022].
193 The lecture performance was performed by Susan Aasman, Andreas Fickers, Tom Slootweg, Tim van der Heijden and Guy Edmonds on 31 March 2014 at the 9th International Orphan Film Symposium at the Eye Filmmuseum Amsterdam. The performance was recorded on video; see Tim van der Heijden, *Staging the Amateur Film Dispositif* (Vimeo, 2014), https://vimeo.com/ 95314562 [last accessed 26.07.2022].

The Speaking Arc and the Singing Arc

The demonstration of *The Speaking Arc and Singing Arc* experiment, conducted by Paolo Brenni, Roland Wittje and Anna Giatti, is one of over a hundred videos made by Brenni, a historian of science at the Fondazione Scienza e Technica Firenza, and his team. They document historical experiments using original and functioning scientific instruments from the museum's collection, which serves as a source for historical research and teaching purposes (see also Chapter 3).[194] Carbon arc lamps were used for street lighting ca. 1900, and created light via an electrical arc between two carbon electrodes, which often produced audible sounds. The demonstration followed contemporary experiments by W. B. Dudell and H. T. Simon in making the arc speak and sing, functioning both as a microphone and a loudspeaker. Although it was not commercially exploited and largely confined to scientific demonstrations, the speaking arc is seen as a forerunner to wireless telephony and the thermionic valve or vacuum tube. Brenni and Wittje described the major challenges they faced in their experiments, using an original electric arc from the early 1900s. As well as posing unforeseen questions that had not arisen in previous research, operating the arc provided new experiences in the field of electro-acoustics that are far removed from modern domestic hi-fi electronics. In order to replicate the singing and speaking arc experiments, Brenni and Wittje referred to original documents and employed apparatus made in the early twentieth century, including items manufactured by Max Kohl and Ernst Ruhmer.[195]

3) Recorded Simulated or Re-enacted Practice

Media archaeological performances can also occur in the form of a recorded simulated practice, in which the media historical object is demonstrated. Simulated practices are meant to simulate or re-enact past user practices and experiences. They are usually performed either by users who may have worked with the object in the past, or contemporary experts who have knowledge about the object and its user practice from the perspective of the present. Examples of simulated practices were the previously discussed ADAPT project on analogue television production practices and cultures by John Ellis, the keyhole surgery project by Roger Kneebone, and Anna Harris' project "Making Clinical Sense"

---

194 See the Sound & Science database for more videos and information, including two essays: Roland Wittje, "The Speaking and Singing Arc: The Sound of Electricity at the Fin de Siècle," *Sound & Science: Digital Histories* (blog), 19 February 2018, https://soundandscience. de/contributor-essays/speaking-and-singing-arc-sound-electricity-fin-de-siecle [last accessed 26.07.2022]; and Paolo Brenni, "Nineteenth-Century Acoustics and Its Instruments: On the Method of Reenactment," *Sound & Science: Digital Histories* (blog), 14 January 2020, https:// soundandscience.de/contributor-essays/nineteenth-century-acoustics-and-its-instruments-method-reenactment [last accessed 26.07.2022].
195 Fondazione Scienza e Tecnica, *Speaking Arc and Singing Arc*, 2016, https://www.youtube. com/watch?v=cCEU3ShVE2E [last accessed 26.07.2022].

about how doctors learn sensory skills and diagnosis. In these projects, simulation served as a heuristic instrument for understanding past (media) practices.

Sean Williams' "Bandpass filters in Stockhausen's Sternklang"

Sean Williams' video demonstration "Bandpass filters in Stockhausen's Sternklang" gives an account of the technical challenges he dealt with in realising a performance of the titular piece in Hanover, in August 2020. The piece, conceived for the open air, has had only a dozen performances since its premiere in 1971. Five groups of musicians – each having a vocalist, instrumentalists and live electronics – are dispersed in a park. The piece is based around vowel sounds and phonemes that are produced or mimicked by the vocalists and instrumentalists. Specific harmonics have to be emphasised using vocalisation, extended techniques and electronic filtering. The analogue low-pass filters used at the time the piece was composed are limited in that they cannot adequately manipulate the sound in order to produce the desired harmonics as notated in the score. Another difficulty arose in achieving accuracy with the foot pedal operation of the filter, which was circumvented by using a control knob on the filter itself. In rehearsal and particularly in the performance itself the operator really had to be self-evaluative and understand the feasibility of controlling the devices to achieve the requirements of the score, by performing with the vocalists and instrumentalists in the "heat of battle". This shows the value of doing such research projects in live public performances – the pressure of a performance situation can illuminate certain questions, in this case around performance practices in electronic music.[196]

---

196 The video from Sean Williams was presented at the DEMA workshop 2020; see Kolkowski and Van der Heijden, "Performing Media Archaeological Experiments."

Fig. 66: Rehearsal image from Karlheinz Stockhausen's "Sternklang" (2020), showing an analogue filtering device (left of Laptop computer) designed by Otto Kränzler ca. 1980, specifically for performances of Sternklang. Courtesy of Sean Williams.

4) Reflexive Performance

The last category of media archaeological performance is the reflexive kind. These performances reflect on the experimental process and/or the results themselves. They may take the form of a video essay, art installation or "making of" video. Reflexive media archaeological performances are usually performed by artists, educators and researchers.

Tennis for Two: Performing the First Electronic Video Game

In this reflexive video, media archaeologists Stefan Höltgen and Shintaro Miyazaki reflect on a re-enactment of *Tennis for Two* – one of the very first electronic video games. The re-enactment was conducted by Höltgen and his students at the Media Archaeological Fundus of the Humboldt-Universität, Berlin. *Tennis for Two* was originally introduced in 1958 at the Brookhaven National Laboratory, New York, by the American physicist William Higinbotham. Unlike *Pong*, the digital computer game from the early 1970s, *Tennis for Two* implemented analogue electronic technologies. On the basis of circuit diagrams from an original manual of the first Telefunken analogue computer, Höltgen was able to reconstruct the three parts of the analogue computer's circuitry. The upper part steers the vertical direction of the ball (up and down), the middle part its horizontal direction (left and right), and the bottom part builds a circle on the screen. The operational amplifiers – arguably the core item of an analogue computer – are illustrated in the form of triangles in the circuit diagram. Their function is to steer the signals within the analogue computer's circuitry, which ultimately leads to the creation of the picture on the oscilloscope. The original analogue computer uses around twenty of such operational amplifiers.

To experience and re-enact how *Tennis for Two* enabled some interactive elements, Höltgen and Miyazaki could have followed William Higinbotham's original circuitry from 1957. However, they decided to go one step further. The original idea for the game came from a "ball in the box" demonstration program that Higinbotham aimed to open up or "hack". Higinbotham wanted to let the ball no longer rebound from the walls – going left and right – but instead make this an interactive element, in which a player presses a button to control the electronic signal. While pressing the button, the player controls the electronic signal by creating an invisible wall related to the ball's position in the field, which makes the ball bounce back as an effect. Because Höltgen and Miyazaki did not have enough operational amplifiers at their disposal, they made an adaptation of the original circuit in which the ball became just a point on the oscilloscope that could move in both vertical and horizontal directions. By simulating these movements, Höltgen and Miyazaki implemented actual principles of physics, including gravitation, to achieve a more realistic feeling of playing tennis – similar to that which the inventors of early electronic computer games were attempting to achieve.[197]

4.3 Teaching

In their writings on experimental media archaeology, Fickers and Van den Oever have argued that the "greatest heuristic potential [of experimental media archaeology] may well lie in the didactic, educational front" and that "experimental media archaeology can make a contribution to (media) historical *education*, which expands the conventional forms of historical learning to a sensorial dimension of imagining the past" (▶ Theory, Chapter 2.6). But how to implement experimental media archaeology within teaching and education in practical terms? What is the pedagogical value of doing hands-on experiments for students and scholars interested in the history of media and communication technologies? This section shares recommendations and reflections based on experiences from media archaeological labs and educational institutes, including the Media Archaeological Fundus (MAF) at Humboldt-Universität, Berlin; Film Archive and Media Archaeology Lab of the University of Groningen; Media Archaeology Lab (MAL) at University of Colorado, Boulder; and our DEMA project at the University of Luxembourg.

---

197 The video from Höltgen and Miyazaki was presented at the DEMA workshop 2020, see Kolkowski and Van der Heijden, "Performing Media Archaeological Experiments."

Stentorphone and Auxetophone Replica Projects: Supervising Students in a Collaboration with the University of Luxembourg Department of Engineering
The pneumatic gramophone soundbox replication projects were used by the students of the University of Luxembourg Department of Engineering as case studies for Master's students, lasting three to four months, and final year projects for Bachelor students, typically lasting six months. The individual projects provided students with an opportunity to learn or improve skills in CAD modelling, producing 3D printed models, and testing them for efficiency. It gave the students and staff members a rare opportunity to work directly from rare historical objects loaned to the project, and to produce functioning models as part of a larger project, with possibilities of involvement in co-written academic papers, presentations and public demonstrations.

In replicating a historical design, students learnt about the role and function of the materials used and how substituting them with modern equivalents will affect the behaviour of the object. Additionally, the students were tasked with finding enhancements and modifications to an existing design, deepening their understanding of the technological object and showing possible defects in the original designs that may have contributed to failure and obsolescence. Improvements that could have been introduced in later manifestations of the technological object may be used to demonstrate what might have been accomplished had it been pushed to its limits.

While course work and technical supervision was given by the academic engineering staff, the students were also given support by the lead researcher, who supplied historical and technical background, patents and schematics. The DEMA project also supplied additional funding when specific work had to be carried out by external experts and engineering firms. This form of supervision works both ways. The students receive additional guidance and historical background for their written theses and final presentations, which contextualise the study. The researcher gains the replica model, often together with technical data and analysis that would otherwise have been overlooked, and works together with the students in conducting and documenting the experiments.

4.3.1 Object Lessons

What media historical objects can tell us about the past is one of the central questions in teaching media history and media archaeology. In their introduction to the special issue on experimental media archaeology in the classroom in *Early Popular Visual Culture*, media historians Patrick Ellis and Colin Williamson propose that teachers "think about historical media in the classroom not simply as objects of study but as resources for creating sensorial engagements with film and media history".[198] Attempting to foster discussion on such sensory and

---

[198] Patrick Ellis and Colin Williamson, "Object Lessons, Old and New: Experimental Media Archaeology in the Classroom," *Early Popular Visual Culture* 18, no. 1 (29 April 2020), 2, https://doi.org/10.1080/17460654.2020.1751434.

object-based pedagogies, they take inspiration from what is known in the fields of visual education and art history as the *object lesson*, defining it as "a method of inciting a student's curiosity by stimulating the senses with images or direct engagements with the objects being studied".[199] In other words, in object lessons the objects themselves teach the students. A nineteenth-century zoetrope or phenakistoscope, for example, can be used to demonstrate the basic principles of animation and visual perception. As a performative method, object lessons have a longer tradition in art and art history – see, for instance, the work by the South African artist William Kentridge.[200]

In the field of media archaeology, object lessons are often used by Erkki Huhtamo in his teachings at UCLA. Drawing from his extraordinary collection of media historical objects, his lessons demonstrate how to practise media archaeology with the objects themselves, such as the Spirograph.[201] Object lessons have also been implemented as a teaching method by Lori Emerson, Wolfgang Ernst, Stefan Höltgen, Andrea Mariani, Annie van den Oever, Jussi Parikka, Wanda Strauven, and Charles Tepperman, among others.[202] For the course "Theory and Critique of Media and New Media" – part of the three-year programme DAMS-Gorizia 2018 – the Italian media archaeologist Andrea Mariani, for instance, initiated the *(Un)Dead Media*

---

199 Ellis and Williamson, "Object Lessons," 2. See also Gunning, "Re-Newing Old Technologies"; see also ▶ Theory, Chapter 5.3.

200 Jane Taylor, *William Kentridge: Being Led by the Nose*, (Chicago, IL: University of Chicago Press, 2019). In this context, see also the work of art historian Ann-Sophie Lehmann, who maintains a process-based approach to art and visual material culture in her research: Ann-Sophie Lehmann, "Object Lessons. Material Begreifen in Acht Lektionen," *Werkbundarchiv – Museum Der Dinge* (blog), 2017, https://www.museumderdinge.de/ausstellungen/object-lessons-material-begreifen-8-lektionen [last accessed 26.07.2022].

201 Huhtamo, "The Dream of Personal Interactive Media."

202 See Charles Tepperman, "Taking a Turn on the Rewind: Strategies for Experiential Learning in Nontheatrical Film History, *The Journal of Cinema and Media Studies* 60, no. 6 (Winter 2021), https://doi.org/10.3998/jcms.18261332.0060.605; Wanda Strauven, *Touchscreen Archaeology: Tracing Histories of Hands-On Media Practices* (Lüneburg, Germany: Meson Press, 2021); Annie van den Oever, "Experimental Media Archaeology in the Media Archaeology Lab: Re-Sensitizing the Observer," in *At the Borders of (Film) History: Temporality, Archaeology, Theories*, ed. Alberto Bertrame, Guiseppe Fidotta, and Andrea Mariani, (Udine: Forum, 2015), 43–53; Erkki Huhtamo and Jussi Parikka, *Media Archaeology: Approaches, Applications, and Implications* (Berkeley, CA; London: University of California Press, 2011); Andrea Mariani, "(Un)Dead Media Project," *(Un)Dead Media Project* (blog), 2022, https://andreamariani.info/ [last accessed 26.07.2022]; Lori Emerson and Wolfgang Ernst, "Archives, Materiality and the 'Agency of the Machine': An Interview with Wolfgang Ernst," *The Signal* (blog), 8 February 2013, //blogs.loc.gov/thesignal/2013/02/archives-materiality-and-agency-of-the-machine-an-interview-with-wolfgang-ernst/ [last accessed 26.07.2022]. For the work done at the FUNDUS, see https://www.musikundmedien.hu-berlin.de/de/medienwissenschaft/medientheorien/fundus/media-archaeological-fundus [last accessed 26.07.2022].

Project and its related blog. Students were invited to write blog entries about specific media historical objects they each had a personal connection with, which included a 35mm film photography camera, a Single 8 film camera, a Video8 Handycam, and a *Game Boy*.[203] Several museums, including the National Science and Media Museum in Bradford, the *Deutsches Filmmuseum* in Frankfurt, the *Fondation Jérôme Seydoux-Pathé* in Paris, and the Eye Filmmuseum in Amsterdam, offer hands-on educational activities with media historical objects as well (▶ Theory, Chapter 4.2).

Panorama, Eye Filmmuseum Amsterdam

Since December 2014, the souterrain of the Eye Filmmuseum in Amsterdam hosts a permanent exhibition on the history of cinema represented through the display of highlights from the museum's apparatus collection, including a Magic Lantern with double optical system (ca. 1880), a Mutoscope (ca. 1900), a 35mm Mitchell film camera (ca. 1935), up until the first iPhone that was equipped with a video camera (2008).[204] The material objects are accompanied by short descriptions, which explain the technological object's historical significance and context of use. The permanent exhibition also features various interactive installations, for instance, one in which visitors can make their own flip books or "thumb cinema". The museum also ran a Magic Lantern workshop for children aged 5 to 12. The permanent exhibition's establishment was the outcome of Eye's new collection policy, led by head curator Giovanna Fossati, which brought about a productive collaboration between the Eye Filmmuseum and the Film Archive and Media Archaeology Lab of the University of Groningen.[205]

Meredith Bak's "Play Labs"

In her article "Optical Play and the Expanded Archive", media archaeologist Meredith Bak reflects on her object lessons, which invite students to interact with various optical toys designed for children. The hands-on approach is helpful in stimulating multisensorial forms of engagement and for thinking beyond imagined usages, as she explains: "In my undergraduate class on Toy Design [. . .] students participate in hands-on 'play labs', which require them first to physically engage toys and identify design characteristics such as affordances, constraints, and signifiers, and then to articulate how each toy 'works'. Experiencing these things firsthand, as opposed to reading descriptions, [makes students question] for instance what forms

---

203 Mariani, "(Un)Dead Media Project."

204 See https://www.eyefilm.nl/en/permanent-presentation [last accessed 26.07.2022] and Caylin Smith, "Extending the Archival Life of Film: Presenting Film History with EYE," in *Exposing the Film Apparatus: The Film Archive as a Research Laboratory*, ed. Giovanna Fossati and Annie van den Oever (Amsterdam: Amsterdam University Press, 2016), 323–331.

205 The collaboration resulted in the symposium, "The Film Archive as a Research Laboratory", and book, *Exposing the Film Apparatus: The Film Archive as a Research Laboratory*, intended to foster international discussion and exchange between media scholars and media archivists on the topic of the use of media apparatuses in both research and teaching. See further Giovanna Fossati and Annie van den Oever, eds., *Exposing the Film Apparatus: The Film Archive as a Research Laboratory* (Amsterdam: Amsterdam University Press, 2016).

of engagement toys' material attributes signal or discourage, and consider the affordances and constraints of toys as media or systems. They often note how promises about toys' play values fall short in practice."[206] For the classroom experiments, Bak developed a "Play Lab Report" in which students can fill in various fields, such as an inventory of the assigned toy, photos of the object, a description of the object's affordances and constraints, and (multisensory) feedback on the practice of "playing with the toy". The report includes several tips meant to stimulate the students to reflect on their sensorial interactions and engagement with the historical object at stake.[207]

4.3.2 The Value of Hands-on Enquiry in Teaching

Experimental media archaeology can be a useful method to teach students about the interaction between the media historical object and the (historical) user. As explained in Chapter 1, one of the heuristic potentials of hands-on approaches is the attention it creates regarding the constructivist nature of media technology products, which is helpful for studying the performative dimension of media technologies and the tactile interactions between the user and object. Fickers and Van den Oever argue that it is the "strong aesthetic and performative impact of media devices" that makes them so effective in educational terms (▶ Theory, Chapter 2.6). The hands-on approach invites students to "think differently", media archaeologist Wanda Strauven argues, although she considers the educational value of hands-on activities to be conceptual rather than historical:

> By physically engaging with old artefacts or apparatuses, the intention is not so much to bring the students in contact with the past, but rather to make them think differently, to make them question what is taken for granted, to 'unsettle' them – all this with regard to their present, that is, to their contemporary media use and their actual training as media scholars (and therefore also to their knowledge of media history).[208]

Drawing on the notion of thinkering, we believe that the value of the hands-on approach within education lies exactly in the combination of the conceptual and the historical, the theoretical and the practical, the cognitive and the (multi)

---

206 Meredith Bak, "Optical Play and the Expanded Archive: Mapping Childhood and Media Archaeology," *Early Popular Visual Culture* 18, no. 1 (2 January 2020): 35, https://doi.org/10.1080/17460654.2020.1761602.

207 Meredith Bak, "Play Lab Report – Identifying Design Attributes," 2021, https://domitor.org/wp-content/uploads/2021/08/Bak_Play-Lab-Exercise.docx-1.pdf [last accessed 26.07.2022].

208 Wanda Strauven, "Media Archaeology as Laboratory for History Writing and Theory Making," in *New Media Archaeologies*, ed. Ben Roberts and Mark Goodall (Amsterdam: Amsterdam University Press, 2019), 27.

sensorial/physical, the mind and the body, the reflexive and the embodied. In fact, hands-on experiments in both research and teaching may help to transcend such binary oppositions and categorizations in knowledge production.

Film Archive and Media Archaeology Lab, University of Groningen

During the 2019 DEMA workshop, film scholar Annie van den Oever shared some experiences and lessons learnt as head of the Film Archive and Media Archaeology Lab of the University of Groningen.[209] The collection holds over 2000 film reels, but Van den Oever re-focused on the technological apparatuses in particular, so that the archive would become a laboratory for doing hands-on experiments in both research and teaching. Many film scholars, she noticed, never touch the technological devices, but rather live in a "world of books". This inspired her to invite first-year students to the lab before they start reading about film as a medium and technology. The aim was to let students experience the technologies by allowing them to physically touch and examine the historical objects from the film archive's collection, including a 70mm film reel, a 16mm Bell & Howell Filmo camera from 1937, a Zeiss Ikon 35mm projector. Handing the students these objects, rather than giving lectures or explanations, allows the students to, for example, feel the weight of the camera, smell the vinegar syndrome (caused by the film's acetate base degradation), hear the sound of the *Maltese Cross* and the flapping of the projector's shutter, which is very loud and therefore raises questions about cinema's silent era, for example (▶Theory, Chapter 2). After these encounters with such historical devices, Van den Oever's students go to another room, where they are asked to draw the object that they have just seen and touched, purely based on memory. Interestingly, Van den Oever found that while most of the students had never seen the object or read about it before, they were able to recall a lot of detail during this exercise. More importantly, using the hands-on approach as a didactic tool worked on their historical imagination and so led them to ask different sorts of questions. In other words, working with the collection in a hands-on manner "kick-starts" their reading and even creates a different type of relationship to the film-historical sources. This example demonstrates the heuristic value and pedagogical potential of a hands-on and sensorial approach in teaching film studies.

Use of Hands-on Enquiry in the London Science Museum

Many heritage institutions with a technical or scientific collection shifted their didactic aims from specialists to a much wider (i.e., lay, young) audience during the second half of the twentieth century.[210] An important parallel development in many of these museums was the shift in display techniques (inspired by new conservation theories) from once accessible objects being placed in inaccessible static display cases. Understanding the didactic value of having hands-on access to objects has led to a rising interest in museum displays that offer hands-on access while also conforming to contemporary conservation standards. The Science Museum in

209 For more information about the Film Archive and Media Archaeology Lab of the University of Groningen, see https://filmarchief.ub.rug.nl/Welcome [last accessed 26.07.2022].
210 Andrew Nahum, "Exhibiting Science: Changing Conceptions of Science Museum Display," in *Science for the Nation: Perspectives on the History of the Science Museum*, ed. Peter J. T. Morris (London: Palgrave Macmillan, 2010), 176–193, https://doi.org/10.1057/9780230283145_9.

London has incorporated various displays of this kind into their exhibitions, especially in the Information Age Gallery (opened in 2014), which is divided into six zones and has a multi-layered display "to represent a tactile window into each zone".[211] This includes touchable replicas of (parts of) relevant objects, such as a dial phone and a switchboard where visitors can "plug in" wires to listen to stories from former switchboard operators.

4.3.3 Reflexive Video Essays

While historical imagination plays a crucial role in both the object lessons and hands-on approach in the classroom or media archaeological lab, another approach to teaching experimental media archaeology involves the actual creation of media products, in the form of reflexive video essays or documentaries on specific media historical objects, for instance. As exemplified in Chapter 2.5, there is great potential in artistic approaches for both researching and teaching of historical media technologies and practices. Inviting students to actually create and produce something based on their interactions and experiences with media historical objects within a laboratory setting may serve multiple purposes. Besides being a pedagogical tool that helps students to reflect on their personal or group experiences by means of using different types of media (texts, images and sounds), these creative practices can actually serve the production of knowledge about the objects as well.

Media Archaeology Lab (MAL), University of Colorado, Boulder
The Media Archaeology Lab (MAL) at the University of Colorado, Boulder, serves once more as an inspiring example of implementing creative and artistic approaches in teaching media histories. In addition to general tours in which students visit the lab, the MAL collection is also used as part of an assignment to make short video essays about objects from the lab.[212] A recent example of a reflexive video based on a student's encounter with the MAL collection is the video *The past must live so the present can be seen*, made by Riley Bartlett, a former student of the University of Colorado. The reflexive video essay, drawing on the MAL as a "technological time capsule", presents a "journey through the effects different mediums of technology have on both our heads and hearts".[213]

---

211 For more information about the Science Museum in London, see https://www.sciencemu seum.org.uk/see-and-do/information-age [last accessed 26.07.2022].

212 For more information about the Media Archaeology Lab (MAL), see https://www.me diaarchaeologylab.com/community [last accessed 26.07.2022].

213 Riley Bartlett, *The Past Must Live so the Present Can Be Seen*, 2021, https://vimeo.com/ 653869229 [last accessed 26.07.2022].

4.4 Recommendations and Reflections

Within this chapter, we have discussed various aspects related to the practice of disseminating media archaeological experiments. Based on the examples discussed, we can summarise the following recommendations and reflections:

- Different modes of disseminating media archaeological experiments can be distinguished: on location, online and hybrid. Each mode comes with its own advantages and disadvantages (4.1).
- Different forms for disseminating media archaeological experiments can be distinguished: experimental report, blog post, video demonstration, video essay and media archaeological performances (4.2).
- Object lessons can be used as sensory and object-based pedagogies in teaching experimental media archaeology (4.3).
- The value of the hands-on approach for teaching media histories is that it invites students to "think differently" about the media historical objects and their associated practices (4.3).
- There is great potential in using reflexive video essays as a form of knowledge production and dissemination, both in research and teaching contexts (4.3).

Chapter 5
Conclusions

The aim of this book is to serve as a practical guide for doing experimental media archaeology as an object-oriented and sensorial approach to media historiography. Together, the four chapters provide a systematic and methodological framework for how to prepare, research, analyse, document and disseminate media archaeological experiments. The heuristic potential of experimental media archaeology served as an important starting point for this guide. We have reflected on the main lessons learnt, based on our own hands-on experiments and experiences in relation to experimental work done by other researchers, artists and practitioners in and beyond the field of media history. The various examples presented in these chapters have highlighted how doing media archaeological experiments may serve as a heuristic tool for understanding the materiality and functionality of past media technologies and for exploring their histories of use. Doing experimental media archaeology helps to explicate the tacit knowledge involved in past media usages and, as Fickers and Van den Oever argue, to stimulate one's historical imagination (▶ Theory, Chapters 2.6 and 4.2). We have seen how this heuristic value is not necessarily limited to the domain of research, on which we have focused in this guide, which has been principally informed by our DEMA-research projects. It can also be beneficial for education, in which hands-on pedagogies and "learning by doing" approaches provide new ways for students to engage with the past. In this concluding chapter, we provide a brief summary of the main recommendations and reflections from the different chapters and discuss their methodological and epistemological implications.

Synopsis

In Chapter 1, we discussed how the preparation of a media archaeological experiment requires the formulation of a clear and concise research question, and the selection of a suitable method and approach prior to the experiment. Different objectives, types of experiments and experimental settings were considered, as well as how studying historical and modern sources can both inform and be informed by hands-on experimentation. One of the central recommendations was to collaborate with institutional partners, experts and/or collectors, who can help to inform the media archaeological experiments and provide possibilities for their dissemination. Various routes were discussed for gaining access to historical objects for hands-on experimentation, from collaboration with cultural heritage institutions or

∂ Open Access. © 2023 the author(s), published by De Gruyter. [CC] [BY] This work is licensed under the Creative Commons Attribution 4.0 International License.
https://doi.org/10.1515/9783110799767-006

collectors to purchasing the object from an online resource, each coming with its own pros and cons.

In Chapter 2, we discussed how media archaeological experiments can be informed by conventional research methods and, vice versa, how the experiments can inform the reading of traditional historical sources, such as handbooks, magazines and advertisements. By shifting the attention from discourse to practice, experimental media archaeology has the potential to make explicit the tacit knowledge, practical skills and sensorial perception related to historical media usages. A central element of the experiment is the encounter with failure, mistakes and unexpected problems, which can become learning opportunities, as they may produce new insights into actual user practices and experiences of the past. Media archaeological experiments furthermore provide opportunities for examining the role of the senses in performing tasks, operations and other aspects of the "re-enacted" user experience. Finally, it was recommended to involve experts from the field of practice and audiences in the design and performance of media archaeological experiments.

In Chapter 3, we discussed how to choose documentation methods and tools, as each comes with different affordances and limitations. Recommendations were given on the importance of sound synchronisation in case of multiple input sources; data management of documentation materials; and ethical considerations related to documentation practices and General Data Protection Regulation (GDPR). Further, various objectives of documentation practices were discussed and ways to use the method of contextual inquiry for documenting audience behaviour and responses to media archaeological experiments. The chapter describes various challenges of documentation, as well as several strategies on how to deal with these challenges. Re-doing the documentation after the experiment, for instance, can be a strategy to solve the problem of the documentation practice potentially influencing or distracting the experimentation process. This is particularly useful in cases where there is no role division between experimenter and documentalist within the experimental process. Finally, it was recommended not to strive for historical authenticity, as this is by definition impossible, but to use the notion as a heuristic instrument to reflect on and question to what degree the reconstructions represent past media constellations and usages and so mediate between the "old" and the "new". These reflections should be made explicit in both the documentation and dissemination of the media archaeological experiment.

In Chapter 4, we discussed different modes of disseminating media archaeological experiments: on location, online and hybrid. Each mode comes with its own pros and cons. Different ways of disseminating media archaeological experiments were discussed, such as the experimental report, blog post, video demonstration, video essay and media archaeological performances. Recommendations were given on using object lessons as sensory and object-based pedagogies in teaching experimental media archaeology. Finally, the chapter discussed the value of the hands-on approach for teaching media histories and the potential for using reflexive video essays as forms of knowledge production and dissemination in both research and teaching contexts.

Experimental System

Inspired by the work and terminology of the historian of science Hans-Jörg Rheinberger, we have proposed an "experimental system" for doing experimental media archaeology, which involves different types of experiments and various modes of experimentation. Distinguishing between basic, media-technological, and performative experiments has helped us to systematically analyse past media technologies as both epistemic and technical objects. The three types of experiments often form a natural trajectory in our own experimental processes. Generally, we started with the basic experiments, involving the practices of testing, repair and maintenance, described as being part of the preparation phase. Subsequently, the media-technological experiments correspond to the research phase, experimenting with the technological affordances in order to study the relation between the media historical object and its histories of use. Finally, the performative experiments deal with the phases of documentation and dissemination, in which the historical media practice is staged, either in the form of an edited recording of the experiment or as a live re-enactment and performance.

Although we have presented and discussed the phases of preparation, research, documentation and dissemination as four rather distinct phases, they do not always succeed each other in practice. In our experience, for example, some of the documentation practices, such as setting-up the recording equipment and making sure batteries are fully charged, are also part of the preparation phase. Similarly, the dissemination phase sometimes required the re-recording of certain things that were forgotten, or were not successfully captured in the documentation phase. Rather than a straightforward and linear process, the four practices inform each other iteratively. Similarly, overlaps exist between the three types of media archaeological experiments as well as between the different methods of experimentation that we have distinguished. The recordings of a basic experiment or media-technological experiment, for instance, could become part of a performative experiment, or they could even co-exist. The Cartavox Sound Postcard event, for example, tested the technological affordances and user-technology relationship while, at the same time, it performed their practices with an audience present. The methods of simulation and re-enactment may furthermore overlap, as when some of the involved participants have a living memory of the re-enacted media practices. Finally, the method of replication may involve creative or artistic research practices, thus overlapping with this method of experimentation. This happens, for instance, when specific constituents of past media technologies or formats need to be recreated. Nevertheless, distinguishing between the various types and methods of experimentation can help scholarly practitioners to purposefully make choices in relation to the objectives, approach and design of their media archaeological experiments.

Historical Authenticity

In relation to their proposed user typology, Fickers and Van den Oever argue that experimental media archaeology aims to bring forward a new and different type of user: the "re-enacted user". This type of user can provide a different or complementary perspective on past media technologies and user practices compared to other user types represented in historical sources. One of the recurring points of discussion, however, is whether media archaeological experiments aim to authentically recreate past media practices. Fickers and Van den Oever argue that experimental media archaeology is not at all concerned with striving for authenticity. Rather, its potential is to open up a "dialogue with the past", which helps to raise new questions (▶ Theory, Chapter 2.7). While historical authenticity may not be the end goal of the media archaeological experiment, however, it can serve as a reflexive means and heuristic instrument. We found Lesley Carlyle's notion of "historical accuracy" as a continuum and relative concept to be particularly useful for determining the degree of historical authenticity ascribed to the experimental setting, the media historical object itself, and the materials and technical instruments used within the media archaeological experiment. In addition, as we have shown in this guide, the three types of experiments may provide a helpful framework for doing so. The inspection of the media historical object in the basic experiments, for instance, can be used to determine which parts are original and which were modified during the object's lifetime, or are actually modern replacements. In media-technological experiments, the level of historical accuracy can be defined on the basis of the workings of the media technology in use. Further, in performative experiments the authenticity of the experimental setting and the interaction with the environment, including audiences, can be the subject of investigation.

Productive Tensions

This practical guide aims to be complementary or applicable to all kinds of media technologies. While the goal was to systematically reflect on the methodological underpinnings of doing experimental media archaeology, our focus on early to mid-twentieth century visual and sound media technologies makes it naturally biased towards historical *analogue* and *mechanical* media technologies. Therefore, it may not be comprehensive enough for media archaeological experiments that involve later electronic or digital media technologies. Whether the methodological and epistemological implications of the hands-on approach are different for mechanical, analogue electronic and digital media technologies is a moot point and a topic for further research. In addition, this book has presented various other productive tensions that we believe are very much at the heart of hands-on experimentation in media historical research and teaching, including the dynamic relationships between theory and practice, research and teaching, as well as between historical and artistic approaches to past media experiences.

We hope that this book, as a practical compendium to the theoretical volume *Doing Experimental Media Archaeology: Theory*, provides a useful guide for doing media archaeological experiments. It was written as a first exploration and practice-driven step towards a systematic foundation for experimental media archaeology as a methodological framework. We hope that it will inform both theory-driven and practice-based research on media histories, and promote a hands-on approach in both research and education. Furthermore, we hope it will stimulate discussions on best practices in experimentation and documentation across various disciplines in the humanities and social sciences, and lead to new transdisciplinary forms of collaboration between scholars and artists, media theorists and practitioners, and between universities and cultural heritage institutions. It is our conviction that such collaborations and initiatives will provide an important basis not only for demonstrating, but also for validating and valorising the heuristic value of doing experimental media archaeology *in practice*.

Bibliography

Aasman, Susan. *Ritueel van huiselijk geluk: Een cultuurhistorische verkenning van de familiefilm*. Amsterdam: Het Spinhuis, 2004.

Aasman, Susan. "Report 'Staging the Amateur Dispositif'," 27 June 2014. [Online] https://homemoviesproject.wordpress.com/report-staging-the-amateur-dispositif/ [last accessed 26.07.2022].

ADAPT Television History. *16mm Film Crew Prepares to Shoot: Multi-Angle Version*, 2016. [Online] https://www.youtube.com/watch?v=BDlKVGtxXpo [last accessed 26.07.2022].

Ambrosini, Véronique, and Cliff Bowman. "Tacit Knowledge: Some Suggestions for Operationalization." *Journal of Management Studies* 38, no. 6 (2001): 811–829. DOI: https://doi.org/10.1111/1467-6486.00260.

An Expert. *The Art of Projection and Complete Magic Lantern Manual*. London: E. A. Beckett, 1893.

Anderson, Jane, Kelly Bannister, Emma Feltes, Ellen Frankenstein, Kate Hennessy, Julie Hollowell, Jock Langford, Silke von Lewinski, and Douglas Trainor. "Using Video in Research and Documentation: Ethical and Intellectual Property Issues to Consider – Fact Sheet," 2013. [Online] https://summit.sfu.ca/item/16151 [last accessed 26.07.2022].

Anthony, Barry. *The Kinora: Motion Pictures for the Home 1896-1914: A History of the System*. London: The Projection Box, 1996.

Bak, Meredith. "Optical Play and the Expanded Archive: Mapping Childhood and Media Archaeology." *Early Popular Visual Culture* 18, no. 1 (2 January 2020): 29–43. DOI: https://doi.org/10.1080/17460654.2020.1761602.

Bak, Meredith. "Play Lab Report – Identifying Design Attributes," 2021. [Online] https://domitor.org/wp-content/uploads/2021/08/Bak_Play-Lab-Exercise.docx-1.pdf [last accessed 26.07.2022].

Bartlett, Riley. *The Past Must Live so the Present Can Be Seen*, 2021. [Online] https://vimeo.com/653869229 [last accessed 26.07.2022].

Beyer, Hugh, and Karen Holtzblatt. *Contextual Design Defining Customer-Centered Systems*. San Francisco, CA: Morgan Kaufmann, 2000.

Bienek, Karin, and Ludwig Vogl-Bienek. *Media-Archaeological Experiments with 'Improved Phantasmagoria Lanterns' (1820–1880)*. Frankfurt am Main, 2020. [Online] https://player.vimeo.com/video/489306344 [last accessed 26.07.2022].

Blijleven, Klazina Johanna. "Conveying Histories of Use to Science Museum Audience Via Object-based Re-enactment: Practical and Ethical Considerations." Master's thesis, University of Groningen, 2020. [Online] https://arts.studenttheses.ub.rug.nl/25117/ [last accessed 26.07.2022].

Breidbach, Olaf, Peter Heering, Matthias Müller, and Heiko Weber. "Experimentelle Wissenschaftsgeschichte." In *Experimentelle Wissenschaftsgeschichte*, edited by Olaf Breidbach, Peter Heering, Matthias Müller, and Heiko Weber, 13–72. Munich: Fink, 2010.

Brenni, Paolo. "Nineteenth-Century Acoustics and Its Instruments: On the Method of Reenactment." *Sound & Science: Digital Histories* (blog), 14 January 2020. [Online] https://soundandscience.de/contributor-essays/nineteenth-century-acoustics-and-its-instruments-method-reenactment [last accessed 26.07.2022].

Brylawski, Samuel, Maya Lerman, Robin Pike, and Kathlin Smith, eds. *ARSC Guide to Audio Preservation*. Eugene, Washington: Association for Recorded Sound Collections, Library of Congress, and Council on Library and Information Resources, 2015.

∂ Open Access. © 2023 the author(s), published by De Gruyter. [(cc) BY] This work is licensed under the Creative Commons Attribution 4.0 International License.
https://doi.org/10.1515/9783110799767-007

Carlyle, Leslie. "Reconstructions of Oil Painting Materials and Techniques: The HART Model for Approaching Historical Accuracy." In *Reconstruction, Replication and Re-enactment in the Humanities and Social Sciences*, edited by Sven Dupré, Anna Harris, Julia Kursell, Patricia Lulof, and Maartje Stols-Witlox, 141–168. Amsterdam: Amsterdam University Press, 2020.

Carpenter, Philip. *Elements of Zoology: Being a Concise Account of the Animal Kingdom According to the System of Linnaeus*. London: Rowland Hunter, 1823.

Collingwood, R. G. *The Idea of History*. Oxford: Oxford University Press, 1946.

Collins English Dictionary. "Definition of 'Experimental'," 29 June 2022. [Online] https://www.collinsdictionary.com/dictionary/english/experimental [last accessed 26.07.2022].

DeMarinis, Paul. "Installations 1973–2010." In *Paul DeMarinis: Buried in Noise*, edited by Ingrid Beirer, Sabine Himmelsbach, and Carsten Seiffairth, 105–200. Heidelberg, Berlin: Kehrer Verlag, 2010.

Derrida, Jacques. *Archive Fever: A Freudian Impression*. Translated by Eric Prenowitz. Chicago, London: University of Chicago Press, 1996.

Drever, John Levack. "Soundscape Composition: The Convergence of Ethnography and Acousmatic Music." *Organised Sound* 7, no. 1 (2002): 21–27. DOI: https://doi.org/10.1017/S1355771802001048.

Dreyfus, Stuart E. "The Five-Stage Model of Adult Skill Acquisition." *Bulletin of Science, Technology & Society* 24, no. 3 (2004): 177–181. DOI: https://doi.org/10.1177/0270467604264992.

Dupré, Sven, Anna Harris, Julia Kursell, Patricia Lulof, and Maartje Stols-Witlox, eds. *Reconstruction, Replication and Re-enactment in the Humanities and Social Sciences*. Amsterdam: Amsterdam University Press, 2020.

Eastman Kodak Company. "Instructions for Use of the Ciné-Kodak Eight, Models 20 and 25," 1934. [Online] https://www.browniecam.com/brownie_user_manuals/cine-kodak-20-25.pdf [last accessed 26.07.2022].

Eastman Kodak Company. "Making Titles with the Ciné-Kodak Titler," n.d.

Edmonds, Guy. *Vibrating Existence: Early Cinema and Cognitive Creativity*. Plymouth: University of Plymouth, 2020. [Online] http://hdl.handle.net/10026.1/16096 [last accessed 26.07.2022].

Ellis, John. *Visible Fictions: Cinema, Television, Video*. London, New York: Routledge, 1992.

Ellis, John. "Filming for Television: How a 16mm Film Crew Worked Together." *VIEW Journal of European Television History and Culture* 8, no. 15 (27 October 2019): 1–19. DOI: https://doi.org/10.18146/2213-0969.2019.jethc167.

Ellis, John. "Why Hands on History Matters." In *Hands on Media History: A New Methodology in the Humanities and Social Sciences*, edited by Nick Hall and John Ellis, 11–25. London: Routledge, 2019.

Ellis, Patrick, and Colin Williamson. "Object Lessons, Old and New: Experimental Media Archaeology in the Classroom." *Early Popular Visual Culture* 18, no. 1 (29 April 2020): 1–13. DOI: https://doi.org/10.1080/17460654.2020.1751434.

Emerson, Lori, and Wolfgang Ernst. "Archives, Materiality and the 'Agency of the Machine': An Interview with Wolfgang Ernst." *The Signal* (blog), 8 February 2013. https://blogs.loc.gov/thesignal/2013/02/archives-materiality-and-agency-of-the-machine-an-interview-with-wolfgang-ernst/ [last accessed 26.07.2022].

Emerson, Lori, and libi rose striegl. "Slow Networks Experiment 1: Over-the-Air TV Transmission." Loriemerson.net, 14 December 2020. [Online] https://loriemerson.net/2020/12/14/slow-networks-experiment-1-over-the-air-tv-transmission/ [last accessed 26.07.2022].

Emery, Kate Meyers. "A Whole New (Digital) World: Online Experiences at the Eastman Museum during 2020." *George Eastman Museum* (blog), 20 May 2021. [Online] https://medium.com/george-eastman-museum/a-whole-new-digital-world-online-experiences-at-the-eastman-museum-during-2020-8c352494bba2 [last accessed 26.07.2022].

Ferguson, Jeffrey, ed. *Designing Experimental Research in Archaeology: Examining Technology through Production and Use.* Boulder: University Press of Colorado, 2010.

Fickers, Andreas. "Experimental Media Archaeology: A Plea for New Directions." In *Technē/Technology: Researching Cinema and Media Technologies – Their Development, Use, and Impact*, edited by Annie van den Oever, 272–278. Amsterdam: Amsterdam University Press, 2014.

Fickers, Andreas, Andy O'Dwyer, and Alexandre Germain. "'On the Road Again': An Experimental Media Archaeology Journey to the Origins of Transnational Television in Europe." *VIEW Journal of European Television History and Culture* 7, no. 13 (16 May 2018): 142–147. DOI: https://doi.org/10.18146/2213-0969.2018.jethc148.

Fickers, Andreas, and Annie van den Oever. "(De)Habituation Histories: How to Re-Sensitize Media Historians." In *Hands on Media History: A New Methodology in the Humanities and Social Sciences*, edited by Nick Hall and John Ellis, 58–75. London: Routledge, 2019.

Fickers, Andreas, and Annie van den Oever. "Doing Experimental Media Archaeology: Epistemological and Methodological Reflections on Experiments with Historical Objects of Media Technologies." In *New Media Archaeologies*, edited by Ben Roberts and Mark Goodall, 45–68. Amsterdam: Amsterdam University Press, 2019.

Fickers, Andreas, and Annie van den Oever. *Doing Experimental Media Archaeology: Theory.* Berlin: De Gruyter, 2022.

Fondazione Scienza e Tecnica. *Speaking Arc and Singing Arc*, 2016. [Online] https://www.youtube.com/watch?v=cCEU3ShVE2E [last accessed 26.07.2022].

Fossati, Giovanna, and Annie van den Oever, eds. *Exposing the Film Apparatus: The Film Archive as a Research Laboratory.* Amsterdam: Amsterdam University Press, 2016.

Fung, F. M. "Seeing through My Lenses: A GoPro Approach to Teach a Laboratory Module." *Asian Journal of the Scholarship of Teaching and Learning* 6, no. 1 (2016): 99–115.

Gale, David. "Cornelia Parker." *Strength Weekly* (blog), 1997. [Online] https://strengthweekly.com/cornelia-parker/ [last accessed 26.07.2022].

Gaydon, H. A. "Improvements in Sound Producing Devices [GB Patent 16,934]," 24 July 1911.

Gaydon, H. A. *The Art and Science of the Gramophone.* London: Dunlop, 1928.

Geertz, Clifford. "Thick Description: Towards an Interpretive Theory of Culture." In *The Interpretation of Cultures*, edited by Clifford Geertz, 3–30. New York: Basic Books, 1973.

Grant, Catherine. "The Audiovisual Essay as Performative Research." *NECSUS. European Journal of Media Studies* 5, no. 2 (2016): 255–265. DOI: https://doi.org/10.25969/mediarep/3370.

Greenberg, Alan D., and Jan Zanetis. "The Impact of Broadcast and Streaming Video in Education." Report commissioned by Cisco Systems Inc. to Wainhouse Research, LLC. San Jose, CA: Cisco Systems, 2012. [Online] https://www.cisco.com/c/dam/en_us/solutions/industries/docs/education/ciscovideowp.pdf [last accessed 26.07.2022].

Gunning, Tom. "Re-Newing Old Technologies: Astonishment, Second Nature, and the Uncanny in Technology from the Previous Turn-of-the-Century." In *Rethinking Media Change: The Aesthetics of Transition*, edited by David Thorburn and Henry Jenkins, 39–59. Cambridge, MA: MIT Press, 2003.

Hagener, Malte. "Divided, Together, Apart: How Split Screen Became Our Everyday Reality." *Pandemic Media: Preliminary Notes Toward an Inventory*, edited by Philipp Dominik Keidl, Laliv Melamed, Vinzenz Hediger, and Antonio Somaini, 33–40. Lüneburg, Germany: Meson Press, 2020. [Online] https://pandemicmedia.meson.press/chapters/time-temporality/divided-together-apart-how-split-screen-became-our-everyday-reality/ [last accessed 26.07.2022].

Hall, Nick. "Bringing the Living Back to Life: What Happens When We Reenact the Recent Past?" In *Hands on Media History: A New Methodology in the Humanities and Social Sciences*, edited by Nick Hall and John Ellis, 26–42. London: Routledge, 2019.

Hall, Nick, and John Ellis, eds. *Hands on Media History: A New Methodology in the Humanities and Social Sciences*. London: Routledge, 2019.

Harkema, Gert Jan, and André Rosendaal. "From Cinematograph to 3D Model: How Can Virtual Reality Support Film Education Hands-On?" *Early Popular Visual Culture* 18, no. 1 (2 January 2020): 70–81. DOI: https://doi.org/10.1080/17460654.2020.1761598.

Harper, A. C. *Lo-Fi Aesthetics in Popular Music Discourse*. Oxford: Oxford University, 2016. [Online] https://ora.ox.ac.uk/objects/uuid:cc84039c-3d30-484e-84b4-8535ba4a54f8 [last accessed 26.07.2022].

Harris, Anna. *A Sensory Education*. London: Routledge, 2021.

Heering, Peter, and Roland Wittje, eds. *Learning by Doing: Experiments and Instruments in the History of Science Teaching*. Stuttgart: Franz Steiner Verlag, 2011.

Heller, Franziska. *Update!* Paderborn, Germany: Wilhelm Fink Verlag, 2020. DOI: https://doi.org/10.30965/9783846764602.

Henderson, Noah. "Analog Resurgence – YouTube," 2018. [Online] https://www.youtube.com/c/AnalogResurgence/about [last accessed 26.07.2022].

Hendriksen, Marieke M. A. "Rethinking Performative Methods in the History of Science." *Berichte Zur Wissenschaftsgeschichte* 43, no. 3 (September 2020): 313–322. DOI: https://doi.org/10.1002/bewi.202000017.

Herbert, Stephen. "Animated Portrait Photography." *History of Photography* 13, no. 1 (1989): 65–78.

Herbert, Stephen. "Stephen Herbert – YouTube," 2006. [Online] https://www.youtube.com/user/horipet/about [last accessed 26.07.2022].

Holtzblatt, Karen, and Hugh Beyer. *Contextual Design: Evolved*. Synthesis Lectures on Human-Centered Informatics 24. San Rafael, CA: Morgan and Claypool, 2015. DOI: https://doi.org/10.2200/S00597ED1V01Y201409HCI024.

Hopwood, Henry V. *Living Pictures: Their History, Photoproduction and Practical Working*. London Optician and Photographic Trades Review, 1899.

Huhtamo, Erkki. "Thinkering with Media: On the Art of Paul DeMarinis." In *Paul DeMarinis: Buried in Noise*, edited by Ingrid Beirer, Sabine Himmelsbach, and Carsten Seiffairth, 33–46. Heidelberg, Berlin: Kehrer Verlag, 2010.

Huhtamo, Erkki, and Jussi Parikka. *Media Archaeology: Approaches, Applications, and Implications*. Berkeley, CA; London: University of California Press, 2011.

Huhtamo, Erkki. "The Dream of Personal Interactive Media: A Media Archaeology of the Spirograph, a Failed Moving Picture Revolution." *Early Popular Visual Culture* 11, no. 4 (November 2013): 365–408. DOI: https://doi.org/10.1080/17460654.2013.840247.

Huhtamo, Erkki. "Art in the Rear-View Mirror: The Media-Archaeological Tradition in Art." In *A Companion to Digital Art*, edited by Christiane Paul, 69–110. Chichester, West Sussex: Wiley, 2016. DOI: https://doi.org/10.1002/9781118475249.ch3.

illuminago. "Improved Phantasmagoria Lanterns [Experimental Report]," 2022.

Ingold, Tim. *Making: Anthropology, Archaeology, Art and Architecture*. London, New York: Routledge, 2013.

Insta360. "Insta360 ONE – A Camera Crew in Your Hand," 2022. [Online] https://www. insta360.com/product/insta360-one/ [last accessed 26.07.2022].

Jackson, Steven J. "Rethinking Repair." In *Media Technologies*, edited by Tarleton Gillespie, Pablo J. Boczkowski, and Kirsten A. Foot, 221–240. Cambridge, MA: MIT Press, 2014. DOI: https://doi.org/10.7551/mitpress/9780262525374.003.0011.

Kattelle, Alan. *Home Movies: A History of the American Industry, 1897-1979*. Nashua, NH: Transition Pub., 2000.

Keathley, Christian, and Jason Mittell. *The Videographic Essay: Criticism in Sound & Image*. Kino-Agora 9. Montreal: Caboose, 2016.

Keathley, Christian, Jason Mittell, and Catherine Grant. *The Videographic Essay: Practice and Pedagogy*. Montreal: Caboose, 2019. [Online] http://videographicessay.org [last accessed 26.07.2022].

Kneebone, Roger, and Abigail Woods. "Recapturing the History of Surgical Practice Through Simulation-Based Re-enactment." *Medical History* 58, no. 1 (January 2014): 106–121. DOI: https://doi.org/10.1017/mdh.2013.75.

Koepnick, Lutz. *Resonant Matter: Sound, Art, and the Promise of Hospitality*. London: Bloomsbury Academic, 2021.

Kolkowski, Aleksander. *The Wax Cylinder Phonograph in the Age of Digital Reproduction: Music-Making, Music Technology and the Aura of Obsolescence*. London: Brunel University, 2011.

Kolkowski, Aleksander, and Alison Rabinovici. "Bellowphones and Blowed Strings: The Auxeto-Instruments of Horace Short and Charles Algernon Parsons." In *Material Culture and Electronic Sound*, Series Artefacts: Studies in the History of Science and Technology 8, edited by Frode Weium and Timothy Boon, 1–42. Washington, D.C.: Smithsonian Scholarly Press, 2012.

Kolkowski, Aleksander. "In Search of Perfect Sound." *Science Museum Blog* (blog), 24 April 2014. [Online] https://blog.sciencemuseum.org.uk/in-search-of-perfect-sound-introducing-britains-largest-horn-loudspeaker/ [last accessed 26.07.2022].

Kolkowski, Aleksander, Duncan Miller, and Amy Blier-Carruthers. "The Art and Science of Acoustic Recording: Re-enacting Arthur Nikisch and the Berlin Philharmonic Orchestra's Landmark 1913 Recording of Beethoven's Fifth Symphony." *Science Museum Group Journal* 3, no. 3 (2015). DOI: http://dx.doi.org/10.15180/150302/001.

Kolkowski, Aleksander. "The Cartavox Machine: Self-Recordable Sound Postcards. Experimental Report No. 1." DEMA documentation, January 2021.

Kolkowski, Aleksander, and Tim van der Heijden. "Performing Media Archaeological Experiments." *DEMA* (blog), 23 May 2021. [Online] https://dema.uni.lu/performing-media-archaeological-experiments-report/ [last accessed 26.07.2022].

Krebs, Stefan. "'Glanz und Elend der Kunstkopf-Stereophonie'. Eine technik- und medienarchäologische Ausgrabung." In *Jeux sans Frontières? – Grenzgänge der Geschichtswissenschaft*, edited by Andreas Fickers, Rüdiger Haude, Stefan Krebs, and Werner Tschacher, 57–69. Bielefeld: Transcript, 2017. DOI: https://doi.org/10.14361/9783839441053.

Lehmann, Ann-Sophie. "Object Lessons. Material Begreifen in Acht Lektionen." *Werkbundarchiv – Museum Der Dinge* (blog), 2017. [Online] https://www.museumderdinge. de/ausstellungen/object-lessons-material-begreifen-8-lektionen [last accessed 26.07.2022].

Liesegang, Paul E., and Franz P. Liesegang. *Die Projektions-Kunst für Schulen, Familien und öffentliche Vorstellungen: mit einer Anleitung zum Malen auf Glas und Beschreibung chemischer, magnetischer, optischer und elektrischer Experimente.* Leipzig: Liesegang, 1909.

Lumière, Auguste, Louis Lumière, and Benjamin Joseph Barnard Mills. "Kinora Lumière Patent: 'Apparatus for the Direct Viewing of Chrono-Photographic or Zoetropic Pictures'. British Patent No: 23,183," 1896.

Lupu, Ruxandra. *The Home Movie 4.0: (Co)Creative Strategies for a Tacit, Embodied and Affective Reading of the Sicilian Home Movie Archive.* Leeds: University of Leeds, 2020. [Online] https://etheses.whiterose.ac.uk/27966/ [last accessed 26.07.2022].

Mariani, Andrea. "(Un)Dead Media Project." *(Un)Dead Media Project* (blog), 2022. [Online] https://andreamariani.info/ [last accessed 26.07.2022].

McCarty, M. "Introduction to Vintage Electronic Equipment Restoration." Vintage Radio and Phonograph Society website, Dallas/Fort Worth, Texas, 2004. [Online] http://vrps.org/ documents/IntroRestoration/IntroRestoration.html [last accessed 26.07.2022].

McCaslin, Sara, Marilyn Young, and Adarsh Kesireddy. "Using GoPro Hero Cameras in a Laboratory Setting." In *Proceedings of the 2014 ASEE Gulf-Southwest Conference.* Tulane University, New Orleans, LA: American Society for Engineering Education, 2014. [Online] http://asee-gsw.tulane.edu/pdf/using-gopro-hero-cameras-in-a-laboratory-setting.pdf.

Merleau-Ponty, Maurice. *Phenomenology of Perception.* Translated by Colin Smith. New York: Routledge, 2007.

Moigno, Abbé François. *L'art des projections.* Paris: Gauthier-Villars, 1872.

Nahum, Andrew. "Exhibiting Science: Changing Conceptions of Science Museum Display." In *Science for the Nation: Perspectives on the History of the Science Museum,* edited by Peter J. T. Morris, 176–193. London: Palgrave Macmillan, 2010. DOI: https://doi.org/ 10.1057/9780230283145_9.

National Film and Sound Archive of Australia (NFSA). "Vinegar Syndrome." Canberra: National Film and Sound Archive of Australia, 8 July 2010. [Online] https://www.nfsa.gov.au/preser vation/preservation-glossary/vinegar-syndrome [last accessed 26.07.2022].

N. N. "Make the Phonograph Record Loud or Soft." *Popular Science Monthly,* September 1921.

N. N. "Direct Comparison (Letter to the Editor)." *The Gramophone,* London, April 1933.

N. N. "Études Expérimentales de l'activité Nerveuse Pendant La Projection Du Film." *Revue Internationale de Filmologie* 16 (March 1954).

Odin, Roger. *Le film de famille: usage privé, usage public.* Paris: Méridiens Klincksieck, 1995.

Oppenheim, A. N. *Questionnaire Design and Attitude Measurement.* London: Heinemann, 1966.

Parikka, Jussi. *What Is Media Archaeology?* Cambridge; Malden, MA: Polity Press, 2012.

Pink, Sarah. *Doing Sensory Ethnography.* London: Sage, 2009.

Polanyi, Michael. *The Tacit Dimension.* [1966]. Chicago, London: University of Chicago Press, 2009.

Rheinberger, Hans-Jörg. *Experiment, Differenz, Schrift: Zur Geschichte Epistemischer Dinge.* Marburg an der Lahn: Basilisken-Press, 1992.

Rheinberger, Hans-Jörg. *Toward a History of Epistemic Things: Synthesizing Proteins in the Test Tube.* Stanford, CA: Stanford University Press, 1997.

Rheinberger, Hans-Jörg. "Epistemics and Aesthetics of Experimentation: Towards a Hybrid Heuristics?", edited by Philippe Sormani, Guelfo Carbone, and Priska Gisler, 236–248. New York: Routledge, 2019.

Rice, Tom. "Acoustemology." In *The International Encyclopedia of Anthropology*, edited by Hilary Callan. Hoboken, NJ: Wiley-Blackwell, 2018. DOI: https://doi.org/10.1002/9781118924396.

Roepke, Martina. *Privat-Vorstellung: Heimkino in Deutschland vor 1945*. Hildesheim: G. Olms, 2006.

Roy, R. A. J. "Procédé de Fabrication de Cartes Postales, Photographies et Imprimés Parlants [FR Patent 1.124.915]," 5 August 1955.

Sendra, Estrella, and Bartolomeo Meletti. "Introduction to Video Essays: Studying and Researching Film through Film." *Learning on Screen*, 2022. [Online] https://learningonscreen.ac.uk/guidance/introductory-guide-to-video-essays/introduction-to-video-essays-studying-and-researching-film-through-film/ [last accessed 26.07.2022].

Sibum, H. Otto. "Science and the Knowing Body: Making Sense of Embodied Knowledge in Scientific Experiment." In *Reconstruction, Replication and Re-enactment in the Humanities and Social Sciences*, edited by Sven Dupré, Anna Harris, Julia Kursell, Patricia Lulof, and Maartje Stols-Witlox, 275–294. Amsterdam: Amsterdam University Press, 2020. DOI: https://doi.org/10.1515/9789048543854-012.

Slugan, Mario. "Film Studies and the Experimental Method." *NECSUS_European Journal of Media Studies* 9, no. 2 (2020): 203–224. DOI: http://dx.doi.org/10.25969/mediarep/15317.

Smith, Caylin. "Extending the Archival Life of Film: Presenting Film History with EYE." In *Exposing the Film Apparatus: The Film Archive as a Research Laboratory*, edited by Giovanna Fossati and Annie van den Oever, 323–331. Amsterdam: Amsterdam University Press, 2016.

Stols-Witlox, Maartje. "Flour and Starch in Preparatory Layers for Oil Painting: Reconstructions Based on Historical Recipes (Sixteenth to Nineteenth Centuries)." In *Painting Techniques: History, Materials and Studio Practice: 5th International Symposium*, edited by A. Wallert, 79–84. Amsterdam: Rijksmuseum, 2016.

Strauven, Wanda. "Media Archaeology as Laboratory for History Writing and Theory Making." In *New Media Archaeologies*, edited by Ben Roberts and Mark Goodall, 23–43. Amsterdam: Amsterdam University Press, 2019.

Strauven, Wanda. *Touchscreen Archaeology: Tracing Histories of Hands-On Media Practices*. Lüneburg, Germany: Meson Press, 2021.

Talbot, Frederick A. *Moving Pictures: How They Are Made and Worked*. Philadelphia, PA: J. B. Lippincott Co., 1914.

Taylor, Jane. *William Kentridge: Being Led by the Nose*. Chicago, IL: University of Chicago Press, 2019.

Tepperman, Charles. "Taking a Turn on the Rewind Strategies for Experiential Learning in Nontheatrical Film History." *The Journal of Cinema and Media Studies* 60, no. 6 (Winter 2021). DOI: https://dx.doi.org/10.3998//jcms.18261332.0060.605.

Theisen, Thomas. *Testing of Original and Replica Stentorphone Soundboxes*, 2021. [Online] https://www.youtube.com/watch?v=CWSubuug5rc [last accessed 26.07.2022].

Theisen, Thomas. *Working Function of a Stentorphone Soundbox*, 2021. [Online] https://www.youtube.com/watch?v=NfNpah8U3Yg [last accessed 26.07.2022].

Tilmans, Karin, Frank van Vree, and Jay Winter. *Performing the Past: Memory, History, and Identity in Modern Europe*. Amsterdam: Amsterdam University Press, 2010.

Tolk, Andreas. *Ontology, Epistemology, and Teleology for Modeling and Simulation: Philosophical Foundations for Intelligent M & S Applications*. Berlin, Heidelberg: Springer, 2013.

UCLA DMA. *The Magic Lantern – Professor Huhtamo's Cabinet of Media Archaeology: Part 1*, 2017. [Online] https://www.youtube.com/watch?v=V37S95AE3Pc [last accessed 26.07.2022].

UCLA DMA. *Peep Media – Professor Huhtamo's Cabinet of Media Archaeology: Part 2*, 2018. [Online] https://www.youtube.com/watch?v=CRb8Ius0e6A [last accessed 26.07.2022].

Van den Oever, Annie, André Rosendaal, and Bernd Warnders. "Media Heritage – Final Report," 2010. [Online] https://www.researchgate.net/publication/331283592_Media_Heritage_-_Final_Report [last accessed 26.07.2022].

Van den Oever, Annie. "Experimental Media Archaeology in the Media Archaeology Lab: Re-Sensitizing the Observer." In *At the Borders of (Film) History: Temporality, Archaeology, Theories*, edited by Alberto Bertrame, Guiseppe Fidotta, and Andrea Mariani, 43–53. Udine: Forum, 2015.

Van der Heijden, Tim. *Staging the Amateur Film Dispositif*. Vimeo, 2014. [Online] https://vimeo.com/95314562 [last accessed 26.07.2022].

Van der Heijden, Tim. "Hybrid Histories: Historicizing the Home Movie Dispositif." In *Materializing Memories: Dispositifs, Generations, Amateurs*, edited by Susan Aasman, Andreas Fickers, and Joseph Wachelder, 35–50. New York: Bloomsbury Academic, 2018.

Van der Heijden, Tim. *Hybrid Histories: Technologies of Memory and the Cultural Dynamics of Home Movies, 1895–2005*. Maastricht: Maastricht University, 2018.

Van der Heijden, Tim, and Aleksander Kolkowski. "Documenting Media Archaeological Experiments." *DEMA* (blog), 15 July 2020. [Online] https://dema.uni.lu/documenting-media-archaeological-experiments-report/ [last accessed 26.07.2022].

Van der Heijden, Tim, Aleksander Kolkowski, Stefan Krebs, and Andreas Fickers. "Images of Invisible Traces: Documenting and Re-enacting an 18th Century Experiment." *C²DH / Luxembourg Centre for Contemporary and Digital History* (blog), 16 July 2020. [Online] https://www.c2dh.uni.lu/thinkering/images-invisible-traces-documenting-and-re-enacting-18th-century-experiment [last accessed 26.07.2022].

Van der Heijden, Tim, and Claude Wolf. "Replicating the Kinora: 3D Modelling and Printing as Heuristics in Digital Media History." *Journal of Digital History*, no. 2 (2022). [Online] https://journalofdigitalhistory.org/en/article/33pRxE2dtUHP [last accessed 26.07.2022].

Vogl-Bienek, Ludwig. "Performative Configurations of the Historical Art of Projection. A Media-Archaeological Approach to the History of the Magic Lantern and the Screen in Live Performance." *eLaterna*, 2022. [Online] http://elaterna-companion.uni-trier.de/en/sections/performance/performative-configurations-of-the-historical-art-of-projection-a-media-archaeological-approach-to-the-history-of-the-magic-lantern-and-the-screen-in-live-performance [last accessed 26.07.2022].

Wersher, Darren, Lori Emerson, and Jussi Parikka. *The Lab Book: Situated Practices in Media Studies*. Minneapolis, MN: University of Minnesota Press, 2022.

Williams, Sean. "Stockhausen Meets King Tubby's: The Stepped Filter and Its Influence as a Musical Instrument on Two Different Styles of Music." In *Material Culture and Electronic Sound*. Series Artefacts: Studies in the History of Science and Technology 8, edited by Frode Weium and Tim Boon, 163–188. Washington, D.C.: Smithsonian Institution Scholarly Press, 2013. [Online] http://oro.open.ac.uk/48770/ [last accessed 26.07.2022].

Windsor, W. Luke. "Data Collection, Experimental Design, and Statistics in Musical Research."
In *Empirical Musicology: Aims, Methods, Prospects*, edited by Eric Clarke and Nicholas
Cook, 197–222. Oxford: Oxford University Press, 2004.

Wittje, Roland. "The Speaking and Singing Arc: The Sound of Electricity at the Fin de Siècle."
Sound & Science: Digital Histories (blog), 19 February 2018. [Online]
https://soundandscience.de/contributor-essays/speaking-and-singing-arc-sound-
electricity-fin-de-siecle [last accessed 26.07.2022].

Wolf, Claude, and Tim van der Heijden. *Kinora Replica 3D Model*. Sketchfab, 2022. [Online]
https://sketchfab.com/3d-models/kinora-replica-3d-model-
2a189b74c5c34c0c9918c10644c1e8b8 [last accessed 26.07.2022].

Wright, Alison. "Festival: The Art of Sound." *Nature Physics* 8, no. 6 (June 2012): 441. DOI:
https://doi.org/10.1038/nphys2349.

Index of Names*

*The Index of Names includes references to both volumes of this twin publication:
    VT = *Doing Experimental Media Archaeology: Theory*
    VP = *Doing Experimental Media Archaeology: Practice*

∂ Open Access. © 2023 the author(s), published by De Gruyter. [(cc) BY] This work is licensed under the Creative Commons Attribution 4.0 International License.
https://doi.org/10.1515/9783110799767-008

Index of Subjects*

*The Index of Subjects includes references to both volumes of this twin publication:

VT = *Doing Experimental Media Archaeology: Theory*

VP = *Doing Experimental Media Archaeology: Practice*

Bold = main section that discusses entry

Italics = footnote section that discusses entry

3D
- Modelling VP 4, 5, 8, 10, 18, 32, 33, 47, 60, 61, 74, 85, 107, 108, 134, 139, 150, 151, 159, 176
- Printing VP 4, 8, 10, 18, 74, 85, 107, 108, 139, 150, 176
- Replication VT 16, 20, 23, 42, 43, 61, 69, 70, 72, 73, 76, 78, 82, 109, 117   VP 5, 18, **32–33**, 48, 60, 61, 74, 85, 91, 107, 139, 150, 153, 176

Acoustic recording VP 17, 28, 31, 80, 88, 98, 144, 148
Acoustics
- Acoustic properties VP 88
- Resonators VP 35, 104
- Room acoustics VP 28, 35, 88
- Science of VT 94   VP 31, 144, 148
Acoustemology VP 98, 99
Aesthetic(s)
- of Astonishment VT *65, 99*
- Aesthetic qualities VP 14, 38
- Anaesthetics VT 20–22
- Experimentation VT 44, 70
Affordances VT 11, 16, 17, 76–78, 96   VP 14, 23, 25, 27, 33, 38, 39, 73, 75, 76, 110, 135, 148, 154, 158, 178, 184, 185
Amateur
- Film VT 45–47, 50, 84, 90   VP 4–6, 49, 57, 101, 171
- User VT 34, 37, 45–47, 65, 84, 101   VP 45, 46, 56, 57, 60, 62
Amplification
- Acoustic VP 8, 9
- Electrical VP 8, 9
- Pneumatic VP 28, 80

Analogue
- Electronics VP 103, 173–175, 187
- Film VP 4–7, 67, 111, 163, 172
- Sound VP 2, 8–12, 17, 23, 40, 84, 103, 124, 173–175
Anamorphic lens VT 43, 44, *57*   VP 25
Animated photography VP 5, 83
Apparatus theory VT 4, 7, 8, *27*
Art history VT 5, 60, **96–101**, 104, 108   VP 3, 177
Archives
- Archive-driven research VT 6, 117   VP 52
Artefact
- Conceptual VT 4, *27*
- Historical VT 19   VP 1, 13–15, 21, 36, 52, 77, 97, 179
- Material VP 1 *see also* Materiality
- Technological VT 31   VP 14, 38, 77
Artifact *see* Artefact
Artistic
- Experimentation VT 36, 78, 96–101   VP 77
- Practices VT 100, 101   VP 15, 26, **33–35**, 108, 181
- Research VT 78, 96–101   VP 33–35, 77, **89–94**, 108, 181, 186
Astonishment
- Aesthetics of VT *65, 99*
- Hermeneutics of VT 23, 105
Audience
- Collaboration VT 69, 90   VP **85**
- Observation VP 87–89, 100, 122, 142, 143
- Participation VT 48, 76–78, 90   VP 71, **85**, 86
Aura
- Auratic objects VT 3
- De-auratisation VT 25–28
- Re-auratisation VT 26

𝟄 Open Access. © 2023 the author(s), published by De Gruyter. (CC) BY ▮▮▮▮ This work is licensed under the Creative Commons Attribution 4.0 International License.
https://doi.org/10.1515/9783110799767-009

www.ingramcontent.com/pod-product-compliance
Lightning Source LLC
Chambersburg PA
CBHW070408100426
42812CB00005B/1668

* 9 7 8 3 1 1 0 7 9 5 8 1 3 *